Mastering gRPC
Strategies for Developing Scalable and Efficient APIs

Nova Trex

© 2024 by Wang Press. All rights reserved.

No part of this publication may be reproduced, distributed, or transmitted in any form or by any means, including photocopying, recording, or other electronic or mechanical methods, without the prior written permission of the publisher, except in the case of brief quotations embodied in critical reviews and certain other noncommercial uses permitted by copyright law.

Published by Wang Press

For permissions and other inquiries, write to:
P.O. Box 3132, Framingham, MA 01701, USA

Contents

1 Introduction to gRPC and High-Performance APIs — 11
- 1.1 The Evolution of Remote Procedure Calls — 12
- 1.2 Why gRPC for Modern Applications — 15
- 1.3 Core Components of gRPC — 19
- 1.4 Synchronous vs Asynchronous Communication — 23
- 1.5 gRPC in the Ecosystem — 27
- 1.6 Performance Benefits of gRPC — 31

2 Setting Up Your Development Environment — 35
- 2.1 Choosing the Right Tools and IDE — 35
- 2.2 Installing Protocol Buffers Compiler — 40
- 2.3 Setting Up gRPC Libraries — 45
- 2.4 Creating Your First gRPC Project — 52
- 2.5 Configuring Your Development Environment — 58
- 2.6 Troubleshooting Setup Issues — 65

3 Protocol Buffers: Defining Your Data — 71
- 3.1 Understanding Protocol Buffers — 71
- 3.2 Creating a .proto File — 75

3.3	Syntax and Structure of Protocol Buffers	78
3.4	Compiling Protocol Buffers	82
3.5	Versioning and Evolving Protocol Buffers	87
3.6	Extensions and Advanced Features	91

4 Understanding gRPC Architecture and Concepts 97

4.1	Core Architecture of gRPC	98
4.2	Communication Patterns in gRPC	102
4.3	HTTP/2 Underpinning gRPC	107
4.4	Data Serialization with Protocol Buffers	112
4.5	Naming and Discovery Concepts	117
4.6	Load Balancing and Scalability	121

5 gRPC in Action: Implementing Unary and Streaming APIs 127

5.1	Implementing Unary RPCs	128
5.2	Server Streaming RPCs	133
5.3	Client Streaming RPCs	139
5.4	Bidirectional Streaming RPCs	145
5.5	Handling Streaming Errors	152
5.6	Optimizing Streaming Performance	157

6 Error Handling and Debugging in gRPC 163

6.1	Understanding gRPC Status Codes	163
6.2	Implementing Error Handling in gRPC	168
6.2.1	The Necessity of Structured Error Handling	168
6.2.2	Client-Side Error Handling	169
6.2.3	Server-Side Error Handling	170
6.2.4	Advanced Error Handling Strategies	171

	6.2.5	Conclusion	173
	6.3	Debugging gRPC Applications	173
	6.4	Handling Deadlines and Timeouts	180
	6.5	Using Interceptors for Error Management	185
	6.6	Testing gRPC Error Scenarios	190

7 gRPC Security and Authentication — 195

	7.1	Overview of gRPC Security	195
	7.2	Transport Security with TLS	200
	7.3	Authentication Mechanisms	204
	7.4	Using OAuth2 and JWT	209
	7.5	Role-Based Access Control	214
	7.6	Securing Data with Encryption	219

8 Advanced gRPC Features and Techniques — 225

	8.1	Custom Metadata in gRPC	226
	8.2	Interceptor Design Patterns	230
	8.3	Load Balancing Strategies	235
	8.4	gRPC with HTTP/2 Features	241
	8.5	Asynchronous Programming Models	246
	8.6	Reflection and Dynamic Service Discovery	251

9 gRPC for Microservices and Distributed Systems — 257

	9.1	Integrating gRPC with Microservices	258
	9.2	Service Discovery in Distributed Systems	263
	9.3	Handling Failures and Retry Policies	267
	9.4	Distributed Tracing and Monitoring	272
	9.5	Load Balancing in Distributed Applications	276
	9.6	Real-time Data Streaming with gRPC	280

10 Case Studies and Best Practices in gRPC   **285**
    10.1 Successful gRPC Implementations 285
    10.2 Transitioning from REST to gRPC 290
    10.3 Ensuring Backward Compatibility 295
    10.4 Optimizing gRPC for Cloud Environments 299
    10.5 Lessons Learned from gRPC Failures 305

Introduction: Mastering gRPC for Scalable and Efficient API Development

In the constantly evolving realm of software engineering, the demand for efficient and high-performance communication solutions has never been greater. As applications become increasingly distributed and interconnected, developers need robust systems to handle remote procedure calls (RPCs) effectively. gRPC, an open-source universal RPC framework developed by Google, stands at the forefront of this technological evolution, addressing these precise needs with remarkable proficiency.

This book, "Mastering gRPC: Strategies for Developing Scalable and Efficient APIs," serves as a comprehensive guide for developers eager to dive deep into the intricacies of gRPC. Our objective is to equip you with both the theoretical understanding and the practical skills necessary for leveraging gRPC to build high-performance APIs capable of meeting the demands of today's diverse and complex application landscapes.

gRPC capitalizes on the advanced features of HTTP/2—such as multiplexing, header compression, and bidirectional streaming—which collectively mark a substantial leap over traditional RESTful architectures.

These features, combined with the efficacious serialization capabilities of Protocol Buffers, translate into reduced latency and bandwidth consumption, making gRPC particularly suitable for real-time communication and processing.

In recent years, gRPC has gained momentum, largely fueled by the rising interest in microservices architecture and distributed systems. It presents a unified solution for designing and maintaining scalable services, boasting language-agnostic support and extensive tooling across various programming languages. This versatility extends gRPC's applicability from backend service communication to mobile and IoT development, establishing it as a cornerstone technology in modern software engineering.

This book is methodically structured to provide a deep dive into the architectural principles of gRPC and its seamless integration into diverse environments. We aim to cater to software architects, developers, and engineers who are determined to optimize system communication. You will explore gRPC's core components and concepts, embark on step-by-step setup instructions, and engage with practical implementation examples that mirror real-world scenarios.

As the chapters progress, you'll be introduced to advanced features that enhance gRPC's utility further, such as load balancing, service discovery, and error handling. Security remains a crucial focus throughout, ensuring you can build APIs that are not only efficient but also secure. Our detailed examination culminates in case studies and best practices drawn from real-world applications, underscoring gRPC's effectiveness in tackling performance-critical challenges across different domains.

Ultimately, "Mastering gRPC: Strategies for Developing Scalable and Efficient APIs" seeks to empower developers with a nuanced comprehension of gRPC, transforming it into a vital tool in the API developer's arsenal. Whether you're configuring your development environment with the requisite tools and libraries or implementing secure, scalable APIs, this book provides the insights and guidance necessary for success.

By the book's end, you will be equipped with the knowledge and skills to harness the full potential of gRPC, creating APIs that not only meet today's requirements but are engineered to withstand the demands of

CONTENTS

the future software ecosystem.

CONTENTS

Chapter 1

Introduction to gRPC and High-Performance APIs

gRPC, developed by Google, is an open-source framework designed for high-performance communication in distributed systems. It leverages HTTP/2 for enhanced speed and efficiency, utilizing Protocol Buffers for effective data serialization. This chapter explores gRPC's capabilities in creating robust, scalable APIs, highlighting its advantages over traditional methods like REST. It sets the stage for understanding how gRPC facilitates modern application architectures, particularly in environments where low latency and high throughput are essential. By examining core components and communication patterns, this chapter provides foundational insights into why gRPC is becoming integral in contemporary software development.

1.1 The Evolution of Remote Procedure Calls

Remote Procedure Calls (RPC) have become a cornerstone in distributed systems, enabling communication between different software components across diverse networked environments. The evolution of RPC has been shaped by technological advancements, changes in application architecture, and the increasing need for efficient, scalable communication mechanisms. This section delves into the historical progress of RPC, providing insights into its transformation and setting the framework for modern protocols like gRPC.

RPC originated as a means to simplify the process of calling a function on a remote server by abstracting the complexities of network communication. The concept builds on the foundation of local procedure calls, allowing developers to execute program subroutines in different address spaces — a critical capability in distributed computing.

The earliest implementations of RPC can be traced back to the seminal paper by Andrew Birrell and Bruce Nelson at Xerox PARC in 1984, which formalized the RPC model for distributed systems. Their work laid the groundwork by introducing key concepts such as stub generation and marshalling, which automate the process of preparing and packaging the remote call and response data for network transmission.

```
/* Example of a simple RPC implementation using C */

typedef struct {
    int param1;
    char param2[256];
} Request;

typedef struct {
    int result;
} Response;

Response remote_procedure(Request req);
```

In this early stage, RPC systems had several limitations. They were tightly coupled with specific operating systems and hardware configurations, often running over simple transport protocols without any standardized model. The focus was primarily on achieving basic functionality rather than optimizing performance or scalability.

1.1. THE EVOLUTION OF REMOTE PROCEDURE CALLS

The introduction of the Open Network Computing (ONC) RPC by Sun Microsystems in the 1980s marked a significant step forward, offering a more standardized approach to RPC implementation. It utilized the eXternal Data Representation (XDR) for data serialization, which improved compatibility and cross-platform data exchange.

During this period, RPC mechanisms started to gain popularity in enterprise settings, primarily due to the increased demand for client-server architectures, where applications were being decomposed into logically separated layers. The ONC RPC capitalized on this trend and was incorporated into various UNIX operating systems, further establishing RPC as a viable communication model.

Subsequent developments introduced more robust and versatile RPC systems. The Distributed Computing Environment (DCE) RPC from the Open Software Foundation (OSF) introduced support for authentication and encryption, increasing the security of remote communications. DCE RPC addressed interoperability across different systems by supporting multiple transport protocols, making it suitable for diverse network environments.

As distributed systems grew more complex, the need for flexible and scalable solutions became apparent. Microsoft introduced the Component Object Model (COM) and later the Distributed Component Object Model (DCOM), extending the RPC capabilities to support object-oriented paradigms and network transparency over various protocol stacks.

With the advent of the Internet and the rise of web-based services, the Simple Object Access Protocol (SOAP) emerged as a widely used RPC framework. SOAP leveraged the standard HTTP protocol and XML for message format, making it firewall-friendly and web compatible. However, SOAP's verbosity and complexity often resulted in performance bottlenecks, setting the stage for the development of lighter alternatives.

```xml
<!-- Example of a SOAP message structure -->
<soap:Envelope xmlns:soap="http://www.w3.org/2003/05/soap-envelope">
  <soap:Body>
    <m:RemoteProcedure xmlns:m="http://www.example.org/remoteproc">
      <m:Param1>ExampleValue</m:Param1>
    </m:RemoteProcedure>
  </soap:Body>
</soap:Envelope>
```

The mid-2000s saw significant shifts fueled by the rise of microservices architectures and the need for highly efficient, low-latency communication protocols. REST (Representational State Transfer) architecture became predominant, emphasizing resource-oriented rather than action-oriented principles, which departs from traditional RPC. However, due to REST's dependency on HTTP/1.1, its performance in high-throughput scenarios was suboptimal.

Google's internal projects and the prevailing trends for lightweight, efficient communication led to the development of Protocol Buffers (Protobuf) by Google. Protobuf offered concise data serialization, serving as a catalyst for gRPC's development. gRPC emerged in 2015 as an open-source RPC platform designed to exploit the full capabilities of HTTP/2, providing multiplexed connections and binary data framing, which ensure high performance and low latency.

Central to gRPC's design is its support for multiple types of streaming: unary, server streaming, client streaming, and bidirectional streaming. This flexibility allows gRPC to adapt to a wide array of scenarios, such as real-time data processing or interactive client-server operations.

The introduction of gRPC was further bolstered by its compatibility with various programming languages and its extensive tooling support, which includes features like code generation and service discovery. gRPC's architecture is inherently suited for cloud-native environments, aligning well with the demands of microservices by providing efficient service-to-service communication.

The adoption of gRPC has also inspired the exploration of transport-level optimizations and efficiency improvements in other RPC frameworks, fostering an era of rapid evolution and innovation in distributed communication protocols. The broad support for OAuth and JWT within gRPC provides enhanced security and authentication, addressing prior concerns in cross-platform RPC implementations.

```
// gRPC service definition using Protocol Buffers
syntax = "proto3";

service RemoteService {
  rpc Unary(RequestMessage) returns (ResponseMessage);
  rpc StreamData (stream RequestMessage) returns (stream ResponseMessage);
}

message RequestMessage {
  int32 param1 = 1;
```

```
  string param2 = 2;
}
message ResponseMessage {
  int32 result = 1;
}
```

As a comprehensive and high-performance framework, gRPC continues to underscore the iterative nature of RPC development, reflecting ongoing trends in software engineering and system design. Its robust architecture exemplifies how integration of new technologies like HTTP/2 and Protocol Buffers can drive significant improvements in efficiency and performance, meeting the evolving requirements of modern distributed systems. The broad community adoption and support by tech giants attest to its importance and effectiveness in streamlining inter-service communication.

Thus, the trajectory of RPC reveals a consistent pattern of growth and refinement, promising continued innovation driven by emerging needs in distributed and cloud computing landscapes. The evolution from early bespoke systems to sophisticated platforms like gRPC illustrates the adaptability and enduring relevance of RPC in continually reshaping the landscape of remote computing.

1.2 Why gRPC for Modern Applications

With the proliferation of complex distributed systems and microservices architectures, the demand for efficient and scalable communication protocols has intensified. gRPC, developed by Google, addresses these challenges head-on by providing a robust framework for building high-performance APIs. The adoption of gRPC in modern applications hinges on several compelling advantages over traditional communication protocols like REST. This section elaborates on these benefits, highlights use cases, and illustrates how gRPC facilitates efficient software development.

The primary advantage of gRPC lies in its use of HTTP/2, a modern transport protocol that supersedes HTTP/1.1. HTTP/2 introduces multiplexed streams, header compression, and binary framing, drastically improving network efficiency and reducing latency. These features enable gRPC to support multiple concurrent requests over a single TCP connection, minimizing the overhead associated with establishing and tearing down connections.

```
/* Sample Proto file demonstrating a gRPC service */
syntax = "proto3";

service Greeter {
  rpc SayHello (HelloRequest) returns (HelloReply);
}

message HelloRequest {
  string name = 1;
}

message HelloReply {
  string message = 1;
}
```

HTTP/2's support for bidirectional streaming is another critical feature leveraged by gRPC. It permits both client-to-server and server-to-client streaming, making gRPC suitable for applications requiring real-time data exchange. The ability to stream data significantly enhances the responsiveness of applications, particularly in scenarios involving large data transfers or interactive client-server dynamics.

gRPC's reliance on Protocol Buffers (Protobuf) for data serialization is another factor contributing to its superior performance. Protobuf is a language-agnostic, binary serialization format known for its efficiency and compactness. Compared to JSON or XML, which are text-based and result in larger payload sizes, Protobuf produces smaller data packets and accelerates parsing and serialization processes. This efficiency is particularly advantageous in mobile and IoT environments, where bandwidth constraints and processing capabilities are limited.

Interoperability across multiple languages and platforms is a cornerstone feature of gRPC. By providing language-specific client and server libraries for many popular programming languages, gRPC simplifies cross-platform development, allowing teams to integrate services written in different languages seamlessly. This capability is vital in heterogeneous system architectures where diverse technologies coexist.

Another key strength of gRPC is its built-in support for deadline and timeout propagation, enhancing the reliability of distributed systems. Deadline propagation ensures that each RPC within a propagated context adheres to a specified duration limit, preventing indefinite re-

1.2. WHY GRPC FOR MODERN APPLICATIONS

source lockup in case of network failures or slow servers. This feature is crucial for maintaining robust system performance, particularly in microservices architectures with potentially lengthy call chains.

Service definition and automatic code generation further streamline development processes in gRPC. A single '.proto' file defines the entire service contract, specifying the RPC methods and associated message types. gRPC's tooling automatically generates client and server code stubs in various supported languages, eliminating boilerplate code and ensuring consistency across different components. This level of automation reduces development effort and errors, allowing developers to focus on implementing core business logic.

```
// Java implementation of a Greeter service using the generated code
public class GreeterImpl extends GreeterGrpc.GreeterImplBase {
    @Override
    public void sayHello(HelloRequest req, StreamObserver<HelloReply>
        responseObserver) {
      HelloReply reply = HelloReply.newBuilder().setMessage("Hello, " + req.
          getName()).build();
      responseObserver.onNext(reply);
      responseObserver.onCompleted();
    }
}
```

Security is another area where gRPC's capabilities excel. The integration with existing security frameworks such as TLS for transport security, along with support for authentication mechanisms like OAuth and JWT, ensures secure communication between clients and servers. This security model is essential in modern applications where sensitive data exchange is prevalent.

The role of gRPC in microservices and cloud-native applications cannot be overstated. In such architectures, services are distributed and deploy independently, necessitating a reliable and efficient communication layer. gRPC not only provides this utility but also integrates with service mesh technologies, such as Istio or Linkerd, which manage service-to-service interactions, policy enforcement, and observability. This integration makes gRPC a natural fit for Kubernetes-based deployments and containerized environments.

Real-world use cases of gRPC cement its reputation as a premier choice for modern applications. Large-scale applications that require scalable, low-latency communication, such as video streaming platforms, use gRPC to manage the high throughput of requests and data. Financial services leverage gRPC's security features and efficient data handling for secure transactions and interactive customer applications. Moreover, IoT applications, which often involve a multitude of devices with constrained resources, benefit from gRPC's compact binary serialization format, allowing for rapid and efficient data processing.

To illustrate, consider an example of a telemetry system that utilizes gRPC's streaming capabilities. IoT devices equipped with sensors generate data continuously and stream this information to a centralized server for analysis. The server processes incoming streams and applies data aggregation or transformation tasks to extract meaningful insights. By harnessing gRPC's bidirectional streaming, the server can also send commands or configuration changes back to the devices in real-time, optimizing the system's adaptability and responsiveness.

```
// Streaming telemetry service example via gRPC
service TelemetryService {
  rpc StreamData (stream TelemetryData) returns (stream ControlCommand);
}

message TelemetryData {
  int64 timestamp = 1;
  double temperature = 2;
  double humidity = 3;
}

message ControlCommand {
  string command = 1;
}
```

Such a system exemplifies how gRPC facilitates seamless, high-performance communication in distributed environments, augmenting the capabilities of IoT systems through enhanced flexibility and data interchange efficiency.

As applications evolve towards more distributed, containerized, and microservices-oriented architectures, gRPC stands out as an optimal RPC framework. Its design leverages HTTP/2's advanced features and Protobuf's compression strengths, providing a rich ecosystem for efficient communication. By supporting a diverse range of platforms and languages, automating service generation, and integrating seamlessly into modern cloud environments, gRPC empowers developers to construct scalable, maintainable, and high-performing APIs.

Consequently, understanding the nuances of gRPC and its application potential becomes increasingly crucial for software engineers striving to build robust modern applications. The adoption of gRPC in an array of industries underscores its versatility and effectiveness in addressing the performance and scalability challenges inherent in contemporary distributed systems. As the landscape of software design continues to shift, gRPC's role will likely expand, further reinforcing its position as an indispensable tool in the development toolkit for high-performance communication in distributed architectures.

1.3 Core Components of gRPC

At the heart of gRPC's functionality lie several core components that collectively enable efficient communication in distributed applications. Understanding these components is crucial for leveraging gRPC's capabilities to their fullest potential. This section provides a detailed examination of the fundamental elements that constitute the gRPC architecture, explaining their roles and interactions within the framework.

The gRPC framework revolves around the concept of services, defined using Protocol Buffers. Services in gRPC represent a collection of remote procedures that can be invoked by clients. The '.proto' file serves as the schema definition for these services, detailing the method signatures and the structured data types exchanged during remote calls.

```
/* Example of a gRPC service definition */
syntax = "proto3";

service UserService {
  rpc CreateUser (UserRequest) returns (UserResponse);
  rpc GetUser (UserId) returns (UserResponse);
  rpc UpdateUser (UserRequest) returns (UserResponse);
  rpc DeleteUser (UserId) returns (Empty);
}

message UserRequest {
  string name = 1;
  int32 age = 2;
}

message UserId {
  int64 id = 1;
}

message UserResponse {
  int64 id = 1;
  string status = 2;
}
```

```
message Empty {}
```

In the above example, the 'UserService' defines a set of operations related to user management. Each RPC is declared with its input and output message types, allowing robust service definition. Once a service is defined, gRPC's tooling generates client and server stubs in various programming languages, significantly reducing manual coding efforts.

The generated stubs act as the fundamental building blocks for implementing and consuming gRPC services. The server stub, which extends the core application logic, handles incoming RPC requests by executing the corresponding method implementations. Conversely, the client stub facilitates remote method invocation, abstracting away the intricacies of network communication.

The gRPC client and server can be configured with various options to optimize their behavior. These options include setting connection timeouts, retry policies, load balancing strategies, and authentication mechanisms. This configurability ensures a flexible deployment tailored to the specific needs of an application.

One of gRPC's distinctive features is its support for multiple communication patterns. These include:

- **Unary RPCs**: A single request is sent from the client, and a single response is returned from the server. This pattern is analogous to a standard function call.

  ```
  // Unary RPC call in a Java client
  UserId userId = UserId.newBuilder().setId(1234).build();
  UserResponse response = blockingStub.getUser(userId);
  ```

- **Server Streaming RPCs**: The client sends a single request to the server and receives a stream of responses. This pattern is useful for scenarios where a large dataset needs to be delivered in segments.

  ```
  // Server streaming call in a Java client
  UserId userId = UserId.newBuilder().setId(1234).build();
  Iterator<UserResponse> responses = blockingStub.streamUserData(userId);
  while (responses.hasNext()) {
      UserResponse response = responses.next();
      // Process each response
  }
  ```

1.3. CORE COMPONENTS OF GRPC

- **Client Streaming RPCs**: The client sends a stream of requests to the server, which returns a single response upon completing the request processing. This pattern is ideal for aggregating data from multiple inputs.

```java
// Client streaming call in a Java client
StreamObserver<UserResponse> responseObserver = new StreamObserver<
    UserResponse>() {
    @Override
    public void onNext(UserResponse value) {
        // Handle server response
    }

    @Override
    public void onError(Throwable t) {
        // Handle error
    }

    @Override
    public void onCompleted() {
        // Completion logic
    }
};
StreamObserver<UserRequest> requestObserver = asyncStub.uploadUserData(
    responseObserver);
for (UserRequest request : requests) {
    requestObserver.onNext(request);
}
requestObserver.onCompleted();
```

- **Bidirectional Streaming RPCs**: Both client and server send a stream of messages to each other. This pattern is highly interactive and supports real-time communication.

```java
// Bidirectional streaming call in a Java client
StreamObserver<UserRequest> requestObserver = asyncStub.chat(new
    StreamObserver<UserResponse>() {
    @Override
    public void onNext(UserResponse value) {
        // Handle response from server
    }

    @Override
    public void onError(Throwable t) {
        // Handle error
    }

    @Override
    public void onCompleted() {
        // Handle stream completion
    }
});

// Sending multiple requests from the client
```

CHAPTER 1. INTRODUCTION TO GRPC AND HIGH-PERFORMANCE APIS

```
requestObserver.onNext(UserRequest.newBuilder().setName("Alice").setAge(30).
    build());
requestObserver.onNext(UserRequest.newBuilder().setName("Bob").setAge(40).
    build());
requestObserver.onCompleted();
```

Communication patterns play a pivotal role in determining how data is exchanged between clients and servers, enhancing the adaptability of gRPC to fulfill diverse application requirements, from simple query-response interactions to complex real-time data flows.

Each gRPC method inherits default settings for response deadlines, but these can be tailored per call to uphold performance or client requirements. This fine-grained control over request handling makes gRPC particularly resilient in environments subjected to variable network conditions or high-latency connections.

Beyond communication patterns, gRPC supports advanced features that augment the framework's core components. Load balancing, for instance, is integral in distributing incoming client requests across multiple server instances to optimize resource usage and ensure high availability.

Authentication is addressed via token-based systems like OAuth2 or through mutual TLS, indelibly integrating security within communication channels. Built-in authentication mechanisms are essential for maintaining integrity and confidentiality within sensitive applications.

gRPC's extensibility is illustrated by its integration with systems like Prometheus and OpenTelemetry for observability, facilitating performance monitoring and diagnostics through telemetry data collection, exposing real-time insights into application behavior and enabling proactive troubleshooting.

While these features define the mechanics of gRPC, proactive best practices around service design and interaction patterns further elevate application architectures. Considerations such as encapsulating business logic within service methods, limiting the granularity of RPC calls to reduce chattiness, and implementing authentication and validation within application layers play significant roles in crafting coherent, efficient microservices.

The interoperability and toolchain support, epitomized through gRPC's autogenerated stubs, significantly bolster productivity, affording developers a comprehensive yet streamlined pathway for implementing services across diverse platforms.

gRPC's role in revolutionizing microservices interconnectivity cannot be overstated. It's a synthesis of performance, flexibility, and developer-friendly design that propels efficient service-to-service communication within modern distributed systems. Through its core components, gRPC forms a unified framework that catalyzes high-performing applications while resisting evolving demands.

By thoroughly grasping the architecture and capabilities of gRPC, developers can better harness its full potential, building resilient systems tailored to tackle the multifaceted challenges of contemporary software development. As a versatile RPC framework, gRPC epitomizes the essence of next-generation, high-throughput, low-latency communications, translating complex network dynamics into a coherent, manageable paradigm.

1.4 Synchronous vs Asynchronous Communication

The effectiveness of gRPC in sophisticated distributed systems is greatly influenced by its support for both synchronous and asynchronous communication styles. Understanding these two communication approaches is vital, as they underpin the design and operational efficiency of modern applications, particularly in environments characterized by high concurrency and diverse service interactions.

Synchronous communication in gRPC is akin to traditional method calls in procedural programming. In this model, the client sends a request to the server and waits, or blocks, for the server's response. The key advantage of synchronous communication is its straightforwardness, offering a predictable and accessible programming model where request-response cycles are tightly coupled. This coupling simplifies error handling and control flow management since responses, errors, and exception handling are immediate.

```
# Python example of synchronous gRPC call
import grpc
import user_pb2
import user_pb2_grpc

def run():
    with grpc.insecure_channel('localhost:50051') as channel:
        stub = user_pb2_grpc.UserServiceStub(channel)
        response = stub.GetUser(user_pb2.UserId(id=1))
        print("User status:", response.status)

if __name__ == '__main__':
    run()
```

While synchronous communication can be straightforward to implement, it introduces restrictions regarding scalability and responsiveness, particularly in high-latency networks or when handling long-running operations. Because the client is blocked until the response is received, the application's concurrency is limited, potentially leading to idle waiting times and increased system inefficiencies.

Conversely, asynchronous communication in gRPC decouples the request initiation from the response processing. The client sends a request to the server but continues executing other operations without waiting for the response. When the server completes processing, it delivers the response to the client through a callback mechanism or a similar non-blocking construct.

```
# Python example of asynchronous gRPC call
import grpc
import user_pb2
import user_pb2_grpc

def handle_response(future):
    try:
        response = future.result()
        print("Asynchronous user status:", response.status)
    except Exception as e:
        print("Error:", e)

def run():
    channel = grpc.insecure_channel('localhost:50051')
    stub = user_pb2_grpc.UserServiceStub(channel)
    future = stub.GetUser.future(user_pb2.UserId(id=1))
    future.add_done_callback(handle_response)
    # Continue doing other operations
    # ...

if __name__ == '__main__':
    run()
```

1.4. SYNCHRONOUS VS ASYNCHRONOUS COMMUNICATION

By allowing asynchronous communication, gRPC maximizes application responsiveness and throughput, facilitating concurrent processing of multiple requests and freeing resources to handle additional tasks. This model aligns well with applications where response times are variable or hard to predict, such as those accessing remote resources or relying on compute-intensive operations.

The choice between synchronous and asynchronous communication should be informed by the specific requirements and constraints of the application. Factors such as the expected workload, concurrency demands, latency tolerance, and the complexity of handling backpressure and retries all influence the decision.

Utilizing asynchronous communication can be particularly beneficial in microservices architectures where various services interact concurrently and need to process a high volume of requests efficiently. In such settings, service interactions can exploit non-blocking IO operations, facilitating horizontal scaling and resource optimization.

gRPC's compatibility with various programming languages further enhances its support for asynchronous operations, offering extensive libraries and concurrency primitives native to specific programming environments. Languages like Java utilize 'CompletableFuture', while Python makes use of 'asyncio' and related constructs to implement asynchronous behavior, empowering seamless integration with existing systems and frameworks.

```java
// Java example of asynchronous gRPC call
ManagedChannel channel = ManagedChannelBuilder.forTarget("localhost:50051").
    usePlaintext().build();
UserServiceGrpc.UserServiceFutureStub futureStub = UserServiceGrpc.newFutureStub
    (channel);

UserId userId = UserId.newBuilder().setId(1).build();

ListenableFuture<UserResponse> futureResponse = futureStub.getUser(userId);

futureResponse.addListener(() -> {
    try {
        UserResponse response = futureResponse.get();
        System.out.println("Asynchronous user status: " + response.getStatus());
    } catch (Exception e) {
        System.err.println("Error: " + e.getMessage());
    }
}, MoreExecutors.directExecutor());

// Additional asynchronous operations can continue here
```

CHAPTER 1. INTRODUCTION TO GRPC AND HIGH-PERFORMANCE APIS

While asynchronous communication promotes enhanced utilization and performance, it also necessitates attention to synchronization, error handling, and potential callback hells, especially in large-scale distributed systems. Production-grade systems often integrate patterns like futures, promises, or reactors to manage these intricacies, achieving scalability without sacrificing reliability and maintainability.

gRPC supports a rich ecosystem that includes sophisticated frameworks and libraries, such as reactive extensions or task management libraries, which provide comprehensive abstractions to manage asynchronous interactions effectively. These tools ensure visibility and control over the execution lifecycle of asynchronous operations, aiding in the orchestration of complex workflows.

In practice, combining synchronous and asynchronous communication methods within the same architecture often yields optimal results. Given diverse service dependencies and interaction patterns, selectively applying each communication model where they fit best can enhance overall application performance. For example, synchronous calls might be preferred for tightly coupled, performance-critical service interactions, while asynchronous calls are suitable for user-facing or batch-processing operations.

A hybrid approach also helps mitigate some intrinsic trade-offs within synchronous and asynchronous paradigms, distributing workloads effectively across system components and maximizing both responsiveness and processing capacity.

Asynchronous techniques inherently align with modern paradigms such as event-driven architectures and serverless computing, supporting stateless interactions and elastic scaling requirements. gRPC's libration of such patterns further reinforces its support for building resilient and high-performing systems, directing innovation towards service responsiveness and elasticity.

Service orchestration platforms, such as Kubernetes, facilitate the effective dissemination of network traffic using asynchronous processing hooks and configurations, highlighting the harmony between gRPC's architectural agility and modern cloud ecosystems.

In summary, mastery of synchronous and asynchronous communication paradigms in gRPC is indispensable for designing applications that efficiently address the demands of modern distributed systems. gRPC's allowances for both paradigms grant unparalleled flexibility in configuring service interactions, laying the groundwork for assemblies that balance reliability, scalability, and performance adeptly. This exploration of communication models arms developers with the insights needed for prudent decision-making, enabling them to harness gRPC's full breadth of capabilities in sophisticated environments.

1.5 gRPC in the Ecosystem

gRPC has emerged as a pivotal framework in the landscape of modern application development, seamlessly integrating into today's ecosystems characterized by microservices, cloud-native architectures, and application decoupling. Its role within these environments is underpinned by its design for high-performance, low-latency communication and its ability to streamline service-to-service interactions. Understanding how gRPC fits into this broader ecosystem is essential for leveraging its strengths to build scalable, resilient, and maintainable distributed systems.

Central to gRPC's integration into the modern software ecosystem is its compatibility with microservices architectures. In such environments, applications are decomposed into finer-grained services, each handling specific business logic and communicating over network boundaries. gRPC's high-throughput, low-latency capabilities make it an ideal choice for these internal service communications, where minimizing overhead is crucial for maintaining system responsiveness and efficiency.

Microservices architectures are often characterized by a service mesh, an infrastructure layer that facilitates service-to-service communication, security, and observability. gRPC integrates seamlessly with popular service mesh solutions such as Istio, Linkerd, and Consul, which provide added functionalities like traffic management, load balancing, and telemetry.

Service mesh frameworks typically use sidecar proxy patterns, injecting proxies like Envoy alongside each service instance. These proxies handle all network traffic, enabling features such as automatic retries, fault injection, and comprehensive logging. gRPC's compatibility with these proxies ensures that organizations can leverage advanced service management features while benefiting from gRPC's streamlined RPC model.

```
# Example of deploying a gRPC service with Istio in Kubernetes
kubectl apply -f user-service.yaml
kubectl apply -f istio-gateway.yaml
```

gRPC's role in cloud ecosystems extends beyond microservices to encompass serverless computing, another pervasive trend in modern development. Serverless platforms such as AWS Lambda, Google Cloud Functions, and Azure Functions provide event-driven, stateless execution environments where resources are dynamically allocated in response to incoming events.

Within serverless paradigms, continuous, efficient invocation of functions is essential, which aligns with gRPC's ability to provide fast communication and lightweight data exchange through its Protocol Buffers serialization. Serverless functions can be triggered by gRPC-based event sources, enabling responsive systems that scale according to workload demands while keeping costs in check.

Moreover, the utility of gRPC extends into container orchestration systems, particularly Kubernetes, the de facto standard for deploying containerized applications. Kubernetes inherently supports extensive service discovery mechanisms, allowing gRPC services to announce themselves and discover other services without requiring manual configuration.

```
# Kubernetes service definition for a gRPC server
apiVersion: v1
kind: Service
metadata:
  name: user-service
spec:
  selector:
    app: user-service
  ports:
    - protocol: TCP
      port: 50051
      targetPort: 50051
```

The confluence of gRPC and Kubernetes facilitates powerful patterns such as rolling updates, canary deployments, and efficient scaling. These patterns are critical for managing the lifecycle of microservices

1.5. GRPC IN THE ECOSYSTEM

in production, ensuring that gRPC services can be evolved and scaled according to incoming demand without downtime.

In data-centric applications, gRPC's impact is further amplified by its compatibility with big data and machine learning platforms. Data pipelines and distributed processing frameworks often require robust communication protocols to manage data flow across diverse components, all of which demand high throughput and low latency.

Tools and frameworks like Apache Kafka, Apache Hadoop, and TensorFlow can rely on gRPC for their RPC needs, enabling a seamless exchange of data and model artifacts. This compatibility allows developers to create complex data-driven workflows where model training, serving, and monitoring are integrated into a cohesive system using gRPC for intercommunication.

Security is another critical aspect where gRPC asserts its efficacy in the ecosystem. Distributed systems require stringent security measures to authenticate and authorize users and services while maintaining data integrity across communication channels. gRPC supports Transport Layer Security (TLS) and allows integration with advanced identity and access management solutions like OAuth2 and JWT, fortifying service interactions.

Security policies and identity providers are often managed through identity-as-a-service platforms or integrated within service meshes, allowing flexible service-to-service authentication and encryption management. This interoperation ensures robust protection for sensitive data traversing gRPC calls.

On the tooling and development front, gRPC's rich ecosystem of libraries and frameworks enhances the efficiency of software development workflows. gRPC's language support encompasses major programming environments, affording developers the flexibility to orchestrate cross-language communication without friction.

Integration with development tools like Visual Studio Code, IntelliJ IDEA, and Docker streamlines the software delivery pipeline, enabling code testing, debugging, and deployment processes. Code generation utilities within gRPC provide necessary stubs and scaffolding, simplifying implementation across client and server components.

Furthermore, observability tools such as Prometheus, Grafana, and

OpenTelemetry provide invaluable insights into gRPC application performance. The ability to track metrics, trace requests, and monitor system health empowers teams to identify and rectify performance bottlenecks proactively.

The intersection of gRPC with DevOps practices fosters enhanced CI/CD pipelines, emphasizing automation, testing, and reliable delivery. These integrations ensure that gRPC services can be updated and deployed rapidly, adapting to evolving business needs with minimal risk and maximum consistency.

```
Pipeline:
  - Build: Compile gRPC service binaries
  - Test: Run unit and integration tests on gRPC endpoints
  - Package: Create Docker images of gRPC service
  - Deploy: Use Kubernetes for canary or blue-green deployments
  - Monitor: Track service performance with Prometheus
```

To maximize gRPC's potential, organizations need to adopt best practices throughout the lifecycle of their services. These best practices may include employing robust API versioning strategies, implementing circuit breaker patterns within service communication flows, and ensuring backward and forward compatibility across evolving service definitions.

gRPC's integration within the ecosystem is a manifestation of its adaptability, enabling it to transcend traditional boundaries of remote procedure calls. Its relevance in contemporary architectures is characterized by its synergy with cloud, container, and DevOps trends, establishing itself as a vital component in the collaborative interplay of various technologies.

The facilitation of cohesive service interactions underscores gRPC's significance in fostering scalable and performant systems, crucial for responding to the dynamic demands of today's digital enterprises. As application ecosystems continue to evolve, gRPC's ongoing development and community support are likely to amplify its role, continuing to redefine the ways distributed systems engage in effective and reliable communication.

By fostering understanding and expertise in leveraging gRPC within the ecosystem, developers and architects will find themselves well-equipped to navigate the complexities of modern cloud-native environments, driving innovation and delivering high-value outcomes in their strategic technological initiatives. As the foundation of many forward-thinking architectures, gRPC signifies not only an advancement in RPC protocols but a paradigm shift in how systems interoperate among the vast networks of an interconnected world.

1.6 Performance Benefits of gRPC

The efficiency and performance of communication protocols play a crucial role in the architecture of modern software systems, particularly those involving distributed components and microservices. gRPC, an open-source framework developed by Google, is designed to offer significant performance advantages over traditional communication methods like REST. This section explores the technical elements contributing to gRPC's high performance and examines real-world applications where these benefits become most apparent.

A fundamental factor in the performance superiority of gRPC is its use of HTTP/2, the latest version of the HTTP protocol. HTTP/2 introduces several enhancements over HTTP/1.1, notably multiplexing, header compression, and stream prioritization, each of which significantly impacts the efficiency of data transmission.

Multiplexing in HTTP/2 allows multiple concurrent requests and responses to be sent over a single TCP connection. This reduces latency and improves throughput by eliminating the need to establish multiple connections for parallel data streams. As a result, gRPC can provide robust and responsive communication even in high-load scenarios where many services interact simultaneously.

Header compression further enhances performance by reducing the overhead of HTTP headers. With HTTP/1.1, verbose headers could contribute significantly to the size of HTTP requests and responses, especially in RESTful architectures where frequent, repetitive exchanges occur. HTTP/2 employs HPACK compression to optimize this, compressing header data and thereby minimizing bandwidth usage. In gRPC, this translates to quicker transmissions and reduced latency, making it well-suited for bandwidth-constrained environments or mobile networks.

Stream prioritization and flow control mechanisms in HTTP/2 also allow gRPC applications to specify the importance and resources allocated to individual streams. This feature is particularly useful in systems that need to manage complex data workflows or prioritize critical operations, ensuring optimal utilization of available network resources.

Another core aspect of gRPC's performance edge is its use of Protocol Buffers (Protobuf) for data serialization. Protobuf is a lightweight, efficient binary serialization format that offers several advantages over traditional text-based formats like JSON or XML. Binary serialization results in smaller message sizes and faster parsing, which enhance overall throughput and reduce the processing load on client and server systems.

```
# Protobuf message example for a gRPC service
syntax = "proto3";

message UserProfile {
  int32 id = 1;
  string name = 2;
  string email = 3;
}

message UserProfileRequest {
  int32 user_id = 1;
}

message UserProfileResponse {
  UserProfile profile = 1;
}
```

The serialization efficiency offered by Protobuf makes gRPC exceptionally well-suited for performance-sensitive applications, such as those in high-frequency trading, gaming, and real-time analytics. These fields demand rapid data processing and minimal latency to deliver timely, actionable outcomes.

In addition to HTTP/2 and Protobuf, gRPC supports efficient client and server streaming communication patterns. Streaming allows for continuous data flow between clients and servers, a marked departure from the strictly unidirectional request-response model of traditional API calls. This capability is integral in scenarios involving real-time data exchange, such as video conferencing or telemetry systems, where data is sent and received continuously over the network.

```
// Java example showing server streaming in gRPC
UserProfileRequest request = UserProfileRequest.newBuilder().setUserId(1).build();
```

1.6. PERFORMANCE BENEFITS OF GRPC

```
Iterator<UserProfileResponse> responses = blockingStub.getUserProfileStream(
    request);

while (responses.hasNext()) {
  UserProfileResponse response = responses.next();
  // Process each response as it arrives
}
```

The stream-based model not only improves latency and responsiveness but also empowers developers to handle large datasets efficiently without overwhelming the client or server resources. By processing data incrementally and asynchronously, gRPC achieves superior performance and adaptability across a wide range of application domains.

In microservices architectures, where numerous services communicate rapidly and frequently, minimizing network latency and maximizing throughput are paramount for maintaining high responsiveness. gRPC's performance capabilities excel in such environments, enabling efficient inter-service communication and scaling of services under variable loads.

Organizations deploying gRPC often report significant improvements in application performance over their previous REST-based architectures, citing faster data interchange, reduced infrastructure cost due to lower data bandwidth consumption, and decreased latency. For instance, companies engaged in the IoT domain have leveraged gRPC's compact message format and efficient streaming to manage vast sensor networks while maintaining swift and reliable data collection and analysis.

Moreover, gRPC's asynchronous capabilities complement its performance benefits by further enhancing resource utilization. Asynchronous communication facilitates the overlap of I/O operations with computation tasks, reducing idle waiting times and exploiting concurrency to accelerate processing pipelines.

The combination of these features ensures that gRPC not only meets the performance requirements of modern applications but often surpasses them, making it an ideal candidate for use cases where speed and efficiency are critical.

Compelling examples of gRPC's employment can be found in scenarios such as:

- Film Streaming Services: gRPC efficiently handles the delivery of video streams and related metadata to millions of users through its server-streaming features, supporting high-quality playback with reduced load latency.

- Real-time Financial Systems: Utilized in trading platforms for securing instant communication among agents, brokers, and markets, where performance dictates the ability to execute timely transactions.

- Online Multiplayer Games: gRPC powers real-time data exchange and rapid responses between game servers and clients, enhancing the gaming experience through lower latencies and richer interactions.

Furthermore, gRPC's performance optimization through settings adjustment, such as gRPC channel parameters, assists developers in fine-tuning connections to enhance network performance further. This fine-granularity control involves tuning settings like timeouts, message sizes, and retry policies to suit specific workloads.

```
// Java configuration of gRPC channel for performance tuning
ManagedChannel channel = ManagedChannelBuilder.forAddress("localhost", 50051)
    .maxInboundMessageSize(10485760) // 10 MB
    .usePlaintext()
    .build();
```

The ability to analyze and optimize these layers allows organizations to cultivate significant gains in performance, achieving the utmost efficiency from the extensive infrastructure investments involved in global-scale software operations.

In summary, gRPC presents a comprehensive solution that delivers performance gains essential for modern distributed systems. By capitalizing on advancements like HTTP/2 and Protobuf, alongside versatile streaming features, gRPC provides unparalleled capabilities for building responsive and scalable applications. Adopting gRPC in systems that require high throughput, low latency, and efficient data interchange equips organizations to meet contemporary challenges, driving technological innovation and delivering value through expertly executed software architectures.

Chapter 2

Setting Up Your Development Environment

This chapter provides a step-by-step guide to establishing a development environment optimized for gRPC applications. It covers the selection of appropriate tools and integrated development environments (IDEs), installation of the Protocol Buffers compiler, and setting up gRPC libraries for various programming languages. Additionally, it walks through creating a basic gRPC project, configuring necessary environment variables, and offers solutions to common setup-related issues. By the end of this chapter, readers will be equipped with a fully functional gRPC development setup, ready for building high-performance APIs.

2.1 Choosing the Right Tools and IDE

Selecting the appropriate tools and Integrated Development Environments (IDEs) is critical for the efficient development of gRPC applications. The landscape of tools and IDEs that cater to various programming languages is vast, necessitating a discerning approach to match your development needs. This section delves into the considerations, options, and best practices for choosing the tools and IDEs that will support your gRPC development journey.

Importance of Choosing the Right Tools The integration of the right tools impacts productivity, code quality, and maintainability of gRPC services. Tools and IDEs should facilitate protocol buffer compatibility, support syntax highlighting, offer auto-completion, and integrate debugging tools. Emphasis on productivity features like integrated command-line interfaces, version control systems, and containerization support are crucial in selecting a toolchain that matches modern development practices.

Criteria for Selecting an IDE When selecting an IDE for gRPC application development, consider the following criteria:

- **Language Support:** Ensure the IDE supports the programming languages you intend to use. Popular languages for gRPC services include Go, Java, Python, C++, and Node.js.

- **Plugin Ecosystem:** A robust plugin ecosystem enhances the IDE's capabilities, allowing integration with gRPC libraries, linters, and formatters.

- **Debugging Tools:** Efficient debugging tools that are integrated into the IDE are crucial for identifying and resolving issues.

- **Performance and Scalability:** The IDE should handle large projects efficiently, maintaining responsiveness.

- **Extensibility:** Functional flexibility to add modules and extensions as project requirements evolve.

Popular IDEs for gRPC Development

1. **Visual Studio Code** Visual Studio Code (VS Code) provides a lightweight, yet powerful environment for editing code. It is highly extensible with a vast marketplace of extensions to enhance its functionality. For gRPC development, consider the following extensions:

```
$ code --install-extension grpc.vscode-grpc-syntax # gRPC Syntax Highlighting
$ code --install-extension xaver.clang-format # Formatter for C++ and Python
$ code --install-extension ms-vscode.cpptools # C++ IntelliSense
```

These extensions enable support for protocol buffer syntax highlighting, gRPC code generation, and language-specific features critical for gRPC services.

2. **IntelliJ IDEA** IntelliJ IDEA is a comprehensive IDE known for its intelligent code completion, coding assistance, and framework support. It supports a plethora of languages and has rich built-in features for gRPC application development:

- **Protocol Buffer Support:** Available plugins enhance protocol buffer files editing capabilities.
- **Integrated Version Control:** Support for Git, SVN and others.
- **Configurable Code Styles:** Allows for enforcement of coding standards.

To work with IntelliJ IDEA, the Protocol Buffers and gRPC plugins offer the required functionalities for compiling protobuf files:

```
# Activating plugins
Go to File > Settings > Plugins > Browse Repositories > Install 'Protobuf Support'
```

3. **PyCharm** PyCharm, particularly useful for Python gRPC development, offers features that support rapid application development:

- **Auto-completion and Refactoring:** Streamlines editing of Python code.
- **Virtual Environment Management:** PyCharm seamlessly manages dependencies.

- **Integrated Test Runner:** For unit testing Python scripts related to gRPC.

To enable gRPC support in PyCharm, developers should install the 'grpcio-tools' Python package for compiling '.proto' files to Python classes:

```
$ pip install grpcio grpcio-tools # gRPC packages for Python
```

Command-Line Tools for gRPC Development While IDEs provide a graphical interface and additional tooling, command-line tools remain essential for many tasks in development. They offer automation capabilities and are vital components of continuous integration pipelines.

Protocol Buffers Compiler (protoc) The Protocol Buffers compiler, 'protoc', is a command-line tool that is paramount in generating code for gRPC:

```
# Generate Python classes from .proto file
$ protoc --proto_path=. --python_out=. example.proto

# Generate Go classes from .proto file
$ protoc --proto_path=. --go_out=. --go-grpc_out=. example.proto
```

Incorporating 'protoc' in automated scripts and build tools such as 'Make' further streamlines the development process.

gRPC Command Line Interface (CLI) The gRPC CLI tool facilitates interaction with gRPC servers, enabling developers to test services independently of the client-side application. It can be used to make calls to gRPC services directly from the command line:

```
# Call a method on the gRPC service
$ grpc_cli call localhost:50051 MyService.MyMethod 'name: "John"'
```

Version Control and Continuous Integration Tools Modern development workflows benefit significantly from version control and continuous integration (CI) tools. Version control systems such as Git allow for managing code changes effectively, providing collaboration capabilities suitable for distributed teams. Integration of CI tools such as Jenkins, Travis CI, or GitHub Actions ensures constant monitoring and validation of the codebase.

Integrating gRPC Code Generation in CI Automating the gRPC code generation as part of the CI process reduces the manual overhead and ensures consistency across builds. Scripts to invoke 'protoc' can be included in CI configuration files.

```
# Sample Travis CI configuration for a Python project
language: python
install:
  - pip install grpcio grpcio-tools
script:
  - protoc --proto_path=. --python_out=. example.proto
  - pytest test/
```

Containerization and Deployment Tools In addition to development tools, understanding containerization and deployment systems is integral to modern gRPC applications. Using Docker, Kubernetes, or similar tools can enhance the deployment process, ensuring consistent environments across development and production systems.

Docker for gRPC Applications Docker provides an isolated environment for building and running gRPC services, becoming a preferred choice for containerization:

```
# Dockerfile for a Python gRPC application
FROM python:3.8-slim

WORKDIR /app
COPY . /app

RUN pip install grpcio grpcio-tools

ENTRYPOINT ["python", "my_grpc_server.py"]
```

Conclusion without Explicit Marker A comprehensive development environment with the right tools and IDE selection significantly impacts the efficiency of building and maintaining gRPC applications. Supported by the flexibility and functionality of command-line utilities, version control, CI/CD integration, and containerization, developers can effectively deliver high-performance, scalable gRPC services. The continuous evolution of these tools and technologies promises ongoing improvements, competency, and adaptation to the complexities and demands of distributed system architectures.

2.2 Installing Protocol Buffers Compiler

The Protocol Buffers compiler, protoc, is a cornerstone tool for developers working on gRPC services. It serves as the main mechanism to transform Protocol Buffers (.proto) files into source code that can be compiled into applications across various programming languages. This section details the installation process for protoc across different operating systems, ensuring developers are equipped with the necessary setup to maximize their gRPC development efficiency.

Overview of Protocol Buffers Protocol Buffers, a language-neutral, platform-neutral extensible mechanism for serializing structured data, is fundamental for gRPC. Defined by Google, Protocol Buffers are utilized to define data structure schemas in .proto files. The protoc compiler reads these schema files and generates data-access classes in the developer's preferred language.

Supported Languages protoc supports code generation for several languages, including:

- C++
- Java
- Python
- Go
- C#
- JavaScript

2.2. INSTALLING PROTOCOL BUFFERS COMPILER

Developers can generate code for any of these languages by specifying the appropriate out directory and language plugin during invocation.

Installation on Windows For users on the Windows platform, installation of protoc can be achieved through both manual download and package managers like Chocolatey.

Manual Installation

- **Download the Compiler:**

    Go to the official Protocol Buffers release page on GitHub, https://github.com/protocolbuffers/protobuf/releases, and download the latest protoc binary suitable for Windows (e.g., protoc-21.0-win64.zip).

- **Extract and Set Environment Variables:**

    Extract the downloaded zip file into a directory such as C:\Program Files\protoc\bin. To ensure protoc is available system-wide, update the PATH environment variable:

    ```
    setx PATH "%PATH%;C:\Program Files\protoc\bin"
    ```

Installation via Chocolatey An alternative is using Chocolatey, a trusted package manager for Windows:

```
choco install protoc
```

Installation on macOS macOS users can install protoc via Homebrew, a package manager that simplifies the installation process significantly.

Installation via Homebrew

- **Install Homebrew:**

    If Homebrew is not already installed, execute the following command in the terminal:

```
/bin/bash -c "$(curl -fsSL https://raw.githubusercontent.com/Homebrew/
install/HEAD/install.sh)"
```

- **Install Protocol Buffers:**

  With Homebrew installed, simply run:

  ```
  brew install protobuf
  ```

The command installs protoc along with any necessary dependencies.

Verification of Installation Verify that protoc has been installed correctly by running:

```
protoc --version
```

The above command should output the version number, confirming proper installation.

Installation on Linux Linux systems, with their wide variety of distributions, offer multiple ways to install protoc, from package managers to building from source.

Installation via APT (Ubuntu/Debian) Ubuntu and Debian users can install protoc using apt:

```
sudo apt update
sudo apt install -y protobuf-compiler
```

Installation via Yum/DNF (CentOS/Red Hat/Fedora) For CentOS, Red Hat, and Fedora distributions, the dnf package manager simplifies installation:

```
sudo dnf install -y protobuf-compiler
```

In systems that still utilize yum:

```
sudo yum install -y protobuf-compiler
```

2.2. INSTALLING PROTOCOL BUFFERS COMPILER

Building from Source In scenarios where package managers do not provide the required version, building protoc from source is an alternative:

- **Install Dependencies:**

    Ensure essential development tools and libraries are in place:

    ```
    sudo apt update
    sudo apt install -y autoconf automake libtool curl make g++
    ```

- **Clone the Repository:**

    Download the Protocol Buffers source code from GitHub:

    ```
    git clone https://github.com/protocolbuffers/protobuf.git
    cd protobuf
    git submodule update --init --recursive
    ```

- **Compile and Install:**

    Run the following commands to compile and install protoc:

    ```
    ./autogen.sh
    ./configure
    make
    make check
    sudo make install
    sudo ldconfig # refresh shared library cache
    ```

This sequence installs the protoc binary on the system, making it accessible via the command line.

Cross-Platform Considerations Developers who aim for cross-platform compatibility should ensure consistent protoc versions across all environments to mitigate potential discrepancies in code generation and dependent libraries. Using containerization with images that come pre-packaged with protoc can resolve such issues, ensuring consistency across development environments.

Integration with IDEs After installation, protoc should be integrated with IDEs for a streamlined development experience. Many

IDEs, such as IntelliJ IDEA and VS Code, have plugins that can automatically invoke protoc during build processes. These integrations permit efficient handling of Protocol Buffers within your IDE's framework, often allowing customization through build tools like Gradle, Maven, Make, or Ninja.

Here is an example configuring protoc with Gradle in a Java project:

```
plugins {
    id 'java'
    id 'com.google.protobuf' version '0.8.12'
}

protobuf {
    protoc {
        artifact = "com.google.protobuf:protoc:3.12.2"
    }
    generateProtoTasks {
        all().each { task ->
            task.builtins {
                remove java
            }
            task.plugins {
                grpc {}
            }
        }
    }
}

sourceSets {
    main {
        proto {
            srcDir 'src/main/proto'
        }
    }
}
```

This build script automates the code generation for Protocol Buffers and gRPC stubs as part of the build process.

Automating Using Docker For developers using Docker, installing protoc in an image enhances reproducibility. Here's a Dockerfile setting up protoc for a Node.js environment:

```
FROM node:14

RUN apt-get update && \
    apt-get install -y unzip && \
    apt-get install -y protobuf-compiler

WORKDIR /app
```

2.3. SETTING UP GRPC LIBRARIES

```
COPY . .
RUN npm install
ENTRYPOINT ["node", "server.js"]
```

Such Docker setups are ideal for continuous integration and deployment pipelines, offering a repeatable and reliable environment.

Potential Issues and Troubleshooting Although installations are generally straightforward, occasionally, developers might encounter issues:

- **Path Issues:** Ensure protoc is added to the system PATH, allowing execution from any directory.

- **Version Mismatches:** Verify that the protoc compiler version corresponds with the Protocol Buffers library version used in your application.

- **Permission Denied Errors:** On Unix-based systems, ensure the executable permissions are correctly set.

- **Dependency Errors:** When building from source, ensure all required dependencies are correctly installed and available.

Successful installation and configuration of the Protocol Buffers compiler are pivotal for the smooth operation of gRPC service development. The encompassing setup ensures a solid foundation for crafting efficient data serialization schemes, vital to advanced inter-service communications.

2.3 Setting Up gRPC Libraries

The effective utilization of gRPC in modern application development requires the correct setup and installation of gRPC libraries, which serve as the cornerstone for implementing remote procedure calls between different services over the network. This section provides an exhaustive look into the setup process for gRPC libraries across multiple programming languages, ensuring seamless integration within diverse development environments.

Understanding gRPC Libraries gRPC is a high-performance, open-source universal remote procedure call (RPC) framework developed by Google. It uses HTTP/2 for transport, Protocol Buffers as the interface description language, and provides features such as authentication, load balancing, and pluggable support for health checks, tracing, and metrics collection. For each supported language, gRPC provides a library that developers can leverage to implement client and server code, handle requests, and manage connections.

Key Languages Supported While gRPC can theoretically be implemented in many programming languages, core support has been established for:

- Go
- Java
- Python
- C++
- Node.js
- C#
- Ruby
- PHP

Each of these languages has its own specific library setup, often with additional dependencies and version restrictions to consider.

Setting Up gRPC for Go The Go programming language is well-suited to leverage gRPC's lightweight and high-performance characteristics. Here is the comprehensive guide to setting up gRPC for Go:

2.3. SETTING UP GRPC LIBRARIES

Installation 1. **Install Go:**

If Go is not already installed, download and install it from the Go official website: https://golang.org/dl/.

2. **Set Up Environment:**

Add Go binary and source directories to your PATH:

```
export PATH=$PATH:/usr/local/go/bin
export GOPATH=$HOME/go
```

3. **Install gRPC and Protocol Buffers:**

Go modules provide a straightforward approach to managing dependencies. Initialize your project:

```
mkdir -p $GOPATH/src/my-grpc-app
cd $GOPATH/src/my-grpc-app
go mod init my-grpc-app
```

Install the necessary gRPC modules:

```
go get google.golang.org/grpc
go get google.golang.org/protobuf
```

4. **Generate Go Code from .proto Files:**

Assuming protoc and the protoc-gen-go plugin are installed, execute:

```
protoc --go_out=plugins=grpc:. *.proto
```

Setting Up gRPC for Java The Java gRPC library facilitates the development of highly performant and scalable gRPC services.

Installation and Configuration 1. **Environment Setup:**

Ensure Java Development Kit (JDK) 8 or later is installed:

```
java -version
```

If necessary, download the JDK from https://www.oracle.com/java/technologies/javase-jdk11-downloads.html or use sdkman:

```
sdk install java 11.0.10-open
```

2. **Using Maven or Gradle**

Integrating gRPC library for Java in Maven:

Add the following dependencies in pom.xml:

```
<dependency>
    <groupId>io.grpc</groupId>
    <artifactId>grpc-netty-shaded</artifactId>
    <version>1.33.0</version>
</dependency>
<dependency>
    <groupId>io.grpc</groupId>
    <artifactId>grpc-protobuf</artifactId>
    <version>1.33.0</version>
</dependency>
<dependency>
    <groupId>io.grpc</groupId>
    <artifactId>grpc-stub</artifactId>
    <version>1.33.0</version>
</dependency>
```

For Gradle projects, amend the build.gradle by including:

```
implementation 'io.grpc:grpc-netty-shaded:1.33.0'
implementation 'io.grpc:grpc-protobuf:1.33.0'
implementation 'io.grpc:grpc-stub:1.33.0'
```

3. **Generate Java Code from .proto Files:**

Execute the following Maven command:

```
mvn protobuf:compile
mvn protobuf:compile-custom
```

Setting Up gRPC for Python   Python's gRPC is best utilized for its simplicity and rapid development capabilities.

Environment Preparation   Ensure Python 3 is installed, and virtual environments are employed to manage dependencies efficiently:

```
python3 -m venv grpc-env
source grpc-env/bin/activate
```

Installing gRPC Libraries   Install the gRPC tools as follows:

```
pip install grpcio
pip install grpcio-tools
```

2.3. SETTING UP GRPC LIBRARIES

Compiling Protocol Buffers Compile .proto files to Python modules:

```
python -m grpc_tools.protoc -I. --python_out=. --grpc_python_out=. my_service.
    proto
```

Setting Up gRPC for C++ C++ offers perhaps the most performance-centric gRPC library setup, suitable for high-load, low-latency conditions.

Installation Steps 1. **Install Prerequisites:**

Ensure cmake, git, build-essential, and autoconf are in place:

```
sudo apt update
sudo apt install -y build-essential autoconf libtool pkg-config
```

2. **Building from Source**

Clone the gRPC repository:

```
git clone -b $(curl -L https://grpc.io/release) https://github.com/grpc/grpc
cd grpc
git submodule update --init
```

Compile gRPC and Protocol Buffers:

```
make
sudo make install
```

3. **Generate C++ Code**

Using protoc, run the following:

```
protoc -I=. --cpp_out=. --grpc_out=. --plugin=protoc-gen-grpc=/usr/local/bin/
    grpc_cpp_plugin my_file.proto
```

Setting Up gRPC for Node.js Node.js' asynchronous nature makes it a strong candidate for building scalable network applications with gRPC.

Installation Process 1. **Preparation:**

Install Node.js and npm if not already present:

```
curl -fsSL https://deb.nodesource.com/setup_16.x | sudo -E bash -
sudo apt-get install -y nodejs
```

2. **Install gRPC Libraries:**

Use npm to add gRPC functionality:

```
mkdir my-grpc-node-app
cd my-grpc-node-app
npm init -y
npm install @grpc/grpc-js
npm install google-protobuf
```

3. **Compile Protocol Buffers:**

You can utilize protoc to generate Node.js code:

```
protoc --js_out=import_style=commonjs,binary:. --grpc_out=. --plugin=protoc-gen
    -grpc=$(which grpc_tools_node_protoc_plugin) libros.proto
```

Setting Up gRPC for C# The integration of gRPC libraries in C#, primarily developed within the .NET ecosystem, uses tools like Visual Studio and dotnet CLI for convenience.

Installation and Configuration 1. **Dotnet Core:**

Ensure you have dotnet installed, which can be achieved by downloading from https://dotnet.microsoft.com/download.

2. **Adding gRPC to a Project:**

Install from the package manager console or use the CLI:

```
dotnet add package Grpc.AspNetCore
```

3. **Compile Protocol Buffers:**

Use the dotnet-grpc tool:

```
dotnet build
```

Here, gRPC libraries are tightly integrated with ASP.NET Core 3.1 and above.

2.3. SETTING UP GRPC LIBRARIES

Library Version Compatibility Careful attention must be paid to library version compatibility. Mismatches between library versions and protoc generated code can result in subtle, hard-to-diagnose issues. Developers should verify that the entire setup from protoc to each language's specific library maintains compatible versioning, often stated in official documentation regarding the ideal pairings for version numbers.

Dockerize Microservices Once libraries are configured and verified to work correctly in the development environment, containerization using Docker ensures dependencies and specific system-level configurations are preserved. Consider using multi-stage builds for lightweight production images:

```
FROM golang:1.15 AS builder
WORKDIR /go/src/app
COPY . .
RUN go get -d -v ./...
RUN go install -v ./...

FROM gcr.io/distroless/base
COPY --from=builder /go/bin/app /app
ENTRYPOINT ["/app"]
```

This Dockerfile ensures builds happen in a Go environment while deploying using a minimal image.

Best Practices Establishing a robust gRPC environment extends beyond simply setting up libraries. Implementing CI/CD pipelines for automated testing and builds, monitoring for runtime diagnostics, and regularly updating to the latest stable releases of gRPC packages are essential to maintaining a high-performing and secure microservices architecture.

Selecting the language-specific libraries, understanding their nuances, and ensuring proper setup aligns with the gRPC vision of efficient, scalable, and high-performance service architectures. Proper setup results in minimized issues and maximized development agility.

2.4 Creating Your First gRPC Project

Embarking on the development of your first gRPC project involves a detailed sequence of steps, ranging from the conceptualization and definition of service contracts to the actual implementation and testing of a functioning service. This section provides a comprehensive walkthrough, focusing on setting up a simple yet illustrative gRPC service that underscores the core principles and features of gRPC, equipping you with a clear understanding and practical skills to initiate your own high-performance applications.

Fundamentals of gRPC Services A gRPC service is defined by Protocol Buffers, which dictate the structure of service contracts and data serialization. Understanding how to define these in '.proto' files and using the 'protoc' compiler to generate code is foundational. Let's explore the precise processes involved.

Designing the .proto File The Protocol Buffers file ('.proto') is where you define the service's remote procedure calls (RPCs) and data types. This definition file establishes the service interface that gRPC uses to automate the generation of both client and server-side code.

Example Service: Consider a basic service, 'Greeter', which includes a simple remote procedure call 'SayHello'.

Content of 'greeter.proto':

```
syntax = "proto3";

option java_package = "com.example.grpc";
option java_outer_classname = "GreeterProto";

package grpc.example;

// The greeting service definition.
service Greeter {
    // Sends a greeting.
    rpc SayHello (HelloRequest) returns (HelloReply) {}
}

// The request message containing the user's name.
message HelloRequest {
    string name = 1;
```

2.4. CREATING YOUR FIRST GRPC PROJECT

```
}
// The response message containing the greetings.
message HelloReply {
   string message = 1;
}
```

Key components of this file include:

- The 'syntax' directive specifies the proto3 version of Protocol Buffers.
- The 'option' directives configure package and class names for generated Java code. These may be omitted or replaced with corresponding options for other languages.
- 'service Greeter': Defines the service, encapsulating one or more 'rpc' methods.
- 'rpc SayHello': A method receiving a 'HelloRequest' and returning a 'HelloReply'.
- 'message HelloRequest' and 'message HelloReply': Define the data structures for incoming and outgoing messages.

Compiling the .proto File Once the '.proto' file is correctly defined, the next step is to compile it using the 'protoc' compiler, translating the '.proto' definitions into language-specific code.

Installation and Execution of protoc: Ensure 'protoc' is installed along with language-specific plugins. Once ready:

```
# For Java
protoc --java_out=./build --proto_path=. greeter.proto
# For Python
python -m grpc_tools.protoc -I. --python_out=. --grpc_python_out=. greeter.proto
# For Go
protoc --go_out=plugins=grpc:. --proto_path=. greeter.proto
```

This process generates the necessary classes and files tailored to the specific language environment, adhering to gRPC's interconnectivity standards across clients and servers.

Building the Server The gRPC server listens for requests on defined RPC methods, processing input and returning results. Implementing a simple gRPC server consolidates understanding of the framework's asynchronous communication architecture.

Implementing a Server in Go: Below is a succinct Go server implementation for the previously outlined Greeter service:

```go
package main

import (
  "context"
  "log"
  "net"

  "google.golang.org/grpc"
  pb "path/to/generated/greeter_proto"
)

type server struct {
  pb.UnimplementedGreeterServer
}

func (s *server) SayHello(ctx context.Context, in *pb.HelloRequest) (*pb.HelloReply, error) {
  log.Printf("Received: %v", in.GetName())
  return &pb.HelloReply{Message: "Hello " + in.GetName()}, nil
}

func main() {
  lis, err := net.Listen("tcp", ":50051")
  if err != nil {
    log.Fatalf("failed to listen: %v", err)
  }

  s := grpc.NewServer()
  pb.RegisterGreeterServer(s, &server{})

  log.Printf("gRPC server listening on %v", lis.Addr())
  if err := s.Serve(lis); err != nil {
    log.Fatalf("failed to serve: %v", err)
  }
}
```

Insights into the Go Server Implementation:

- The 'SayHello' method contains the server logic for handling incoming requests and forming responses based on input data.
- A 'gRPC server' object is created which binds the 'net.Listener' to listen for incoming calls and links the generated service interface

through 'RegisterGreeterServer'.

- Logging within the handler captures client interaction, aiding in debugging and telemetry.

Developing the Client   The client aspect of the service interface involves issuing requests to the gRPC server, utilizing the protocol and data serialization generated by 'protoc'.

Example Client in Python: Illustrating a simple client within the Python environment unveils the ease of which API calls can be constructed to interact with the gRPC server.

```python
from __future__ import print_function
import logging

import grpc
import greeter_pb2
import greeter_pb2_grpc

def run():
    with grpc.insecure_channel('localhost:50051') as channel:
        stub = greeter_pb2_grpc.GreeterStub(channel)
        response = stub.SayHello(greeter_pb2.HelloRequest(name='World'))
    print("Greeter client received: " + response.message)

if __name__ == '__main__':
    logging.basicConfig()
    run()
```

Key Workflow in this Python Client:

- Establishes a 'grpc' channel directed towards the server endpoint, wherein insecure communication is allowed to facilitate unencrypted data transfer in environments without stringent security needs.

- Instantiates a 'GreeterStub', as defined in 'greeter.proto', enabling calls to remote procedures defined in the service.

- The 'SayHello' method is employed, sending a 'HelloRequest' message to the server and receiving a 'HelloReply'.

Testing the gRPC Service Effectively implemented gRPC services require thorough testing, ensuring the detailed operationality across different conditions and edge cases expected in production environments.

Using gRPC CLI for Testing: For quick verification without writing manual test cases, the gRPC command line interface allows for direct interaction with services in development and debug scenarios.

```
grpc_cli call localhost:50051 SayHello "name: 'TestUser'"
```

Results from this call provide immediate feedback from the service, valuable in validating newly introduced service logic or troubleshooting known issues within the deployment environment.

Enhancements and Advancements in Design Consider adding the following enhancements for a more complex, robust application architecture:

- **Authentication and Security:** Introduce SSL/TLS encrypted channels, ensuring data privacy and security.

- **Error Handling:** Implement explicit error handling strategies, using gRPC's status and error messaging utilities to relay clear diagnostic information to clients.

- **Load Balancing and Scalability:** Utilize native gRPC features that cater to load balancing, like Envoy, facilitating service scalability.

Enabling SSL/TLS Encryption: Implementing channel security involves certificates to ensure secure client-server communications.

```
creds, err := credentials.NewServerTLSFromFile(certFile, keyFile)
if err != nil {
  log.Fatalf("failed to load credentials: %v", err)
}
s := grpc.NewServer(grpc.Creds(creds))
```

2.4. CREATING YOUR FIRST GRPC PROJECT

To secure the channel, employing 'grpc.WithTransportCredentials' client-side ensures that data exchanges adhere strictly to the defined security protocols.

Orchestration with Containerization With Docker, encapsulating a gRPC server and its dependencies guarantees a consistent runtime environment, promoting reliability during deployment across varying infrastructures.

Example Dockerfile for Go gRPC Service:

FROM golang:1.15-alpine
WORKDIR /app
COPY . .
RUN go build -o server
EXPOSE 50051
CMD [". /server"]

Containerization affords scaling opportunities through orchestration solutions like Kubernetes, enabling service replication and load distribution to meet demand fluctuations.

Summary Insights in gRPC Project Creation Creating an initial gRPC project epitomizes the potency of distributed systems communication. Innovative advancements in RPC transform the potential and flexibility of networked applications. Forward-thinking iterations should focus on continuous development, using comprehensive testing and sustainable integration practices to achieve real-world, production-grade deployments.

Empowering subsequent iterations through modular expansions, developers maintain agility and adaptability, harnessing full gRPC capabilities to deliver robust, high-performant service architectures tailored to modern technological landscapes.

2.5 Configuring Your Development Environment

A well-configured development environment is pivotal in accelerating software development, enhancing productivity, and minimizing setup-related issues. In creating gRPC applications, configuring your environment correctly integrates various development tools, libraries, paths, and supporting infrastructure necessary for compiling, testing, and deploying services efficiently. This section details the comprehensive setup of a gRPC-compatible development landscape, providing insights into tools and configurations spanning across multiple operating systems and languages.

Core Considerations in Environment Configuration Effective configuration involves several key components:

- IDE Setup: Selecting and configuring an Integrated Development Environment (IDE) that aligns with your chosen programming language and development workflow.

- Toolchain Integration: Ensuring compatibility and accessibility of necessary compilers, build tools, and linters.

- Version Control: Integrating robust version control systems to track changes and collaborate within teams.

- Environment Variables: Correctly configuring PATH and other environment variables required for seamless command-line utilities accessibility.

- Containerization and Virtualization: Assessing the use of Docker or virtual environments to ensure consistent environments across development stages.

Configuring the Integrated Development Environment (IDE)
A well-chosen IDE accelerates code writing with features like autocomplete, syntax highlighting, and debugging tools interpretable within the context of gRPC and Protocol Buffers.

IntelliJ IDEA Configuration for Java Developers For Java developers, IntelliJ IDEA serves as an optimal choice, providing abundant plugin support for gRPC, Java debugging, and comprehensive integration for tools and frameworks.

- Installing Required Plugins:
    - Navigate to 'File > Settings > Plugins' and install the plug-ins:
    - Protocol Buffer Support
    - gRPC Kotlin/Java support
- Configuring Project SDK:
  Ensure the correct Java SDK is aligned with your project:

  File > Project Structure > Project > Project SDK

- Customization and Optimization:
    - Enable 'Inspections' to catch potential issues.
    - Customize keyboard shortcuts for frequent actions.

Enhancing an IDE's native functionality with plugins and configurations tailors the development environment to the unique needs of gRPC projects, reducing syntactical errors and increasing efficiency.

Setting Environment Variables Environment variables are crucial for defining the development path and utilizing system-wide tools efficiently. Setting these variables varies slightly depending on the operating system in use.

Configuration on Unix-based Systems Configuration on Linux/Mac:

Open the terminal and edit your shell profile file (e.g., '.bashrc', '.bash_-profile', '.zshrc') to include your environment variables. For instance:

```
export PATH="$PATH:/usr/local/go/bin"
export GOPATH="$HOME/go"
```

After adding, apply changes:

```
source ~/.bashrc
```

Configuration on Windows Systems Modify environment variables by navigating to 'Control Panel > System and Security > System > Advanced system settings > Environment Variables'. Then, append to the 'Path' variable:

```
C:\Program Files\protoc\bin;C:\Go\bin
```

Setting these paths ensures globally available executable commands for 'protoc', 'go', and other tools.

Toolchain Integration and Installation Integrating the necessary toolchain is pivotal to ensuring functionality across different layers of the software stack.

Using Package Managers Employing package managers streamlines the installation process of necessary libraries and dependencies:

- Homebrew (MacOS):

  ```
  /bin/bash -c "$(curl -fsSL https://raw.githubusercontent.com/Homebrew/install/HEAD/install.sh)"
  brew install protoc
  brew install go
  ```

- Chocolatey (Windows):

  ```
  choco install protoc
  choco install golang
  ```

- APT/YUM (Linux):

  ```
  sudo apt update
  sudo apt install -y protobuf-compiler golang
  ```

Package managers facilitate version control and dependency management, easing the complexity of maintaining development environments, especially when switching across different machine setups.

2.5. CONFIGURING YOUR DEVELOPMENT ENVIRONMENT

Version Control Systems (VCS) Setup Version control is non-negotiable in today's collaborative coding environments, providing mechanisms for managing code changes and enabling seamless collaboration.

Setting Up Git

- Installing Git:

    - MacOS/Windows: Utilize [Git's official page](https://git-scm.com/downloads) to download and install.
    - Linux: Install via apt:

    ```
    sudo apt install -y git
    ```

- Configuring Git:

    After installation, configure user information:

    ```
    git config --global user.name "Your Name"
    git config --global user.email "you@example.com"
    ```

- Creating a Repository:

    Navigate to your project directory and initialize git:

    ```
    git init
    git add .
    git commit -m "Initial commit"
    ```

Integrating VCS within the IDE allows automatic tracking of code changes and seamless push/pull operations with remote repositories.

Containerization and Virtualization Techniques Leveraging containerization aids in mitigating inconsistencies between different environments, ensuring a uniform build process.

Docker Environment Setup For gRPC applications, Docker serves as a reliable solution to isolate services and package dependencies:

CHAPTER 2. SETTING UP YOUR DEVELOPMENT ENVIRONMENT

- Installation:

    - Windows/MacOS: Download [Docker Desktop](https://www.docker.com/products/docker-desktop).

    - Linux:
        ```
        sudo apt update
        sudo apt install -y docker.io
        ```

- Using Docker Compose:

    With 'docker-compose', running multi-container applications becomes straightforward. Here's a simple compose setup to run a gRPC service:

    'docker-compose.yml':
    ```yaml
    version: '3.7'
    services:
      grpc-server:
        build: .
        ports:
          - "50051:50051"
    ```

    Executing 'docker-compose up' launches defined services, managing the entire lifecycle of applications efficiently.

- Building Images and Running Containers:

    Create a 'Dockerfile':
    ```
    FROM golang:1.15-alpine
    WORKDIR /app
    COPY . .
    RUN go build -o my_grpc_server .
    CMD ["./my_grpc_server"]
    ```

    Build and run:
    ```
    docker build -t my_grpc_server .
    docker run -p 50051:50051 my_grpc_server
    ```

Docker simplifies complex environment setups for gRPC interfaces, paving ways for CI/CD pipeline integrations ensuring consistent implementations across development teams.

2.5. CONFIGURING YOUR DEVELOPMENT ENVIRONMENT

Efficient Debugging and Testing Practices Achieving an effective development setup not only involves solving technical hurdles but also incorporates reliable testing methodologies and systematic approaches to debugging:

IDE Integrated Debugging Utilizing IDE-integrated debugging tools assists in real-time analysis and resolution of runtime issues. Setting breakpoints, examining variable states, and stepping through code can be achieved within IDE landscapes such as IntelliJ IDEA, Visual Studio Code, and PyCharm, aligning with developer preferences across languages.

Automated Testing Framework Integration Testing frameworks, essential for reliable and fault-tolerant codebases, form the backbone of well-managed development environments.

- For Go:

  Go projects rely on the built-in testing framework:
  ```
  go test ./...
  ```
  Incorporate mock libraries to simulate gRPC-client interactions.

- For Python:

  Use unittest or pytest to implement and run tests:
  ```
  pytest test_folder/
  ```

- For Java:

  Combine JUnit with Mockito for tests:
  ```xml
  <dependency>
      <groupId>junit</groupId>
      <artifactId>junit</artifactId>
      <version>4.13</version>
  </dependency>
  ```

Testing interfaces capture intricate behavior reconciliations, promoting sustainable and adaptable development lifecycles.

Continuous Integration and Delivery Pipeline Further refine the development landscape through automated builds and deployment pipelines, fostering productivity and decreasing manual errors.

CI Pipeline with GitHub Actions

- Setup CI Workflow:

    Choose GitHub Actions to process builds and tests automatically upon code integration:

    '.github/workflows/main.yml':

    ```yaml
    name: Go gRPC CI

    on: [push]

    jobs:
      build:
        runs-on: ubuntu-latest
        steps:
        - uses: actions/checkout@v2
        - name: Set up Go
          uses: actions/setup-go@v2
          with:
            go-version: 1.15
        - name: Build
          run: go build
        - name: Test
          run: go test ./...
    ```

- Deployment Automation:

    With Jenkins or similar tools, orchestrate deployment processes, integrating seamlessly with containers for large, service-oriented architectures.

Optimizing for Collaboration Mapping configurations across a team involves sharing setup files and employing environment setup scripts to ensure nomenclature consistency and dependency management.

Vagrant or Similar Tools for Consistent Environments Encapsulate environment configurations:

```
vagrant init hashicorp/bionic64
vagrant up
```

These virtualized environments host the entire stack of an application's configuration, encouraging collaborative development and consistency across global teams.

Together, these methodologies and configurations yield an optimized, error-resilient development environment suitable for nurturing continuous innovation in gRPC service design, adapting to the dynamically evolving software development ecosystem.

2.6 Troubleshooting Setup Issues

Setting up a development environment for gRPC can occasionally present challenges due to the myriad of components and configurations involved. This section provides a meticulous guide on diagnosing and resolving common issues encountered during the setup process. Developers using systems as diverse as Windows, macOS, and Linux can encounter unique challenges. By comprehensively understanding potential pitfalls and leveraging systematic troubleshooting techniques, developers can mitigate disruptions, streamline setup processes, and maintain a functional development environment.

Common Issues in gRPC Development Setup   Development setups often involve integration points among the Protocol Buffers compiler, different programming languages, and libraries, potentially leading to the following common issues:

- Path and Environment Variables Misconfigurations: Incorrectly set paths can prevent tools like protoc or build utilities from being accessible.

- Version Mismatches: Using incompatible versions of gRPC libraries, Protocol Buffers, and language runtime environments causes numerous subtle errors.

- Missing Dependencies: Failing to install necessary packages or binaries that libraries rely upon.

- Network and Firewall Issues: Impacting download and install processes or blocking communication between microservices during development.

- Compatibility Issues with IDEs or Plugins: Resulting in unsynchronized loads, incorrect syntax highlighting or erroneous build processes.

Identifying and Resolving Common Setup Problems Some of these issues can hinder the development process, but with a structured approach to troubleshooting, they can be efficiently resolved.

Path and Environment Variables Misconfigurations Incorrectly set environment paths prevent systems from accessing necessary executable files:

1. Ensure the Environment Path includes Essential Binaries:

Use commands like `echo $PATH` (Linux/macOS) or `echo %PATH%` (Windows) to verify if paths such as those for `protoc` are included.

2. Correcting Path Variables:

Example correction for Unix-based systems:

```
export PATH="$PATH:/usr/local/go/bin:/usr/local/bin/protoc/bin"
```

3. Verifying Path Variables Changes:

Re-load configurations using the appropriate command for your shell, e.g., `source /.bashrc`.

4. Windows Environment Variable Adjustment:

Navigate to Environment Variables settings and append missing paths directly using GUI tools provided by Windows under System properties.

Version Mismatches Library version conflicts can manifest as runtime errors or failed builds:

2.6. TROUBLESHOOTING SETUP ISSUES

1. Documentation Consultation:

Always refer to the official package documentation for version compatibility notes. For example, ensure Protocol Buffers version corresponds with the installed gRPC library version.

2. Installing the Correct Version of gRPC Libraries:

Use version specifiers when installing packages.

Python example:
```
pip install grpcio==1.42.0 grpcio-tools==1.42.0
```

Node.js example:
```
npm install @grpc/grpc-js@1.3.4
```

3. Upgrade or Downgrade as Needed:

Use package manager tools such as `pip`, `npm`, or `go get` to upgrade or downgrade libraries according to project specifications.

Missing Dependencies Necessary dependencies require installation to ensure correct library function and compatibility:

1. Reading Build Logs Carefully:

Error messages frequently indicate missing libraries or dependencies. For example, a missing shared library in C++ will log details in compilation logs.

2. Using Package Managers for Dependency Management:

Run system-specific commands:

- For Debian-based systems:
```
sudo apt-get install -y build-essential autoconf libtool pkg-config
```

- For CentOS:
```
sudo yum install -y epel-release
sudo yum install -y autoconf automake libtool
```

3. Verify Dependency Installation:

Commands like `ldconfig -p | grep name` (Linux) verify shared libraries, identifying unmet dependencies facilitating draws.

4. Leveraging Docker for Consistency:

Build and maintain a Docker image with all dependencies, minimizing dependency-related issues across environments.

Network and Firewall Issues Network issues might impede downloads or hinder microservices communication:

1. Verifying Internet Connection:

Basic connectivity tests using `ping` show if internet connection issues are causing hindrance:

```
ping google.com
```

2. Modifying Firewall Rules:

Add exceptions to local firewalls, allowing necessary network traffic for gRPC ports (normally TCP 50051/50052):

```
sudo ufw allow 50051 # Ubuntu
netsh advfirewall firewall add rule name="gRPC" dir=in action=allow protocol=TCP localport=50051 # Windows
```

3. Examining Proxy Configuration Issues:

Proxy configurations impacting `curl` or package managers can occur; configure them via .bashrc (Linux) or network settings panel (Windows/macOS).

Compatibility Issues with IDEs or Plugins IDE mismatches lead to build failures or inconsistencies in code representation:

1. Updating IDE and Plugins:

Regular updates solve numerous syntactic and language support issues. Errors may decrease updating to latest versions:

- IntelliJ IDEA: Help > Check for Updates

- Visual Studio Code: Through Marketplace extensions auto-updates.

2.6. TROUBLESHOOTING SETUP ISSUES

2. Checking Plugin Dependency and Compatibility:

Verify all required plugins are active and set to the correct version. Often cross-compatible plugins overlay unintended configurations.

3. Manual Reinstallation of Plugins:

Plugin removal and reinstallation solve persistent loading issues or incorrect configurations leading to IDE restart.

Advanced Debugging for Complex Issues When issues expand beyond initial troubleshooting and persist despite basic interventions, advanced debugging tools and tactics might be required.

Using Logs and Diagnostic Tools: 1. Enable Extensive Logging:

Set services to verbose—or debug—modes for comprehensive logging:

Example: Java gRPC logging root level set to debug. - Add to logback.xml:

```
<logger name="io.grpc" level="DEBUG"/>
```

2. Utilize Protocol Analyzer Tools:

Tools like Wireshark track gRPC traffic over networks, identifying bottlenecks or miscommunications:

- Filter gRPC packets for detailed inspection using expressions like http2.streamid $<= 0$.

3. Profilers and Performance Tools:

Analyze performance and resource utilization, diagnosing inexplicable slowdowns or memory leaks under specific testing conditions: - VisualVM, Go pprof, Python cProfile for insight-gathering into high-level resource discrepancies.

4. Memory Leak Identification:

Use language-specific tools (Valgrind for C++, Java Memory Analysis Tool for Java) to pinpoint memory mismanagement issues producing side effects during setup phases.

5. Application Performance Management (APM) Tools:

Integrate tools like New Relic, Datadog to monitor dynamic microservice ecosystem interactions, unveiling insights inaccessible from code alone.

Documentation and Community Resources Leveraging community-driven knowledge bases and official documentation aids swift problem resolution:

1. gRPC Official Documentation:

Abundant resources provide usage diversifications or error-specific searches quickly address plugin errors or syntax deprecations.

2. Relevant Online Forums and Community Support Channels:

Platforms like StackOverflow, GitHub Discussions offer situational resolutions; accurate issue articulation facilitates solution suggestions, tapping into broad developer networks.

3. Knowledge Sharing within Teams:

Maintain an internal wiki or shared repository where encountered issues and solutions are documented, assisting team members facing similar scenarios.

4. Participate in Meetups/Channels:

Engaging in virtual or local meetups and online channels like gRPC Developers (Slack, Discord) grants access to collaborative debugging and updated gRPC methodologies.

Establishing effective troubleshooting protocols underpins the successful setup of a gRPC development environment, empowering developers to discern between easily-fixable problems and more convoluted, deeper-seated configurations requiring strategic interaction with infrastructures and frameworks. Through a combination of proactive problem prevention, diagnostic tooling, community collaboration, and extensive documentation referencing, even the most complex setup issues unravel into manageable paths, enhancing operational excellence and project sustainability.

Chapter 3

Protocol Buffers: Defining Your Data

This chapter delves into Protocol Buffers, the binary serialization format used by gRPC to define structured data schemas. It explains how to create and structure .proto files, covering syntax and key components like messages and services. Readers will learn about the compilation of these files into code compatible with multiple programming languages. Additionally, the chapter addresses strategies for versioning and evolving Protocol Buffers to maintain compatibility. Advanced features, such as extensions and customization options, are also discussed, providing a comprehensive understanding of data definition and management in gRPC.

3.1 Understanding Protocol Buffers

Protocol Buffers, often abbreviated as protobufs, stand as a fundamental component in the realm of gRPC communication. They serve as a language-agnostic binary serialization format that facilitates the efficient and reliable definition of structured data. This section elucidates the intricacies of Protocol Buffers, illuminating their critical role in enabling the serialization, deserialization, and transmission of data across different programming languages and platforms.

At their core, Protocol Buffers define interfaces in a declarative manner resembling Interface Description Languages (IDLs). This structured approach allows developers to specify data structures once, and then utilize the Protocol Buffer compiler to generate source code compatible with various programming languages. Such versatility is valuable in heterogeneous system environments where interoperability is essential.

In the development of distributed systems, consistent data serialization is imperative. Protocol Buffers efficiently address this requirement by providing a robust framework that ensures data integrity and preservation of structure during transmission. Data serialization primarily refers to the process of encoding structured data into a format that can be transmitted or stored and subsequently reconstructed. Unlike traditional human-readable formats like JSON or XML, Protocol Buffers employ a compact binary format which conserves bandwidth and enhances performance.

Protocol Buffers encompass the definition of *messages*, the building blocks that represent structured data in the format. Messages consist of fields where each field corresponds to an individual piece of data. Each piece of data in a message is typed, and Protocol Buffers support multiple data types including int32, int64, float, double, string, as well as more complex custom message types.

Consider the following example of a Protocol Buffer message definition in a .proto file:

```
syntax = "proto3";

message Person {
  int32 id = 1;
  string name = 2;
  string email = 3;
}
```

This succinct definition declares a message Person comprising three fields: an integer id, and two string fields for name and email. The numbering of fields, such as id = 1, establishes a unique tag for each field within a message. These tags are integral in the encoding and

3.1. UNDERSTANDING PROTOCOL BUFFERS

decoding process, enabling the efficient and consistent identification of fields.

The choice of data format in Protocol Buffers is immensely optimized for both CPU utilization and network bandwidth. The binary encoding allows Protocol Buffers to serialize data significantly faster than textual formats. This improvement in serialization performance is particularly crucial in use cases involving large-scale data transfers, such as in microservices communication or real-time streaming applications.

Underpinning the binary serialization is the concept of *varint encoding*, which effectively compresses data into a variable-length format. The use of a varint allows for the efficient encoding of integers, with smaller values occupying fewer bytes. This mechanism contrasts with fixed-size integers in other formats, providing enhanced flexibility and less susceptibility to wasteful overhead.

To understand the practical impact of Protocol Buffers, consider a simple serialization process in different scenarios. Here is an example of encoding a Person message instance using a generated Protocol Buffers class in Python:

```
import person_pb2

p = person_pb2.Person()
p.id = 123
p.name = "Alice"
p.email = "alice@example.com"

serialized_data = p.SerializeToString()
```

The method SerializeToString() executes the binary serialization of the data, preparing it for efficient transmission or storage. Reconstruction of the data is performed via deserialization, as demonstrated below:

```
received_data = serialized_data # typically this comes from a network or file

p2 = person_pb2.Person()
p2.ParseFromString(received_data)

print("ID:", p2.id)
print("Name:", p2.name)
print("Email:", p2.email)
```

The above snippets reveal how Protocol Buffers abstract away the complexity of low-level data handling, offering a streamlined interface to developers. The immediate gain from employing Protocol Buffers extends beyond serialization efficiency; it encompasses improvements in maintainability and evolution of data structures, aspects further explored in subsequent sections of this chapter.

Protocol Buffers also feature mechanisms for evolution and versioning, accommodating changes in data schemas over time. This ability is vital in real-world applications, where maintaining backward compatibility is a common necessity when updating data models. A pivotal guideline in evolving Protocol Buffers is to avoid reusing or renumbering fields within a message. Deleting fields is permissible but encouraged to use reserved tags to prevent future accidental reuse which could lead to deserialization incompatibilities.

In other advanced scenarios, one might need to perform more than just simple encoding and decoding - Protocol Buffers support complex data hierarchies and nested data, addressed through composition of messages within other messages. For example:

```
message AddressBook {
  repeated Person people = 1;
}
```

This proto definition illustrates a message *AddressBook* containing a repeated list of Person messages, exhibiting the Protocol Buffer's capability to manage collections of messages in a single construct.

The developer's toolkit for working with Protocol Buffers typically includes a diverse set of programming language support, encompassing C++, Java, Python, Go, JavaScript, and more. This cross-language portability ensures that distributed systems constructed with diverse stacks can seamlessly exchange data with minimal friction.

In summary, understanding Protocol Buffers involves appreciation for their concise syntax, efficient serialization, and broad cross-platform applicability. These attributes collectively make Protocol Buffers an indispensable element in modern software architectures. As the chapter progresses, further details on creating, structuring, and evolving these protobuf schemas will deepen the comprehension and operational capabilities of readers in practically applying Protocol Buffers in distributed and scalable communication scenarios.

3.2 Creating a .proto File

The creation of a .proto file is a fundamental step in leveraging Protocol Buffers to define structured data schemas for gRPC services. These files serve as the blueprint from which source code is generated, irrespective of the target programming language. This section provides an in-depth exploration into how to effectively craft .proto files, delineating the syntax and semantics that characterize message definitions and service interfaces.

Typically, a .proto file comprises the following key components:

- syntax declaration,
- package declaration,
- import statements,
- message definitions,
- service definitions.

Each of these components integrates into the broader schema to describe how data is structured, encoded, and transmitted.

The composition of a .proto file begins with declaring the syntax version. The syntax version ensures that the Protocol Buffer compiler interprets the source file correctly. Protocol Buffers support two syntax versions: proto2 and proto3, with proto3 being the latest standard that simplifies protocol buffers by removing certain features of proto2, such as optional and required fields.

```
syntax = "proto3";
```

Following the syntax declaration is the package declaration. Typically optional, the package declaration organizes Protocol Buffer definitions, preventing naming conflicts particularly when multiple .proto files are compiled into the same target language. Consider the following:

```
package tutorial;
```

In this example, the package tutorial encapsulates the defined messages and services. The utility of naming packages manifests particularly in programming languages where namespaces or modules group related classes or functions.

For projects utilizing multiple .proto files, import statements allow message types from one file to be used in another. This modular structure enhances reusability and maintainability of message definitions, preventing redundancy across .proto files. Import statements reflect basic file dependencies:

```
import "google/protobuf/timestamp.proto";
```

With foundational aspects outlined, the crafting of message definitions forms the core activity within a .proto file. Messages are the fundamental units of data that can be serialized, encompassing fields and data types. Each field within a message is tagged with a unique number, acting as a field identifier for encoding and decoding purposes.

Consider an illustrative message structure:

```
message Student {
  int32 id = 1;
  string name = 2;
  bool enrolled = 3;
  repeated string courses = 4;
}
```

In this example, the message Student comprises four fields: an integer id, a string name, a boolean enrolled, and a repeated field courses which represents a list of strings. The repeated field enables encoding of a list or array of values within a single message field.

For proto3, all fields are optional by default; absence of field values indicates their default values, thus simplifying the declaration by removing optional and required field qualifiers present in proto2.

Advanced definitions may include nested messages, facilitating the encapsulation of hierarchical data. Nested messages are embedded directly within other message definitions:

```
message School {
  string name = 1;
  message Department {
    string name = 1;
  }
  repeated Department departments = 2;
```

3.2. CREATING A .PROTO FILE

```
}
```

In crafting .proto files, it is essential to ensure fields have unique tag numbers. Tag numbers from 1 to 15 are encoded using a single byte; for efficiency, frequently used fields should use these lower numbers. Additionally, field numbers above 15 are encoded using twos complement encoding to extend byte usage.

Once the data structures, represented as message definitions, are defined, the .proto file may articulate service definitions. Service definitions outline the RPC methods exposed by the service, identifying input and output message types. Here's the basic structure of a service definition:

```
service UniversityService {
  rpc GetStudent(StudentRequest) returns (StudentResponse);
}
```

Here, UniversityService exposes an RPC method GetStudent, which accepts a StudentRequest message and returns a StudentResponse message. Such declarations, when compiled, generate both client and server code stubs, simplifying integration into gRPC services.

Completeness of field definitions within .proto files demands adherence to established best practices, emphasizing considerations such as backwards compatibility, succinctness, and logical separation of concerns. This entails reserving previously used field numbers or renaming fields judiciously over time.

Let us consider complexity management in field evolution. Here's an example showcasing field reservation:

```
message Course {
  reserved 5, 9, 15;
  reserved "oldCourseCode";

  int32 id = 1;
  string name = 2;
  string description = 3;
}
```

By reserving field numbers and names, future additions avoid unexpected clashes that could compromise backward compatibility and data integrity upon message evolution.

Lifecycle management of .proto files necessitates meticulous planning of field tags, particularly when services are incrementally expanded. Frequent revision of these designs, accompanied by automated unit tests, mitigates potential risks caused by inadvertent field alterations.

Generating code from .proto files involves using the Protocol Buffers compiler, known as protoc. The protoc compiler translates the succinct message and service definitions into corresponding classes or types in the target language, supporting multiple languages including but not limited to C++, Java, Python, Go, and Dart.

Here's a simple command for generating Python code:

```
protoc --python_out=. student.proto
```

The specific python_out option specifies the directory to which the generated Python files are written. The resulting classes provide functions for serialization, deserialization, and field manipulation.

The creation of .proto files not only represents a technical constraint but also embodies deeper design philosophy about the system under construction. Placing emphasis on clear communication and consistency among development teams, the .proto files serve as both documentation and implementation guide, bridging the gap between conceptual design and practical application.

Collectively, these aspects emphasize that creating a .proto file involves a deliberate attempt to anticipate future needs, integrate with existing systems, and address complex data interactions. Protocol Buffers, by emphasizing clarity, performance, and cross-language interoperability, streamline the pathways through which modern distributed systems are imagined, designed, and realized.

3.3 Syntax and Structure of Protocol Buffers

Protocol Buffers, a powerful tool for serializing structured data, employ a compact and efficient syntax that is vital for defining message structures and services. Understanding the syntax and structure of Protocol Buffers is essential for leveraging their full capabilities in gRPC and beyond. This section dissects the various elements of Protocol Buffers

3.3. SYNTAX AND STRUCTURE OF PROTOCOL BUFFERS

syntax and provides comprehensive insights into its structural facets to facilitate the creation of robust and interoperable data models.

Fundamental Syntax Overview

The syntax of Protocol Buffers is designed to be concise and clear, focusing on the definition of messages and services. Each .proto file begins with a specified syntax version, which informs the Protocol Buffer compiler about the parsing standards to adhere to. This versioning is crucial for maintaining compatibility across different iterations of Protocol Buffer protocols.

```
syntax = "proto3";
```

Present in both proto2 and proto3, the syntax version declaration should be the initial line in the file, preceding any other definitions or declarations. The pivot to proto3 introduced simplifications to the language, notably in field handling, which will be elaborated upon further in this section.

Defining Packages and Imports

Following the syntax declaration, the package declaration establishes a namespace for the .proto definitions, helping prevent naming collisions in the generated code, especially in large-scale projects.

```
package my.example;
```

Here, my.example defines a hierarchically structured package. Structuring the package name in this manner reflects typical domain naming conventions, conveying a sense of organization and context.

Imports are used to incorporate definitions from external .proto files. This feature promotes modularity and code reuse, allowing developers to manage complex data structures efficiently.

```
import "google/protobuf/timestamp.proto";
```

This import statement integrates the pre-defined timestamp message from Google's protobuf library, extending the .proto file's capabilities to include standardized time-typing.

Message Structure and Field Types

Central to Protocol Buffers are *messages*, which define structured data entities, composing one of the main elements of serialization. Messages consist of fields, each with a unique tag number, a data type, and an identification name. The syntax under proto3 denoted elegantly:

```
message Car {
  string model = 1;
  int32 year = 2;
  string manufacturer = 3;
}
```

In this example, Car is a message with three fields: model (a string), year (a 32-bit integer), and manufacturer (also a string). Each field type plays an essential role in optimizing the efficiency and speed of serialized data.

Field numbers are crucial for encoding wire format efficiently and uniquely identify fields within a message. It is standard practice to assign field numbers between 1 and 15 to those expected to frequently appear, as these field numbers are encoded in a single byte for maximum storage efficiency.

The various data types available include:

- int32, int64: For signed integers of 32 and 64 bits respectively.
- uint32, uint64: Unsigned integer variants.
- float, double: Representing floating-point numbers.
- bool: A Boolean data type encoding true or false values.
- string: A UTF-8 encoded string.
- bytes: For raw arbitrary byte data.
- Composite types: Custom message types defined elsewhere within the .proto file or imported from other files.

The flexibility in defining custom messages enriches the ability to model complex data structures, supporting nested messages within envelopes or envelopes within envelopes, akin to the following structure:

```
message Address {
  string street = 1;
  string city = 2;
  string state = 3;
```

3.3. SYNTAX AND STRUCTURE OF PROTOCOL BUFFERS

```
  string postal_code = 4;
}
message Person {
  string name = 1;
  int32 age = 2;
  Address address = 3; // Nested message
}
```

Here, the Person message includes a nested Address message, demonstrating the seamless incorporation of structured data into larger entities.

Under proto3, it is noteworthy that all fields are implicitly optional, and unset fields default to their zero-valued equivalents: numbers to 0, strings to "" (empty string), booleans to false, and bytes to empty.

Enumerations for Controlled Value Sets

Protocol Buffers support enumerations to define a set of named constants which an integer field can take. Enumerations are beneficial when the data model inherently involves a limited set of values:

```
enum CarType {
  UNKNOWN = 0;
  SEDAN = 1;
  SUV = 2;
  TRUCK = 3;
}
```

The enumeration CarType defines possible types of cars. Enums simplify both human understanding and data handling, inherently restricting values to valid choices while maintaining readability.

Service Definitions for RPC Communication

In service-oriented architectures, gRPC leverages Protocol Buffers not only to define message structures but also to delineate service endpoints that espouse Remote Procedure Call (RPC) methods. These methods establish the interface through which client-server communication occurs.

```
service VehicleService {
  rpc GetCar (CarRequest) returns (CarResponse);
}
```

This service VehicleService exposes a method GetCar, which accepts a CarRequest and returns a CarResponse. Despite conceptual simplicity, RPC service declarations hide extensive automated processes that generate client and server stubs across all supported languages, which abstract method invocation details and facilitate seamless communication.

Performance Considerations and Best Practices

Optimizing the syntax and structure of Protocol Buffers directly affects serialization efficacy. Design decisions include judiciously assigning field numbers, preemptively considering field deprecation and evolution, and organizing .proto files for clarity and scalability. Here are some pragmatic guidelines:

- Regularly review and reserve obsolete field numbers to prevent accidental reuse, establishing a backward compatibility protocol.

- Prioritize ordering fields such that frequently altered or accessed fields conform to optimal tag numbers, minimizing serialization size.

- Abstract related messages into separate domains or .proto files to establish modular microservices architectures, supporting parallel development and system expansion.

The adoption of Protocol Buffers inherently entails understanding and navigating trade-offs related to efficiency gains from binary serialization and the developmental agility afforded through widely supported cross-language compatibility.

Protocol Buffers' syntax and structure offer a robust framework to articulate high-performance data models that cater to diverse application requirements across distributed systems. As we delve deeper into this chapter, the construction and evolution of these complex schemas become clearer reflections of their immense potential in modern data-driven infrastructures.

3.4 Compiling Protocol Buffers

Compiling Protocol Buffers is a pivotal step that transforms abstract data definitions from .proto files into operational code across a variety

3.4. COMPILING PROTOCOL BUFFERS

of programming environments. This process is facilitated by the Protocol Buffer compiler, known as protoc, which generates source code tailored to specific languages, enabling integration into diverse applications and services. An understanding of the intricacies involved in compiling Protocol Buffers offers significant insight into the deployment and utilization of Protocol Buffers within software projects.

The compilation of Protocol Buffers begins with the construction of .proto files that adhere to defined syntax and structure. These files encapsulate message definitions and, if applicable, service definitions, which the protoc compiler uses to generate source code artifacts. The execution of the compiler involves specifying target languages, output directories, and the input .proto files.

To illustrate, consider the following command used to generate Python code from a file named example.proto:

```
protoc --python_out=. example.proto
```

This command instructs protoc to compile example.proto, outputting generated Python source code into the current directory. The –python_out flag specifies the desired output language and location for the generated code.

The protoc utility supports a vast array of languages, including but not limited to C++, Java, Python, Go, C#, Ruby, JavaScript, and more. By providing the language-specific output flag in conjunction with language-specific plugins, the protoc compiler generates classes or types and code structures that allow developers to use defined messages and services seamlessly.

Installation and Setup

To compile Protocol Buffers, the first step is to install the Protocol Buffers compiler and language-specific plugins. Installation methods vary depending on the system's operating environment. For instance, on Unix-based systems, the compiler can be installed via package managers:

```
# On Ubuntu/Debian
sudo apt-get install protobuf-compiler

# On MacOS using Homebrew
brew install protobuf
```

Each target language may necessitate the installation of additional dependencies or plugins. For example, generating Java source code often requires setting up the protobuf Maven plugin, whereas generating code for JavaScript might involve npm packages. C++ developers need to link against the protobuf library during compilation of code utilizing Protocol Buffers.

To ensure readiness for all supported languages, consult the official Protocol Buffers documentation for comprehensive installation guidelines tailored to specific languages and platforms.

Understanding Generated Code Artifacts

Upon successful compilation, protoc produces language-specific code artifacts that represent defined messages and services. These artifacts include classes or data structures corresponding to messages, with methods for serialization, deserialization, and manipulation of data fields.

For languages like C++ and Java, the generated code closely aligns with object-oriented paradigms, featuring classes with member variables corresponding to each field in the .proto message:

Consider the following C++ example generated from a Car message:

```
#include "example.pb.h"

Car car;
car.set_model("Sedan");
car.set_year(2020);

std::string output;
car.SerializeToString(&output);
```

This snippet demonstrates initializing a Car object, setting field values, and serializing the object to a binary string. The generated .pb.h header file and associated .cc source file embody method definitions that facilitate these operations.

For dynamically typed languages such as Python, the generated classes also include methods like MergeFrom() for populating message fields from another message instance or ToDict() for converting messages to dictionary representations.

The encapsulation of serialization logic within the generated classes abstracts serialization mechanics from developers, promoting ease of

3.4. COMPILING PROTOCOL BUFFERS

use and minimizing boilerplate code.

Compiler Options and Customization

The protoc compiler accommodates numerous command-line options to fine-tune the compilation process, including directives for specific import paths (–proto_path), descriptor sets (–descriptor_set_out), and more:

```
protoc --proto_path=./protos --java_out=./gen/java ./protos/example.proto
```

In this command, –proto_path specifies the directory where the compiler should search for import statements within example.proto, while –java_out directs Java-generated code to the ./gen/java directory.

The use of –descriptor_set_out proves beneficial when sharing compiled descriptors across services deployed in microservices architectures. Descriptor sets are binary files encapsulating protocol buffer definitions, which gRPC services can use to dynamically understand service methods and payloads without access to the original .proto files.

Handling Advanced Compilation Scenarios

Advanced use cases might involve more extensive compilations, such as compiling multiple interdependent .proto files, integrating custom options, or dealing with nested data structures. Modularization of .proto files, facilitated through effective use of import statements, supports scalable compiler execution without redundancy or duplication.

Additionally, the compiler's extensibility through custom plugins enables developers to target unique code generation requirements not natively supported by protoc. For instance, generating custom serialization mechanisms or integrating with proprietary data-processing pipelines.

For performing compilations on complex projects or integrating Protocol Buffers into automated build systems like Makefiles or CMake for C++, or using Gradle and Maven for Java, it is necessary to script these processes explicitly, wielding compiler flags and options to meet specific project needs.

Cross-Language Interoperability

A fundamental strength of Protocol Buffers, realized through protoc, is cross-language interoperability. By targeting multiple language outputs from a single set of .proto files, developers can employ consistent data structures for client-server communication, both in backend microservices and front-end applications.

For example, generating client code in JavaScript and server code in Go allows an application to maintain consistency in terms of message formats and service expectations across inherently different ecosystems. The uniformity in data representation ensures clear communications protocols and reduces the risk of serialization incompatibility.

Common Pitfalls and Best Practices

Several common pitfalls may surface when compiling Protocol Buffers, including version inconsistencies, missing import paths, or misconfigured compiler flags. Addressing these challenges entails rigorous attention to:

- Verifying consistent usage of proto3 syntax when compiling across different projects or teams to avert version conflicts.
- Clearly structuring .proto file hierarchies to ensure all imports are resolvable during compilation.
- Systematically upgrading protoc and related plugins to avoid deprecated options or unsupported language targets.
- Utilizing a version control system to manage .proto files along with generated source code, ensuring transparency and traceability in code changes.

In composite projects, establishing compilation pipelines in Continuous Integration (CI) environments may increase reliability, providing real-time feedback on integration status and compilation success.

Conclusion on Compiling Protocol Buffers

Compiling Protocol Buffers effectively transforms intricate .proto definitions into tangible code artifacts, effectively bridging conceptual data models and software implementations across multiple programming languages. Mastering the compilation process, alongside knowledge of protoc's capabilities and constraints, stands as a cornerstone of modern software system design, enabling dynamic, efficient, and interoperable data serialization in an ever-expanding technological landscape.

The following sections advance the understanding by discussing versioning protocols and advanced feature utilization in Protocol Buffers, enriching the comprehensive applicability discovered herein.

3.5 Versioning and Evolving Protocol Buffers

The evolution and versioning of Protocol Buffers are critical processes for maintaining compatibility and functionality across distributed systems, where changes in data structures necessitate backward and forward compatibility. This section delves into best practices and methodologies for effectively versioning and evolving Protocol Buffers, ensuring stability across applications as data requirements grow and transform over time.

In complex and evolving software systems, changes to data formats are inevitable. Whether adding new features, accommodating additional data fields, or refactoring existing data models, developers must manage these evolutions without disrupting the systems that depend on them. Protocol Buffers provide mechanisms to deftly handle these transformations, minimizing the impact on existing infrastructures.

Field Additions and Deletions

Among the simplest operations, adding fields to messages ensures backward compatibility. When adding a new field in Protocol Buffers, simply define the additional tag number, ensuring it does not conflict with existing field numbers. For example, consider expanding a message ContactInfo to include a phone number:

```
message ContactInfo {
  string email = 1;
  string phone_number = 2; // Newly added field
}
```

Clients and servers using older versions of the ContactInfo message without this new field phone_number will not face issues. During serialization, any fields not known to an older version default to unset, thereby upholding backward compatibility.

Conversely, when fields become obsolete or redundant, the recommended approach is to mark them as reserved rather than remove them outright. This precaution prevents their accidental reuse, which could lead to serious compatibility issues.

```
message ContactInfo {
  string email = 1;
  reserved 3, 4; // Reserving previously used fields
}
```

By reserving field numbers, developers can safely evolve schemas, facilitating both backward and forward compatibility within evolving systems.

Changing Field Types and Names

Adjustments to field types or names require careful consideration. While changing a field's name poses no compatibility risk, altering a field's data type can break backward compatibility. To accommodate such changes, introduce a new field with a different number and desired type, eventually phasing out the old field:

```
message User {
  int32 user_id = 1;
  string old_field = 2;
  bool active = 3; // Type change: was previously string
}
```

In this example, if the field old_field needed to be updated to a boolean from a string, the prudent approach is to add a new field, retaining both during a transitional period while systems adapt.

Field Number Reservations and Reuse

Consistently reserving and avoiding reuse of field numbers is essential in the lifecycle of Protocol Buffers. Reusing field numbers presents a high risk of misinterpretation, as the same binary identifier would correspond to different data fields across versions. Hence, reserved statements act as safeguards against accidental reuse:

```
message Product {
  string name = 1;
  int32 price = 2;
  reserved 10 to 20; // Previously used range
}
```

Marking deprecated or discarded fields remains vital to long-term schema integrity, preventing older programs from experiencing incom-

3.5. VERSIONING AND EVOLVING PROTOCOL BUFFERS

patible data.

Advanced Field Management Through Extensions

Extensions facilitate dynamic schema alterations, allowing applications to incorporate supplementary data without altering the original message schema. Through extensions, third-party developers can veritably extend protocol structures:

To illustrate, consider defining an extendable message:

```
message BasicInfo {
  string first_name = 1;
  string last_name = 2;
  extensions 100 to 199;
}
```

Third-party developers can add fields within the defined extension range:

```
extend BasicInfo {
  string middle_name = 100;
}
```

Extensions are especially advantageous for scenarios necessitating a separation of core data and optional enhancements, where core message structures remain untouched while enabling new functionalities.

Maintaining Compatibility in Distributed Systems

Version evolution in distributed systems extends beyond singular data models. The intricate web of interdependent microservices results in scenarios where different services operate on disparate versions of Protocol Buffers. Ensuring compatibility across such boundaries typically involves:

- Concurrent support for multiple generations of messages, allowing different modules to process data according to their respective version understandings while converging on serialized/deserialized data states.

- Establishing robust testing and deployment strategies to ensure modifications to Protocol Buffers propagate successfully without unanticipated disruptions.

- Leveraging feature toggles and gradual rollouts, enhancing the deployment process by easing change adoption incrementally.

Version Management Strategies with gRPC Services

With gRPC services adding another layer of complexity, managing versioning gets intertwined with how services expose and consume APIs. Services should be versioned at the API level, entailing explicit endpoint versioning strategies, such as:

```
service UserServiceV1 {
  rpc GetUserDetails (UserRequest) returns (UserResponse);
}

service UserServiceV2 { // Updated interface version
  rpc GetUserDetails (UserV2Request) returns (UserV2Response);
}
```

By distinctly delineating service versions, systems effectively route end-user requests against stable, legacy-supported versions while gradually introducing enhancements.

Moreover, client-side utility tools and libraries that interact with version-controlled gRPC APIs should adopt evolutionary designs to seamlessly cater to new message fields or service methods without error propagation or crash risks.

Documentation and Tooling for Schema Evolution

Aiding schema evolution in Protocol Buffers demands emphasis on meticulous documentation, change logs, and compatibility analysis. Establishing a versioning policy ensures cohesive progress across teams, guiding them through field addition, deprecation, and future-proofing.

Alongside human-readable insights, investing in tooling to automate schema validations, diff comparisons between versions, and regression tests complements a formal versioning strategy. Such tools can regularly assess forward and backward compatibility, proactively identifying potential disruptions before deployment.

Conclusion of Evolving Protocol Buffers

Evolving Protocol Buffers commands a structured approach, balancing the need for enhancement against the necessity for stability and dependability. Developers must proactively engage with evolving schemas, capitalizing on Protocol Buffers' intrinsic adaptability while upholding compatibility across multifaceted orchestration. As modern challenges in distributed architectures intensify, astute mastery over protobuf versioning distinguishes systems resilient to volitions of change from those vulnerable to obsolescence. The building blocks establish prominence in the paradigm of scalable, reliable, evolving microservices and data-centric facets of contemporary software development.

3.6 Extensions and Advanced Features

Protocol Buffers, widely recognized for their efficiency in serializing structured data, also encompass a suite of advanced features designed to enhance data models and streamline communication in complex systems. Extensions represent one such powerful feature, allowing developers to extend existing messages dynamically without altering their definitions. Beyond extensions, this section delves into advanced features such as options, packed repeated fields, oneof fields, and custom options, each offering unique capabilities to tailor Protocol Buffers to specific requirements.

Understanding Extensions

Extensions offer a method to augment predefined Protocol Buffer messages, providing increased flexibility for developers who need to add custom fields without modifying the original message schema. This can be particularly useful when messages are defined by external libraries or third-party systems.

The process begins by reserving a range of tag numbers for extensions in the original message definition. Consider the following message Person that is made extensible:

```
message Person {
  string name = 1;
  int32 id = 2;
  extensions 100 to 199;
}
```

With extensions declared, developers can augment the Person message within the reserved range:

```
extend Person {
```

```
string middle_name = 100;
string email = 101;
}
```

Through extensions, applications maintain backwards compatibility while incorporating new data elements. Such flexibility fosters the co-existence of core functionalities and custom enhancements, gratifying disparate requirements across heterogeneous systems without sacrificing protocol conformance.

Extensions have been deprecated in proto3 in favor of better practices like introducing new fields, adjusting schemas when necessary, or utilizing a feature like Any, providing similar dynamic message behavior.

Options for Customizing Definitions

Options in Protocol Buffers afford developers the means to modify how fields, messages, enums, and services behave, tailoring their representation and application behavior. Among the prominent options is packed, applicable to repeated fields to enable efficient encoding.

A packed field is stored using fewer bytes, compressing repeated scalar values into a single wire entry:

```
message IntList {
  repeated int32 numbers = 1 [packed = true];
}
```

In this example, list elements numbers take advantage of packing, considerably reducing serialization size when the repeated field encompasses numerous elements.

Options extend beyond packing. Custom options allow developers to define domain-specific metadata, encapsulated as protocol buffer extensions. Deployment of custom options promotes semantic richness, propelling domain-specific annotations over data definitions within .proto files.

Defining a custom option entails the following protocol scheme:

```
extend google.protobuf.MessageOptions {
  optional string custom_description = 51234;
}

message Example {
  option (custom_description) = "An extended message option";
}
```

3.6. EXTENSIONS AND ADVANCED FEATURES

Custom options exemplify a method to annotate messages with additional metadata, delivering context-specific insights to developers or automation tools that process these .proto files, promoting advanced introspection or validation activities.

Utilizing Oneof Fields

The oneof field provides a mechanism to express union-like semantics in Protocol Buffers, where only one of several defined fields within the oneof construct may be set at any given time. The exploitation of oneof fields optimizes memory usage and enforces exclusivity among mutually exclusive data attributes:

```
message Contact {
  oneof contact_method {
    string email = 1;
    string phone = 2;
    string mailing_address = 3;
  }
}
```

Only one method of contact—email, phone, or mailing address—is appropriate within a single Contact message instance. This exclusivity not only economizes serialization but also enforces logically correct and consistent message configurations.

Protocols imbued with oneof semantics advantages encompass lean wire formats and assured single-field assignment. Moreover, they prevent users from encountering invalid state conditions that could arise should multiple options be unwittingly set.

The Any Field for Dynamic Typing

Another advanced feature within Protocol Buffers is the Any type. Introduced with proto3, the Any type allows for any arbitrary message to be embedded within another, akin to dynamic typing. It encodes a reference to another message, providing a universal container facilitating message inclusions of diverse types without prescriptive coupling.

Usage of the Any type imitates the following structure:

```
import "google/protobuf/any.proto";

message Event {
  string event_name = 1;
  google.protobuf.Any event_data = 2;
}
```

Embedding Any allows dynamic message dispatch, supporting operations like logging, auditing, and eventing where message structures are not fixed at compile time. Invoking Any fields in applications grants flexibility unsusceptible to schema rigidity while maintaining Protocol Buffers' efficiency and compactness.

Security Implications and Best Practices

Despite their substantial advantages, the use of Protocol Buffers' advanced features necessitates careful security consideration. For example, the indiscriminate use of Any could theoretically introduce polymorphic attacks, driving the need for robust validation and strict message type management during deserialization.

One of the best practices involves constraining the message types conveyable within Any by maintaining a whitelist of approved message types and conducting validation before processing.

In environments where backward compatibility and extensibility converge, leveraging oneof semantics more effectively delineates criteria boundaries within messages, mitigating risks posed by undefined or transitionary state junctions—central in concurrent and distributed ecosystems where protocols play an amplified role.

Scalability and Interoperability Enhancement

Protocol Buffers' advanced features capacitate scalable systems. Smaller, more compact serialized forms emerged from practices like packing and oneof fields arbitrate resource-efficient operation, steering protocols seamlessly into performance-critical applications.

The advanced way of configuring Protocol Buffers through extensions and custom options further strengthens the framework for cross-organizational or cross-service interoperability, affording systems developers to derive cohesive schema paradigms while independently embedding proprietary logic and implementations.

As organizations architect increasingly multifaceted and distributed systems, the intrinsic flexibility and modularity enabled by these Protocol Buffers' advanced and nuanced features present developers with the tools to craft extensible, efficient, and future-proof solutions.

Protocol Buffers thus emerge as the pivotal data interchange standard, equipping developers with a composing toolkit capable of handling so-

3.6. EXTENSIONS AND ADVANCED FEATURES

phisticated data scenarios while fortifying the principled disciplines of serialization best practices demanded in today's high-stakes data environments. The correct usage of these advanced features enhances both functional depth and adaptability, ensuring alignment with enterprise-grade data strategies and seamless technology landscapes.

Chapter 4

Understanding gRPC Architecture and Concepts

This chapter offers a detailed exploration of the core architecture and concepts underpinning gRPC. It covers the client-server model and the different communication patterns supported, including unary and streaming RPCs. The integration of HTTP/2 features, such as multiplexing and server push, is examined to highlight gRPC's performance advantages. The chapter also discusses data serialization via Protocol Buffers, service naming, and discovery, as well as strategies for load balancing to ensure scalability. By understanding these foundational elements, readers will gain insight into the efficient implementation and management of gRPC services.

4.1 Core Architecture of gRPC

gRPC is a high-performance, open-source, universal remote procedure call (RPC) framework initially developed by Google. Its core architecture is founded on the client-server model, ensuring efficient interprocess communication (IPC) with language-agnostic support. At a foundational level, the gRPC framework facilitates the execution of method calls remotely, similar to a local function invocation, abstracting away the complexities of network communication.

The client-server model in gRPC delineates clear roles and responsibilities across distributed applications. In this model, the server application defines the available service methods, which clients can invoke. By utilizing the power of protocol buffers as an interface definition language (IDL) and the underlying HTTP/2 protocol, gRPC achieves a robust and scalable architecture.

The server in a gRPC setup must implement specified service methods aligning with the definitions provided in protocol buffer files. Protocol buffers, a key element in gRPC, offer a structured way to define services and associated message types. The server listens for and handles incoming requests, processes them, and returns the corresponding response messages to the client.

A typical protocol buffer file, which serves as the contract between client and server, might look like the following:

```
syntax = "proto3";

package example;

service ExampleService {
  rpc ExampleMethod (ExampleRequest) returns (ExampleResponse);
}

message ExampleRequest {
  string name = 1;
}

message ExampleResponse {
  string message = 1;
}
```

In this example, the 'ExampleService' defines a single RPC method named 'ExampleMethod', which takes 'ExampleRequest' as an input

4.1. CORE ARCHITECTURE OF GRPC

and returns 'ExampleResponse'. This definition is leveraged by both the client and server to ensure consistent interaction.

Upon defining the protocol buffer, the gRPC tools auto-generate client and server code snippets in the chosen programming languages. This code provides the necessary infrastructure to marshal and unmarshal the protobuf-encoded messages, seamlessly facilitating client-server communication.

On the client side, the generated code includes a client stub, a critical component allowing clients to perform remote method invocations that appear local. The client stub manages communication intricacies such as serialization, sending requests, and processing responses. Implementing a client typically involves creating a stub instance corresponding to the service of interest and invoking the desired remote methods through this stub. The following Python example demonstrates a client-side invocation:

```python
import grpc
import example_pb2
import example_pb2_grpc

def run():
    with grpc.insecure_channel('localhost:50051') as channel:
        stub = example_pb2_grpc.ExampleServiceStub(channel)
        response = stub.ExampleMethod(example_pb2.ExampleRequest(name='World'))
        print("Client received: " + response.message)

if __name__ == '__main__':
    run()
```

In this example, a 'gRPC' channel is established to the server address, and an 'ExampleServiceStub' is instantiated. The client invokes 'ExampleMethod', passing it an 'ExampleRequest' message, and prints the result from 'ExampleResponse'.

The server-side implementation, however, requires the developer to extend the generated base class, providing concrete implementations for each service method. An example implementation in Python is illustrated below:

```python
from concurrent import futures
import grpc
import example_pb2
import example_pb2_grpc

class ExampleService(example_pb2_grpc.ExampleServiceServicer):
```

CHAPTER 4. UNDERSTANDING GRPC ARCHITECTURE AND CONCEPTS

```
    def ExampleMethod(self, request, context):
        return example_pb2.ExampleResponse(message='Hello, {}'.format(request.
            name))
def serve():
    server = grpc.server(futures.ThreadPoolExecutor(max_workers=10))
    example_pb2_grpc.add_ExampleServiceServicer_to_server(ExampleService(),
        server)
    server.add_insecure_port('[::]:50051')
    server.start()
    server.wait_for_termination()

if __name__ == '__main__':
    serve()
```

The server example employs a 'ThreadPoolExecutor' to handle concurrent requests, allowing multiple gRPC calls to be processed in parallel. The service method 'ExampleMethod' is defined to produce a greeting message, leveraging the input provided by the client.

Beyond the simplicity of basic calls, gRPC architectures support a range of communication patterns: unary, server streaming, client streaming, and bidirectional streaming. Unary calls, as demonstrated in the examples, involve a single request followed by a single response. However, the architecture of gRPC allows leveraging more advanced patterns, where streams of data can be sent between client and server.

- **Server Streaming and Client Streaming:**

In scenarios where large amounts of data need to be moved, server streaming and client streaming provide scalable solutions. Server streaming entails the server returning a stream of responses to a single client request. Conversely, client streaming allows clients to stream messages continuously to the server. Implementation of a server streaming method in the previous 'ExampleService' can showcase its functionality:

```
service ExampleService {
  rpc ExampleStream (ExampleRequest) returns (stream ExampleResponse);
}
```

With this specification, the server implementation alters slightly to handle streaming:

```
class ExampleService(example_pb2_grpc.ExampleServiceServicer):
    def ExampleStream(self, request, context):
```

4.1. CORE ARCHITECTURE OF GRPC

```
        for i in range(5):
            yield example_pb2.ExampleResponse(message='Hello, {}'.format(request.
                name))
```

Conversely, client streaming would modify the protocol buffer to accept a stream of requests:

```
service ExampleService {
  rpc ExampleClientStream (stream ExampleRequest) returns (ExampleResponse);
}
```

Server implementation might aggregate client messages:

```
class ExampleService(example_pb2_grpc.ExampleServiceServicer):
    def ExampleClientStream(self, request_iterator, context):
        messages = []
        for request in request_iterator:
            messages.append(request.name)
        return example_pb2.ExampleResponse(message='Hello, {}'.format(', '.join(
            messages)))
```

- **Bidirectional Streaming:**

Bidirectional streaming, the most advanced model, allows both the client and server to send a stream of messages to each other simultaneously. This bidirectional nature facilitates live communications channels such as chat services or IoT data streams.

For protocol buffers, a bidirectional method is specified similarly:

```
service ExampleService {
  rpc ExampleBidirectionalStream (stream ExampleRequest) returns (stream
      ExampleResponse);
}
```

In implementing bidirectional streaming, the server handles client requests and simultaneously sends responses in a streaming manner:

```
class ExampleService(example_pb2_grpc.ExampleServiceServicer):
    def ExampleBidirectionalStream(self, request_iterator, context):
        for request in request_iterator:
            yield example_pb2.ExampleResponse(message='Hello, {}'.format(request.
                name))
```

The flexibility of these communication patterns highlights gRPC's ability to cater to diverse application needs, emphasizing its core architectural prowess to support a variety of service interactions.

Another pivotal component of gRPC's architecture is its reliance on HTTP/2. The use of HTTP/2 enhances gRPC's ability to perform at scale by supporting multiplexed streams, reducing latency with server push, and using header compression to minimize overhead. Thanks to HTTP/2, gRPC connections can multiplex multiple requests over a single TCP connection, which is particularly beneficial in reducing the cost of connection establishment and improving network utilization.

Security and authentication further deepen gRPC's architecture. Secure connections are generally established using TLS, with mechanisms like token-based authentication or MTLS providing robust security features across client-server interactions.

Ultimately, the gRPC architecture's rigorous emphasis on efficiency, scalability, and flexibility makes it suitable for microservices architecture and real-time data systems. By abstracting complexity, it allows developers to focus on logic rather than transmission, a testament to its capability and significance in modern distributed systems.

4.2 Communication Patterns in gRPC

gRPC supports a range of communication patterns, enabling versatile interactions between distributed services. These patterns cater to different needs and use cases, from simple request-response interactions to complex data streaming. Understanding these communication paradigms, namely unary, server streaming, client streaming, and bidirectional streaming, is crucial for leveraging gRPC's full potential.

- **Unary RPCs**

    Unary RPCs are the simplest form of remote procedure call in gRPC. This pattern involves a single request sent from the client to the server, and a single response sent back from the server to the client. Unary RPCs are analogous to traditional HTTP requests, where the communication is entirely point-to-point for each operation.

    ```
    service UnaryService {
        rpc UnaryCall (UnaryRequest) returns (UnaryResponse);
    }
    ```

4.2. COMMUNICATION PATTERNS IN GRPC

In the example above, the 'UnaryService' defines a 'UnaryCall' method, specifying that it takes a 'UnaryRequest' and returns a 'UnaryResponse'. The corresponding Python client implementation could look like this:

```python
import grpc
import unary_pb2
import unary_pb2_grpc

def call_unary_service():
    with grpc.insecure_channel('localhost:50051') as channel:
        stub = unary_pb2_grpc.UnaryServiceStub(channel)
        response = stub.UnaryCall(unary_pb2.UnaryRequest(data='Hello'))
        print("Unary call response: ", response.data)

if __name__ == '__main__':
    call_unary_service()
```

The simplicity of unary RPC calls makes them ideal for use-cases predominantly characterized by singular requests and responses, such as fetching a single resource or executing a command.

- **Server Streaming RPCs**

    Server streaming RPCs involve the client sending a single request to the server, and the server returning multiple responses. This pattern is useful when a server needs to send a list of responses or continuous data streams back to a client. For example, streaming news updates or sensor data.

    The protobuf definition for a server streaming RPC is as follows:

    ```
    service StreamingService {
      rpc ServerStream (StreamRequest) returns (stream StreamResponse);
    }
    ```

    In this definition, the 'stream' keyword indicates that the method returns an ongoing stream of 'StreamResponse' messages. Below is a sample Python gRPC server implementing a server streaming method:

    ```python
    class StreamingService(streaming_pb2_grpc.StreamingServiceServicer):
        def ServerStream(self, request, context):
            for i in range(10):
                yield streaming_pb2.StreamResponse(data=f"Data chunk {i}")

    def serve():
        server = grpc.server(futures.ThreadPoolExecutor(max_workers=10))
        streaming_pb2_grpc.add_StreamingServiceServicer_to_server(
            StreamingService(), server)
    ```

```
server.add_insecure_port('[::]:50051')
server.start()
server.wait_for_termination()

if __name__ == '__main__':
    serve()
```

The client-side implementation to handle server streaming is also straightforward:

```
def run_server_streaming():
    with grpc.insecure_channel('localhost:50051') as channel:
        stub = streaming_pb2_grpc.StreamingServiceStub(channel)
        responses = stub.ServerStream(streaming_pb2.StreamRequest(query
            ='GetStream'))

        for response in responses:
            print("Server streaming response: ", response.data)

if __name__ == '__main__':
    run_server_streaming()
```

Server streaming RPCs allow clients to begin processing responses while additional data is still being transmitted. This reduces latency and can make applications appear more responsive.

- **Client Streaming RPCs**

In client streaming RPCs, the client sends a stream of requests to the server, and the server responds with a single response message. This pattern is appropriate for situations where the client needs to send a large volume of data over time, and the server only needs to process a final aggregate response.

The client streaming RPC is defined in protocol buffers as follows:

```
service StreamingService {
    rpc ClientStream (stream StreamRequest) returns (StreamResponse);
}
```

For implementation, here is an example of how the server processes client stream data:

```
class StreamingService(streaming_pb2_grpc.StreamingServiceServicer):
    def ClientStream(self, request_iterator, context):
        received_data = []
        for request in request_iterator:
            received_data.append(request.data)
```

4.2. COMMUNICATION PATTERNS IN GRPC

```
        print(f"Received data: {received_data}")
        return streaming_pb2.StreamResponse(data='Processed all data')

def serve():
    server = grpc.server(futures.ThreadPoolExecutor(max_workers=10))
    streaming_pb2_grpc.add_StreamingServiceServicer_to_server(
        StreamingService(), server)
    server.add_insecure_port('[::]:50051')
    server.start()
    server.wait_for_termination()

if __name__ == '__main__':
    serve()
```

In this server implementation, the method 'ClientStream' accumulates client-sent data into a list and processes it upon completion of the stream. A matching Python client example shows how to send data:

```
def client_streaming():
    with grpc.insecure_channel('localhost:50051') as channel:
        stub = streaming_pb2_grpc.StreamingServiceStub(channel)
        def generate_requests():
            for i in range(5):
                yield streaming_pb2.StreamRequest(data=f"Client data {i}")

        response = stub.ClientStream(generate_requests())
        print("Client streaming response: ", response.data)

if __name__ == '__main__':
    client_streaming()
```

Client streaming is effective in scenarios such as uploading large datasets or cases where client-side chunked data needs to be assembled into a singular server-side outcome.

- **Bidirectional Streaming RPCs**

  Bidirectional streaming RPCs enable both client and server to send and receive streams of messages in parallel. This type of communication pattern is akin to duplex communications, where sending and receiving occur simultaneously. It is used in applications requiring real-time feedback or continuous data synchronization.

  In protocol buffers, a bidirectional streaming RPC is defined simply by using 'stream' for both the request and response:

```
service BidirectionalService {
    rpc BidirectionalStream (stream BiRequest) returns (stream BiResponse);
}
```

A Python server example implementing bidirectional streaming is shown below:

```python
class BidirectionalService(bidirectional_pb2_grpc.
        BidirectionalServiceServicer):
    def BidirectionalStream(self, request_iterator, context):
        for request in request_iterator:
            yield bidirectional_pb2.BiResponse(info=f"Echo: {request.data}")

def serve():
    server = grpc.server(futures.ThreadPoolExecutor(max_workers=10))
    bidirectional_pb2_grpc.add_BidirectionalServiceServicer_to_server(
        BidirectionalService(), server)
    server.add_insecure_port('[::]:50051')
    server.start()
    server.wait_for_termination()

if __name__ == '__main__':
    serve()
```

On the client-side, bidirectional streaming can be handled as such:

```python
def bidirectional_streaming():
    with grpc.insecure_channel('localhost:50051') as channel:
        stub = bidirectional_pb2_grpc.BidirectionalServiceStub(channel)

        def generate_requests():
            for i in range(5):
                yield bidirectional_pb2.BiRequest(data=f"Message {i}")

        responses = stub.BidirectionalStream(generate_requests())
        for response in responses:
            print("Bidirectional response: ", response.info)

if __name__ == '__main__':
    bidirectional_streaming()
```

Bidirectional streaming is particularly beneficial in applications needing constant interaction, such as gaming servers, live video broadcasts, collaborative editing, or IoT device management, where real-time bidirectional data flows enhance the functionality and user experience.

The flexibility and variety of gRPC communication patterns support diverse application scenarios and provide developers with the tools for crafting efficient, responsive distributed services. Each pattern leverages gRPC's features, such as HTTP/2's multiplexing and flow control, to optimize network communication and resource management. These patterns provide the foundation for designing robust architectures, adapting to specific requirements of modern distributed systems.

4.3 HTTP/2 Underpinning gRPC

HTTP/2 forms the backbone of the gRPC framework, providing essential features that enhance performance, scalability, and efficiency in remote procedure calls across distributed systems. The adoption of HTTP/2 over the traditional HTTP/1.1 offers numerous advantages due to its design enhancements, well-suited for the needs of gRPC operations in modern microservices architectures.

HTTP/2 was developed to address several inefficiencies in HTTP/1.1. It introduces multiplexing, header compression, prioritization, and flow control—each contributing to improved performance and providing the underpinning mechanisms that enable gRPC's powerful capabilities.

- **Multiplexing:** Multiplexing in HTTP/2 resolves the head-of-line blocking problem encountered with HTTP/1.1. In HTTP/1.1, each connection is bound to a single request-response cycle, meaning concurrent requests require multiple connections. This approach results in considerable overhead and increased latency due to connection management. HTTP/2, however, allows multiple concurrent requests and responses between a client and server to be sent over a single connection.

CHAPTER 4. UNDERSTANDING GRPC ARCHITECTURE AND CONCEPTS

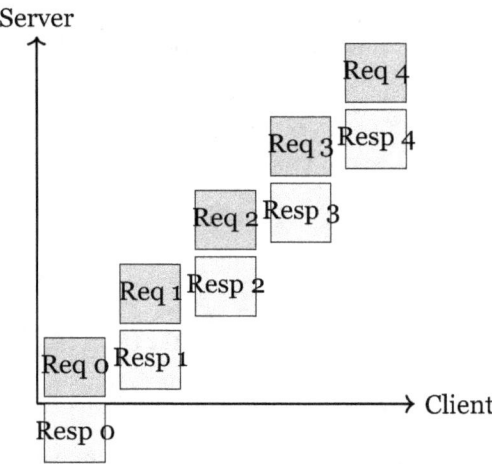

The diagram exemplifies the multiplexing of HTTP/2, where requests and responses can be multiplexed over a single TCP connection, significantly reducing the overhead involved in establishing multiple connections for concurrent communications. This reduction of overhead aligns directly with gRPC's need to support numerous RPCs with low latency.

- **Header Compression:** HTTP/2 introduces the HPACK compression format for header fields, drastically reducing the overhead associated with transmitting HTTP headers. HTTP/1.1 suffers inefficiencies due to repetitive redundant headers being sent with every request and response.

Through HPACK, headers are efficiently compressed and relatively lightweight, employing two primary techniques: static and dynamic tables. The static table includes common header fields pre-defined, while the dynamic table evolves as the connection persists, adapting to utilized headers. This adaptability is crucial for gRPC, which often involves numerous RPCs with similar metadata, such as method and authority headers.

```
Header 1      Header 2
+--------+    +--------+
```

4.3. HTTP/2 UNDERPINNING GRPC

```
| :meth. |   | :path |
| :auth. |   | ...   |
| ...    |-> | ...   |
+--------+   +-------+
```

By compressing HTTP headers, gRPC minimizes bandwidth and processing requirements, which is particularly beneficial in high-throughput applications, directly impacting performance efficiency.

- **Stream Prioritization:** Stream prioritization in HTTP/2 enables clients to assign priority levels to streams, ensuring that essential data is transmitted before less critical information. While gRPC does not explicitly use stream prioritization, multiplexing and efficient use of bandwidth through prioritization mechanisms contribute to overall system performance.

An application could, for example, prioritize updates from real-time sensors over batch data transmission, ensuring that time-sensitive information is transmitted without unnecessary delays:

```
Stream 1: sensor data -- Priority: High
Stream 2: log data    -- Priority: Low
```

The ability to manage and prioritize data streams enhances gRPC's capability to handle diverse and heterogeneous data sources efficiently, particularly in data-intensive environments like IoT.

- **Server Push:** Server push is a notable feature in HTTP/2, allowing servers to initiate data send operations for resources that clients have not requested, preemptively pushing potential resource requirements. Although gRPC does not inherently use server push, the technology enables future enhancements and extensions, encouraging richer interaction models within microservices and client-server communications.

Underlying this feature is the potential for more anticipatory data serving strategies within specific applications where known dependencies exist, effectively preempting cache misses or delays:

Client requests resource A
Server responds with A and pushes resource B

Server push can serve data more strategically, potentially suggesting optimization routes for gRPC applications seeking to implement bespoke communication logic enhancements.

- **Flow Control:** Flow control in HTTP/2 is an integral mechanism allowing both the client and server to manage the amount of data that can be sent or received at any given time, safeguarding against data congestion and buffer overflow. This mechanism ensures that network usage is optimal without overwhelm.

The flow control capability is central to gRPC, especially in streaming scenarios where large payloads or multiple messages are being transmitted. Proper management through flow control ensures smooth data exchange, reducing the likelihood of buffer overflow and optimizing throughput:

```
+--------------------+
| Flow Control       |
+--------------------+
| Receive Window     |
| Update Windows     |
| Time-stamped Ack   |
+--------------------+
```

Flow control distinguishes itself by allowing dynamic data management across connections, attributing to gRPC's claim over reliable and efficient communication protocols in distributed systems.

- **Security:** HTTP/2 mandates the use of Transport Layer Security (TLS) in practical deployments, ensuring communication integrity and confidentiality. gRPC leverages TLS to encrypt data streams between client and server, which is vital for maintaining secure, private communications across potentially untrusted networks.

Adopting strongly integrated security features positions gRPC as a robust solution for sensitive applications like financial services or personal data transfer, expanding its usability across regulated industries.

4.3. HTTP/2 UNDERPINNING GRPC

```
TLS Handshake
 + -- ClientHello
   -- ServerHello
   << Key Exchange >>
   -- Finished (Encrypted)
 + -- Finished (Encrypted)
Data Encrypted
```

TLS, combined with mutual authentication techniques, strengthens gRPC's proposition for securely operating within highly distributed architectures, ensuring both authorized access and encrypted data flow.

- **Implementation and Examples:** Let us examine a practical gRPC implementation using these HTTP/2 enhancements. The example follows the server and client setup using Python gRPC with enforced TLS and HTTP/2 features:

```python
import grpc
from concurrent import futures
import secure_pb2
import secure_pb2_grpc
import ssl

class SecureService(secure_pb2_grpc.SecureServiceServicer):
    def SecureCall(self, request, context):
        return secure_pb2.SecureResponse(message=f'Hello, {request.name}!')

def serve():
    server = grpc.server(futures.ThreadPoolExecutor(max_workers=10))
    secure_pb2_grpc.add_SecureServiceServicer_to_server(SecureService(), server)

    with open('server_cert.pem', 'rb') as f:
        certificate_chain = f.read()
    with open('server_key.pem', 'rb') as f:
        private_key = f.read()

    server_credentials = grpc.ssl_server_credentials([(private_key, certificate_chain)])
    server.add_secure_port('[::]:50051', server_credentials)
    server.start()
    server.wait_for_termination()

if __name__ == '__main__':
    serve()
```

```python
import grpc
import secure_pb2
import secure_pb2_grpc

def run():
    with open('ca_cert.pem', 'rb') as f:
        trusted_certs = f.read()
```

```
credentials = grpc.ssl_channel_credentials(root_certificates=trusted_certs)
channel = grpc.secure_channel('localhost:50051', credentials)

stub = secure_pb2_grpc.SecureServiceStub(channel)
response = stub.SecureCall(secure_pb2.SecureRequest(name='Alice'))
print("Secure Response: ", response.message)

if __name__ == '__main__':
    run()
```

The server configuration displays the use of a secure channel with certificate-based authentication. Both client and server must present valid certificates, affirming mutual authentication that is pivotal for security.

- **Concluding Reflections:** HTTP/2 significantly impacts the design and operation of gRPC by leveraging multiplexing, efficient header compression, prioritization, server push, flow control, and enhanced security through TLS. These features collectively sustain gRPC's capability to offer high-performance solutions suitable for a wide range of applications, particularly those operating in microservices ecosystems or distributed environments with complex data exchange requirements.

Each aspect of HTTP/2 maximized by gRPC plays a cohesive role in advancing reliable, performant, and scalable RPC frameworks, fostering the continuous evolution of modern distributed applications.

4.4 Data Serialization with Protocol Buffers

Protocol Buffers, often referred to as Protobuf, are a language-neutral, platform-neutral, extensible mechanism for serializing structured data. Developed by Google, Protocol Buffers serve as the default serialization mechanism in gRPC, designed to ensure efficient, structured data exchange between services.

Serialization is essential in distributed systems to encode data structures into a format that can be easily stored or transmitted, while deserialization is the process of converting that format back into usable

4.4. DATA SERIALIZATION WITH PROTOCOL BUFFERS

data. Protobuf stands out due to its performance, portability, and ease of use, making it a popular choice for gRPC and other RPC systems.

- Protocol Buffers are fundamentally similar to XML or JSON in purpose but with distinctive efficiencies.

- While XML and JSON focus on readability, Protocol Buffers focus on performance, resulting in smaller message sizes and faster parsing.

- Protocol Buffers utilize a language-neutral interface definition language (IDL) to specify message structures and services, which results in high consistency across diverse platforms.

Here is a simple example of a Protocol Buffer schema:

```
syntax = "proto3";

message Person {
  string name = 1;
  int32 id = 2;
  string email = 3;
}
```

In this snippet, we define a 'Person' message, containing 'name', 'id', and 'email' fields. Each field has a distinct type and a unique numerical tag, used to identify fields in the binary encoding format.

- Protocol Buffers' binary encoding achieves compactness by taking advantage of field numbers and types.

- Fields that have default values or are absent do not get encoded, reducing message size.

- Furthermore, Protobuf employs a technique known as varint encoding for integer types, optimizing the space used based on the actual value. Lower values take fewer bytes to encode.

Numeric Data Encoded as	FieldKey, FieldValue
Where	
FieldKey	FieldNumber « 3 | WireType
FieldValue	Bytes

Through such compact encoding mechanisms, Protobuf minimizes the bandwidth and storage footprint of serialized messages, offering performance advantages over XML and JSON.

One of the most advantageous features of Protocol Buffers is its support for backward and forward compatibility, mitigating issues when evolving schemas. Fields can be added to messages without breaking compatibility with older programs. Conversely, obsolete fields can be marked as reserved to prevent reuse.

The ability to evolve APIs and services over time without breaking compatibility is critical. Here's an extended version of the 'Person' message, illustrating backward compatibility:

```
syntax = "proto3";

message Person {
  string name = 1;
  int32 id = 2;
  string email = 3;
  string phone_number = 4; // Newly added
}
```

In this updated 'Person' message, the field 'phone_number' is added, ensuring older programs that used the prior schema remain functional without modification, as the new attribute is ignored by default. This attribute can be introduced seamlessly into new application versions.

Protocol Buffers are also renowned for automatic code generation. With a simple definition file, developers generate serialization code for multiple programming languages, such as C++, Java, Python, Go, and more, using the Protobuf compiler 'protoc'.

The following command generates Python code from a '.proto' file:

```
protoc --python_out=. addressbook.proto
```

Upon execution, the command creates a Python module containing classes that inherently manage conversion between well-defined Protobuf objects and raw binary data.

The cross-platform capability is extensive, resulting in consistent, compatible messages between services coded in different languages. This property makes Protocol Buffers a desirable data interchange format in polyglot environments typical of microservices.

4.4. DATA SERIALIZATION WITH PROTOCOL BUFFERS

When paired with gRPC, Protocol Buffers bring abstraction levels that enable easy definition of service interfaces alongside the data structures they utilize. Here's how a gRPC service is defined using Protocol Buffers:

```
syntax = "proto3";

package tutorial;

service PersonService {
  rpc GetPerson (PersonId) returns (Person);
}

message Person {
  string name = 1;
  int32 id = 2;
  string email = 3;
  string phone_number = 4;
}

message PersonId {
  int32 id = 1;
}
```

In this example, the 'PersonService' service is defined with a single 'GetPerson' method, taking 'PersonId' as input and returning a 'Person'. gRPC automatically uses Protocol Buffers to serialize input parameters and return values, simplifying the process dramatically.

Here is an example of implementing a simple gRPC service using the previously defined Protocol Buffers:

```
from concurrent import futures
import grpc
import tutorial_pb2
import tutorial_pb2_grpc

class PersonServiceServicer(tutorial_pb2_grpc.PersonServiceServicer):
    def GetPerson(self, request, context):
        return tutorial_pb2.Person(name='John Doe', id=request.id, email='john.
            doe@example.com', phone_number='555-1234')

def serve():
    server = grpc.server(futures.ThreadPoolExecutor(max_workers=10))
    tutorial_pb2_grpc.add_PersonServiceServicer_to_server(PersonServiceServicer(),
        server)
    server.add_insecure_port('[::]:50051')
    server.start()
    server.wait_for_termination()

if __name__ == '__main__':
    serve()
```

```
def run():
    with grpc.insecure_channel('localhost:50051') as channel:
        stub = tutorial_pb2_grpc.PersonServiceStub(channel)
        response = stub.GetPerson(tutcrial_pb2.PersonId(id=1))
    print("Person response: ", response)

if __name__ == '__main__':
    run()
```

This server sends a hardcoded 'Person' message in response to a client request, using Protobuf-serialized messages over the network for efficient data exchange.

While Protocol Buffers provide a compact binary serialization, it is essential to consider security implications such as ensuring data integrity and confidentiality, particularly when transmitting sensitive information. Protobuf data, being binary, might bypass typical textual data inspections, necessitating protective measures like encryption or digital signatures.

Efficiency considerations involve understanding the trade-offs between binary size, parsing speed, and complexity. While Protobuf offers superior space and speed advantages, its binary nature can complicate debugging compared to textual formats like JSON. Consequently, comprehensive logging or equivalent monitoring might be advisable to track operational specifics within serialized communications.

Protocol Buffers continue to evolve, with ongoing enhancements like 'proto3' for simplified syntax and default behaviors. However, limitations such as lack of direct support for schemas or representation of complex structures (for instance, recursive definitions or deeply nested messages) might require thoughtful workarounds.

As Protocol Buffers are augmented over time, potential adaptations and newer Protobuf functionalities offer improved usability and efficiency, paving paths to accommodate emerging technological requirements and more complex data representations typical within dynamic microservices ecosystems.

The choice of Protocol Buffers as the serialization strategy within gRPC underscores its utility in optimizing serialized data exchange in distributed systems. The inherent efficiencies combined with multi-language support, extensibility, and simplistic integration make Protobuf a robust solution fulfilling the requirements of modern high-performance communications across expansive application domains.

4.5 Naming and Discovery Concepts

Naming and discovery are fundamental aspects of distributed systems, facilitating seamless interaction between multiple services. In gRPC, these concepts address the essential need for clients to identify and connect with service instances, supporting scalability and flexibility in dynamic and evolving environments. This section delves into the mechanisms and strategies that govern service naming and discovery within gRPC, providing detailed insights and illustrative coding examples.

Introduction to Naming and Resolution

In distributed architectures, clients must resolve service names to corresponding network addresses. Similarly, when services are scaled horizontally or deployed across multiple instances, it becomes imperative for clients to discover available service endpoints. Naming and discovery mechanisms avoid the need for clients to hardcode endpoint details, minimizing the risk of errors and reducing maintenance overhead.

A typical service name may look like this in a gRPC system:

service.example.com

When a client makes a request, it uses this service name, which is then resolved to the current network address of the available service instances, allowing dynamic updates per changes in service endpoints.

Service Registries

A service registry is a central component that maintains a mapping of service names to available service instances. The registry is responsible for keeping track of services as they start or stop, providing real-time endpoint updates to clients. Popular service discovery tools like Kubernetes, etcd, Consul, and ZooKeeper are commonly integrated with gRPC to handle service registrations and queries.

An example of using Consul for service registration is illustrated below:

```
import consul

c = consul.Consul()

service_id = 'service1-instance3'
service_name = 'service-example'
address = '192.168.1.5'
port = 8080

c.agent.service.register(
    service_name, service_id=service_id, address=address, port=port
)
```

In this example, a service registration includes service ID, name, address, and port. Consul is utilized to update the centralized registry, making it available for discovery by clients.

Client-Side Load Balancing

Once a service address is resolved, gRPC clients can employ load-balancing strategies across the multiple instances returned through the discovery process. This mechanism distributes requests uniformly, optimizing resource utilization and reducing response times.

gRPC supports several load-balancing algorithms, including:

- Round-robin: Distributes requests cyclically across instances.

- Least-connections: Directs requests to instances with fewer active connections.

- Random: Requests are assigned randomly to available instances.

```
import grpc
import service_pb2
import service_pb2_grpc

def channel_with_lb():
    channel = grpc.insecure_channel(
        'service-1.example.com', options=(('grpc.lb_policy_name', 'round_robin'))
    )
    stub = service_pb2_grpc.ExampleServiceStub(channel)
    return stub
```

This code demonstrates creating a gRPC channel configured with a round-robin load-balancing policy, enhancing request distribution across service instances.

4.5. NAMING AND DISCOVERY CONCEPTS

Handling Service Failures

Robust discovery systems must gracefully manage service failures, maintaining seamless operations amidst dynamic conditions. When a service instance fails, clients should automatically retry requests on healthy instances, ensuring high availability and reliability.

Service registries frequently integrate with health checks, enforcing periodic verification of service availability. An unhealthy instance is marked unavailable, preventing client requests until it regains healthy status.

A sample health check configuration using Consul may be as follows:

```
{
    "check": {
        "http": "http://{agent_ip}:8080/health",
        "interval": "10s",
        "timeout": "1s"
    }
}
```

This configuration specifies an HTTP-based health check, conducted every 10 seconds. If the check fails, the service instance is marked unavailable until the check passes, adjusting readiness status dynamically.

Dynamic Configuration Updates

Dynamic updates enable service discovery mechanisms to adapt to live changes in service deployments. Configuration changes, address updates, and instance scaling are seamlessly integrated into the discovery process, offering uninterrupted service access.

Registries like etcd provide watch APIs, enabling services to subscribe to updates and adapt immediately. This is valuable for DevOps environments relying on continuous integration and delivery.

Example code to watch updates in etcd:

```
from etcd3 import Etcd3Client

client = Etcd3Client()
watch_id = client.watch('/services/service-example/', callback=update_handler)

def update_handler(event):
    print("Service update event: ", event.events)
```

The watch method triggers real-time callbacks whenever a service entry is altered, enabling immediate and automated response to changes.

Service Mesh Integration

Service meshes add an additional abstraction layer designed to manage service-to-service communications across microservices. They provide built-in functionalities such as traffic management, policy enforcement, and telemetry in addition to naming and discovery capabilities.

Popular service meshes include Istio, Linkerd, and Consul Connect, incorporating sidecars to offload networking responsibilities from core applications and enhance resilience and observability.

A typical service mesh pattern using Istio involves defining virtual services and destination rules, encapsulating routing details:

```
apiVersion: networking.istio.io/v1alpha3
kind: VirtualService
metadata:
  name: example-service
spec:
  hosts:
  - service.example.com
  http:
  - route:
    - destination:
        host: service-example
        subset: v1
```

The VirtualService specifies which hosts to route traffic to and the criteria controlling this behavior, providing flexible rules for managing service traffic.

Security and Access Control

Naming and discovery integrate tightly with security frameworks, enforcing authentication and authorization rules as part of service interaction policies. Authentication often involves identity providers and tokens, validating service identities and limiting unauthorized access.

The concept of mutual TLS (mTLS) is frequently employed to ensure both client and server authenticate each other, encrypting the communication channels. It is critical to protect service registries from unauthorized queries or updates, supported by authentication mechanisms and encrypted transport layers.

Secure Consul communication, example:

```
consul agent -server -bootstrap-expect=1 -data-dir=data/ \
-encrypt=<base64-key> -config-dir=consul/ -node=<node-name> \
-ca-file=ca.pem -cert-file=server-cert.pem -key-file=server-key.pem
```

Security commands allow encrypted data transmission and management of cryptographic keys to ensure privacy and prevent forged service entries.

Challenges and Considerations

Despite advancements in naming and discovery, they present challenges needing consideration. Network latency, registry consistency, and split-brain conditions are persistent issues that must be addressed. Deployments should ensure synchronized registry state across distributed systems, prevent network isolation from disrupting access, and optimize for low-latency communication.

Ultimately, selecting optimal strategies and technologies for naming and discovery is influenced by architecture constraints, scalability targets, and operational requirements. Each component must harmonize with the broader system architecture, promoting an efficient, reliable, and maintainable service discovery infrastructure.

By leveraging the full spectrum of capabilities service discovery ecosystems offer in conjunction with gRPC, robust architectures emerge capable of adapting to evolving demands, reducing downtime risks, and optimizing microservice interactions. With focused consideration of naming and discovery concepts alongside gRPC, distributed systems can capitalize on the automated orchestration, guided by principles aligned with modern technological-culture advancements.

4.6 Load Balancing and Scalability

Load balancing and scalability are core components of robust distributed systems, pivotal for handling varying workloads and ensuring service availability. gRPC, widely used in microservice architectures, provides support for sophisticated load balancing strategies to facilitate consistent performance and seamless horizontal scaling. This section explores the principles and practices of load balancing and scalability within the context of gRPC, highlighting the techniques and considerations crucial for modern application development.

The Importance of Load Balancing Load balancing distributes incoming network traffic across multiple backend servers, reducing the strain on any single server, maximizing throughput, and ensuring reliability. Without effective load balancing strategies, systems may encounter bottlenecks, resulting in degraded service, latency issues, or even downtime during peak loads.

The primary goals of load balancing include:

- Uniform distribution of client requests: Ensuring no single server becomes overwhelmed.

- Failover capabilities: Redirecting requests from failed instances to operational ones.

- Reduction in latency: Enhancing the user experience by optimizing response times.

- Resource optimization: Effectively utilizing all available resources in a scalable way.

gRPC Load Balancing Models gRPC supports several load balancing models integral to various deployment needs, such as:

- Client-side Load Balancing: Here, the client is responsible for distributing requests across available endpoints. Utilizing a resolver, the client retrieves IPs and ports, while the load balancing policy determines request distribution. This model suits dynamic or frequently changing backends.

- Server-side Load Balancing: With this model, an external load balancer, often managed as part of the network infrastructure, directs requests to services. This approach centralizes control but may introduce additional latency as requests initially traverse the load balancer.

- Proxy-based Load Balancing: Proxies or service meshes distribute incoming requests to pool members. It offers a more

4.6. LOAD BALANCING AND SCALABILITY

holistic solution encompassing security, discovery, and routing, beneficial for complex architectures.

Each model employs distinct strategies and poses unique benefits tailored to deployment environments and operational requirements.

Client-Side Load Balancing in gRPC In gRPC, client-side load balancing integrates tightly with service discovery mechanisms, granting flexibility to directly manage traffic distribution across clients. Implementing client-side load balancing involves:

- Name Resolution: Translating service names into addresses. Typically achieved through DNS or integrated service registries like etcd or Consul.
- Load Balancing Policies: Such as round-robin, pick-first, or custom algorithms, determining how client requests are spread. A sample configuration might appear as follows:

```
import grpc
import service_pb2
import service_pb2_grpc

def create_channel():
    channel = grpc.insecure_channel(
        'service-name', options=(('grpc.lb_policy_name', 'round_robin'),)
    )
    return channel

def run_client():
    channel = create_channel()
    stub = service_pb2_grpc.ExampleStub(channel)
    response = stub.Method(service_pb2.Request(message='Hello'))
    print("Response received: ", response)
```

In this example, the round-robin policy is employed to distribute requests evenly across available instances resolved by the name resolver.

Server-Side Load Balancing Server-side load balancing acts at the network layer, often deployed using load balancers like AWS Elastic Load Balancer (ELB), Google Cloud Load Balancing, or physical hardware balancers. These external entities manage requests and provide unified entry points to the backend servers, ensuring high availability.

A notable advantage of server-side load balancing is simplicity from the client's perspective, where the complexity is abstracted away, allowing centralized management:

- Active Health Checks: Regularly verifies the status of backend servers.

- SSL Termination: Shifts SSL decryption processes to the load balancer.

- Sticky Sessions: Maintains client sessions per specific parameters, enhancing stateful interactions.

Example of configuring a load balancer in a cloud provider like AWS:

```
aws elb create-load-balancer \
  --load-balancer-name my-load-balancer \
  --listeners Protocol=HTTP,LoadBalancerPort=80,InstanceProtocol=HTTP,InstancePort=80 \
  --availability-zones us-east-1a us-east-1b
```

Such configurations, while requiring upfront setup, offload resource distribution into managed services, helping leverage built-in failover and scaling features.

Scalability Considerations Scalability refers to a system's ability to accommodate increases in load and is essential for addressing demand fluctuations without sacrificing performance or reliability.

- Horizontal Scalability: Involves adding service instances. gRPC's stateless design facilitates easy replication across newly provisioned instances.

- Vertical Scalability: Increases resources within the existing nodes, optimizing performance but with potential limits.

The seamless integration of load balancing aids scalability by intelligently routing to less-loaded instances, promoting an effective scale-up or scale-out strategy determined by the workload characteristics.

4.6. LOAD BALANCING AND SCALABILITY

Resilience and Observability Tools Sophisticated gRPC ecosystems supplement load balancing with resilience and observability tools, ensuring sustained operation even under failure scenarios. Techniques such as circuit breakers, retry logic, and rate limiting combat overload conditions, protecting services from cascading failures.

Integration with observability tools such as Prometheus for monitoring or Jaeger for tracing creates actionable insights into load patterns and system behavior, informing data-driven decisions about resource allocation and load distribution tactics.

Example: Implementing client-side retry logic in a gRPC client:

```python
from grpc import StatusCode

def call_with_retry(stub, request):
    attempts = 0
    max_retries = 3
    while attempts < max_retries:
        attempts += 1
        try:
            response = stub.Method(request)
            print("Successful response: ", response)
            break
        except grpc.RpcError as e:
            if e.code() in (StatusCode.UNAVAILABLE,):
                print(f"Retrying {attempts}/{max_retries} due to error: {e}")
            else:
                print("Non-recoverable error occurred: ", e)
                break
```

The retry mechanism aims to mitigate temporary failures, leveraging status codes to identify recoverable errors and attempt reconnections.

Traffic Management with Service Meshes Service meshes further extend the capabilities of load balancing by incorporating advanced traffic management patterns into distributed architectures, employing sidecars to manage connectivity, resilience, and insights, independent of the business logic.

Istio, a prominent service mesh example, introduces Envoy proxies as sidecars, which fortify load balancing with policies covering circuit breaking, mirroring, redirection, and more:

- Traffic Splitting: Divides traffic across versioned services.
- Traffic Shifting: Gradually routes percentages of traffic during

deployments.

Service mesh configurations are usually expressed in YAML for Kubernetes deployments:

```
apiVersion: networking.istio.io/v1alpha3
kind: DestinationRule
metadata:
  name: example-destination-rule
spec:
  host: service-example
  trafficPolicy:
    loadBalancer:
      simple: ROUND_ROBIN
```

The 'DestinationRule' provides fine-grained configurations for traffic routing, underpinned by sophisticated policies managed by the mesh, refining the orchestration of traffic loads to optimize service interactions.

Cost Efficiency and Environmental Impact Efficient load balancing and scalability contribute not only to improved performance but also to optimized operational costs by ensuring resources are utilized effectively without over-provisioning. It aligns with environmentally-conscious computing practices, aiming at reduced energy consumption through efficient resource allocation.

To conclude, the orchestration of load balancing and scalability within gRPC frameworks is essential for building resilient, performant distributed systems. Through strategic alignment with tools for monitoring, resilience, and dynamic adjustments, gRPC applications achieve a scalable and highly responsive architecture. This bricks the foundation, entrenched in best practices of modern software engineering, for enduring systems adaptable to business challenges and technological evolutions.

Chapter 5

gRPC in Action: Implementing Unary and Streaming APIs

This chapter provides practical guidance on implementing gRPC APIs, focusing on unary and streaming communication patterns. It includes a step-by-step walkthrough of creating unary RPCs, where a single request results in a single response, followed by strategies for implementing server streaming, client streaming, and bidirectional streaming RPCs. The chapter also addresses error handling specific to streaming scenarios and offers techniques to optimize the performance of streaming operations. Through these examples, readers will learn how to effectively leverage gRPC for varied real-world communication needs.

5.1 Implementing Unary RPCs

Unary Remote Procedure Calls (RPCs) are the simplest form of communication pattern in gRPC, involving a single request from the client to the server and a corresponding single response back. This mechanism is not unlike traditional HTTP communications but leverages gRPC's advantages such as automatic code generation, built-in load balancing, and HTTP/2 multiplex features.

To begin implementing unary RPCs, it is essential to understand the fundamental components required, starting from the .proto files to the server and client code.

- **Creating the Protocol Buffers Definition**

Protocol Buffers, or proto files, are used to define the gRPC services and the structure of the request and response messages. For unary RPCs, we define a service with methods that take a request message and return a response message.

Below is an example of a basic proto file:

```
syntax = "proto3";

package example;

service UnaryService {
  rpc SayHello (HelloRequest) returns (HelloReply) {}
}

message HelloRequest {
  string name = 1;
}

message HelloReply {
  string message = 1;
}
```

This .proto file defines a service UnaryService with one method called SayHello. It receives a HelloRequest containing a single field name, and it returns a HelloReply which contains a response message.

- **Generating Client and Server Code**

Once the proto definition is ready, we use the Protocol Compiler

5.1. IMPLEMENTING UNARY RPCS

(protoc) to generate the client and server interface code. This ensures that both parties communicate with the same protocol structures.

For instance, using Python:

```
$ protoc -I=. --python_out=. --grpc_python_out=. example.proto
```

This command generates Python modules that can be used to implement client and server logic.

- **Implementing the Server**

The server implementation involves defining the methods specified in the proto file. Consider the following Python server implementation:

```python
import grpc
from concurrent import futures
import example_pb2
import example_pb2_grpc

class UnaryServiceServicer(example_pb2_grpc.UnaryServiceServicer):
    def SayHello(self, request, context):
        return example_pb2.HelloReply(message='Hello, {}'.format(request.name))

def serve():
    server = grpc.server(futures.ThreadPoolExecutor(max_workers=10))
    example_pb2_grpc.add_UnaryServiceServicer_to_server(UnaryServiceServicer(), server)
    server.add_insecure_port('[::]:50051')
    server.start()
    server.wait_for_termination()

if __name__ == '__main__':
    serve()
```

In this example, UnaryServiceServicer implements the SayHello method. The server is set up to listen on port 50051 and is capable of handling incoming unary requests by creating a HelloReply message responding with a greeting.

- **Implementing the Client**

The client part involves creating a stub for the service and making a call to the server. Examine the following client implementation:

```python
import grpc
import example_pb2
```

CHAPTER 5. GRPC IN ACTION: IMPLEMENTING UNARY AND STREAMING APIS

```
import example_pb2_grpc

def run():
    with grpc.insecure_channel('localhost:50051') as channel:
        stub = example_pb2_grpc.UnaryServiceStub(channel)
        response = stub.SayHello(example_pb2.HelloRequest(name='World'))
    print("UnaryService client received: " + response.message)

if __name__ == '__main__':
    run()
```

In the client, a channel is created to communicate with the server, and a stub is used to make RPC calls. The SayHello method is invoked with a HelloRequest instance, and the response message is printed.

- **Exploring the Communication Process**

When the client makes a SayHello request, the gRPC framework handles serialization (using Protocol Buffers) and transmits the request to the server. The server deserializes the request, processes it, and sends back a serialized response. This round-trip is optimized for performance using features of HTTP/2 such as header compression and multiplexing.

- **Error Handling in Unary RPCs**

Error handling in unary RPCs involves managing both network issues and application-level errors. gRPC offers comprehensive status codes to convey error conditions such as UNAVAILABLE for a server that can't be reached, or INVALID_ARGUMENT for application-level validation issues.

Consider enhancing server-side logic for error handling:

```
from grpc import StatusCode

class UnaryServiceServicer(example_pb2_grpc.UnaryServiceServicer):
    def SayHello(self, request, context):
        if not request.name:
            context.abort(StatusCode.INVALID_ARGUMENT, "Name is required.")
        return example_pb2.HelloReply(message='Hello, {}'.format(request.name))
```

In this example, a check ensures the presence of a name field. If absent, the server aborts the request with INVALID_ARGUMENT error.

5.1. IMPLEMENTING UNARY RPCS

- **Testing the RPC Calls**

Testing is a crucial phase to ensure robustness and correctness. Unit tests for gRPC services might involve invoking methods with mocked objects to simulate server responses.

For testing Python gRPC calls, you can employ the unittest framework:

```python
import unittest
from unittest.mock import Mock
import example_pb2
import example_pb2_grpc

class TestUnaryService(unittest.TestCase):

    def setUp(self):
        self.service = example_pb2_grpc.UnaryServiceServicer()
        self.context = Mock()

    def test_say_hello(self):
        request = example_pb2.HelloRequest(name='Tester')
        response = self.service.SayHello(request, self.context)
        self.assertEqual(response.message, 'Hello, Tester')

    def test_say_hello_no_name(self):
        request = example_pb2.HelloRequest(name='')
        with self.assertRaises(grpc.RpcError) as e:
            self.service.SayHello(request, self.context)
        self.assertEqual(e.exception.code(), StatusCode.INVALID_ARGUMENT)

if __name__ == '__main__':
    unittest.main()
```

In this test suite, special attention is given to verifying that the SayHello method produces the correct response and handles errors appropriately.

- **Security Considerations**

For secure communications, gRPC supports TLS to encrypt the data in transit. Server-side configurations must include SSL certificates and enforce secure channel requirements between client and server.

Here is a snippet to enable TLS in the server:

```python
def serve_with_tls():
    server = grpc.server(futures.ThreadPoolExecutor(max_workers=10))
    # Load server credentials
    with open('server.key', 'rb') as f:
        private_key = f.read()
```

```
with open('server.pem', 'rb') as f:
    certificate_chain = f.read()

server_credentials = grpc.ssl_server_credentials(((private_key, certificate_chain),)
    )
example_pb2_grpc.add_UnaryServiceServicer_to_server(UnaryServiceServicer(),
    server)
server.add_secure_port('[::]:50051', server_credentials)
server.start()
server.wait_for_termination()
```

Similar configuration for the client involves specifying a channel credential with the server certificate.

- **Deployment and Scaling**

For production readiness, scaling considerations must include deploying multiple instances of the gRPC server and leveraging gRPC's built-in load balancing for horizontal scaling. Containerization using platforms like Docker can aid in consistent deployment across environments.

```
$ docker build -t grpc-server .
$ docker run -p 50051:50051 grpc-server
```

Additionally, integrating gRPC services with service mesh technologies can provide automatic traffic management, monitoring, and policy enforcement.

- **Debugging and Monitoring**

Effective diagnostics are indispensable. gRPC provides hooks and interceptors for logging metadata, tracing call execution, and exporting metrics for visualization in dashboards like Prometheus or Jaeger.

```
class LoggingInterceptor(grpc.ServerInterceptor):
    def intercept_service(self, continuation, handler_call_details):
        # Extracting and logging metadata
        method = handler_call_details.method
        metadata = dict(handler_call_details.invocation_metadata)
        print(f"Method called: {method}, Metadata: {metadata}")
        return continuation(handler_call_details)
```

Logging interceptors like the above help in recording gRPC requests' metadata and method invocation details to facilitate tracing and debugging efforts.

5.2. SERVER STREAMING RPCS

These strategic implementations result in a robust unary RPC solution that scales, adapts to changing network conditions, and upholds security and reliability principles intrinsic to modern communication frameworks. Through careful design and best practices, unary RPCs harness gRPC's potential to develop resilient, high-performance applications across distributed systems.

5.2 Server Streaming RPCs

Server streaming RPCs in gRPC represent a communication pattern where a client sends a single request to the server and receives a stream of responses back. This pattern is powerful for scenarios where the server needs to asynchronously send multiple messages back to the client in response to a single client request, such as real-time data feeds, notifications, or batch data processing results. Understanding how to implement server streaming RPCs effectively can greatly enhance the capabilities of networked applications.

- **Defining the Protocol Buffers:** As in unary RPCs, the implementation of server streaming RPCs begins with defining the service and messages in a .proto file. The main difference is in the method's return type, which denotes a stream of messages.

    Consider the .proto definition for a weather data streaming service:

```
syntax = "proto3";

package weather;

service WeatherService {
  rpc StreamWeather (WeatherRequest) returns (stream WeatherReport) {}
}

message WeatherRequest {
  string location = 1;
}

message WeatherReport {
  string location = 1;
  string weather_description = 2;
  float temperature = 3;
  uint64 timestamp = 4;
}
```

In this example, the StreamWeather method in the WeatherService is defined to return a stream of WeatherReport messages in response to a single WeatherRequest.

- **Generating Client and Server Code:** Once the proto file is established, the next step is to use the Protocol Compiler (protoc) to generate the required client and server code. For a Python implementation, the following command can be used:

```
$ protoc -I=. --python_out=. --grpc_python_out=. weather.proto
```

This operation generates Python modules that can be further implemented to handle server streaming.

- **Implementing the Server:** The server must implement the streaming logic defined in the proto file. The server-side logic involves generating and sending multiple responses stream to the client.

```python
import grpc
from concurrent import futures
import time
import weather_pb2
import weather_pb2_grpc

class WeatherServiceServicer(weather_pb2_grpc.WeatherServiceServicer):
    def StreamWeather(self, request, context):
        for i in range(5):
            weather_report = weather_pb2.WeatherReport(
                location=request.location,
                weather_description="Sunny",
                temperature=22.5,
                timestamp=int(time.time())
            )
            yield weather_report
            time.sleep(1) # Simulate periodic data production

def serve():
    server = grpc.server(futures.ThreadPoolExecutor(max_workers=10))
    weather_pb2_grpc.add_WeatherServiceServicer_to_server(WeatherServiceServicer(), server)
    server.add_insecure_port('[::]:50051')
    server.start()
    server.wait_for_termination()

if __name__ == '__main__':
    serve()
```

5.2. SERVER STREAMING RPCS

In this server setup, the StreamWeather method uses a generator to yield multiple WeatherReport instances back to the client. Each report is spaced by a time delay using time.sleep(), simulating the periodic generation of weather data.

- **Implementing the Client:** The client code needs to handle incoming streams efficiently, processing messages as they are received.

```
import grpc
import weather_pb2
import weather_pb2_grpc

def run():
    with grpc.insecure_channel('localhost:50051') as channel:
        stub = weather_pb2_grpc.WeatherServiceStub(channel)
        weather_request = weather_pb2.WeatherRequest(location='San Francisco')
        response_iterator = stub.StreamWeather(weather_request)

        for weather_report in response_iterator:
            print(f"Weather in {weather_report.location}: {weather_report.
                weather_description}, "
                f"Temp: {weather_report.temperature}°C, "
                f"Timestamp: {weather_report.timestamp}")

if __name__ == '__main__':
    run()
```

On the client-side, the StreamWeather method returns an iterator (response_iterator) allowing the client to process each WeatherReport as it's streamed from the server.

- **Streaming Concepts and Benefits:** Server streaming utilizes HTTP/2 features to maintain a single connection over which multiple responses are streamed back to the client. This connection reusability reduces overhead, providing efficiency benefits such as lower latency and faster transmission compared to multiple discrete requests.

  Additional benefits include:

- Reduced Network Traffic: Streaming multiple responses over a single connection reduces handshake operations and overhead associated with establishing multiple connections.

- **Real-time Interaction:** Streaming allows ongoing, real-time updates from the server following a single client request.

- **Flow Control and Prioritization:** HTTP/2's built-in flow control features optimize the transmission of streamed data, improving the overall user experience.

- **Handling Errors in Streaming RPCs:** Error handling plays a critical role in streaming RPCs. gRPC provides mechanisms to handle both transport-level errors and application-level errors.

For example, managing errors within a stream involves:

- **Completing the Stream:** If an error occurs, the stream should be properly terminated to allow both server and client to handle the closure gracefully.

- **Error Details:** Using context to provide detailed error codes (e.g., UNSUPPORTED), making it easier for the client to ascertain the cause.

Consider a case where an unsupported location request results in errors:

```
def StreamWeather(self, request, context):
    supported_locations = ["San Francisco", "New York"]
    if request.location not in supported_locations:
        context.abort(grpc.StatusCode.INVALID_ARGUMENT, "Location not
            supported.")

    for i in range(5):
        weather_report = weather_pb2.WeatherReport(
            location=request.location,
            weather_description="Sunny",
            temperature=22.5,
            timestamp=int(time.time())
        )
        yield weather_report
        time.sleep(1)
```

If the location in the request is unsupported, the server stops further processing and aborts with an INVALID_ARGUMENT status.

The client should also be ready to handle such streaming errors gracefully. This involves catching exceptions raised during iteration:

5.2. SERVER STREAMING RPCS

```
try:
    for weather_report in response_iterator:
        print(...)
except grpc.RpcError as e:
    if e.code() == grpc.StatusCode.INVALID_ARGUMENT:
        print("Invalid location.")
```

- **Testing Server Streaming RPCs:** Thorough testing of server streaming RPCs ensures that clients respond correctly to streams and handle interruptions courteously. Integration and unit tests can simulate the entire streaming setup or mock server behaviors in isolation.

Here is an outline for a test using unittest in Python:

```python
import unittest
from unittest.mock import Mock
import grpc
import weather_pb2
import weather_pb2_grpc

class WeatherServiceTest(unittest.TestCase):

    def setUp(self):
        self.service = weather_pb2_grpc.WeatherServiceServicer()
        self.context = Mock()

    def test_stream_weather_valid(self):
        location = "San Francisco"
        request = weather_pb2.WeatherRequest(location=location)
        response_iterator = self.service.StreamWeather(request, self.context)

        for response in response_iterator:
            self.assertEqual(response.location, location)

    def test_stream_weather_invalid_location(self):
        request = weather_pb2.WeatherRequest(location="InvalidCity")
        with self.assertRaises(grpc.RpcError) as e:
            list(self.service.StreamWeather(request, self.context))
        self.assertEqual(e.exception.code(), grpc.StatusCode.INVALID_ARGUMENT)

if __name__ == '__main__':
    unittest.main()
```

This test suite validates both successful and unsuccessful scenarios for streaming RPCs, ensuring the service behavior aligns with expectations.

- **Security in Streaming RPCs:** In server streaming setups, securing the communication channel with TLS is vital to maintain

CHAPTER 5. GRPC IN ACTION: IMPLEMENTING UNARY AND STREAMING APIS

data confidentiality and integrity during streams.

Below is an adaptation of server code to incorporate SSL/TLS for secure communication:

```python
def serve_secure():
    server = grpc.server(futures.ThreadPoolExecutor(max_workers=10))
    # Load server credentials
    with open('server.key', 'rb') as f:
        private_key = f.read()
    with open('server.pem', 'rb') as f:
        certificate_chain = f.read()
    server_credentials = grpc.ssl_server_credentials(((private_key, certificate_chain),)
    )

    weather_pb2_grpc.add_WeatherServiceServicer_to_server(WeatherServiceServicer
        (), server)
    server.add_secure_port('[::]:50051', server_credentials)
    server.start()
    server.wait_for_termination()
```

The client needs to incorporate the same SSL/TLS configurations using appropriate credentials when establishing a channel to the server.

- **Deployment and Optimization:** Deploying server streaming applications requires attention to load balancing and fault tolerance. Supporting scalable, high-throughput workloads necessitates infrastructure that can gracefully handle numerous long-lived connections.

Containers and orchestration tools like Kubernetes can help deploy services that manage resources efficiently and maintain service uptime by automating redundancies and failovers.

Optimizations further extend to:

- Message Granularity: Balancing between detailed information and system load by adjusting message size.

- Nagle's Algorithm: Disable it (using TCP_NODELAY option) to lower latency by transmitting data instantly without aggregation, which is especially useful in scenarios with intermittent data packets.

- **Monitoring and Debugging:** Effective monitoring and debugging in the context of streaming can be realized with logging interceptors, health checks, and telemetry data analytics.

A log interceptor may look like this:

```
class StreamingLoggingInterceptor(grpc.ServerInterceptor):
    def intercept_service(self, continuation, handler_call_details):
        method_name = handler_call_details.method
        print(f"Streaming method {method_name} invoked.")
        return continuation(handler_call_details)
```

This logging mechanism could be expanded to record timestamps, client metadata, and message contents to make troubleshooting more manageable.

By effectively implementing server streaming RPCs, services can be designed to support real-time, low-latency streams that are secure and scalable, making them well-suited for modern, distributed systems that demand interactive, continuous data flows. Through these methodologies, developers gain insights into maximizing the potential of server streaming RPCs within their applications, enhancing their capability to deliver resilient and performant services.

5.3 Client Streaming RPCs

Client streaming RPCs in gRPC provide a flexible and efficient communication pattern where the client sends a stream of requests to the server, which then processes this data and sends a single consolidated response back. This pattern is ideally suited for scenarios where the client has a series of related requests that can be effectively aggregated by the server. Common applications include uploading files in chunks, sending a batch of telemetry data, or uploading streaming analytics events.

- **1. Defining the Protocol Buffers**

The process begins with establishing a .proto file that defines the client streaming service and associated messages. In this structure, the service method receives a stream of messages and returns a single message.

Consider the following .proto file for a file upload service:

```
syntax = "proto3";

package fileupload;

service FileUploadService {
  rpc UploadFile (stream FileChunk) returns (UploadStatus) {}
}

message FileChunk {
  string filename = 1;
  bytes data = 2;
  uint32 chunk_number = 3;
}

message UploadStatus {
  string message = 1;
  bool success = 2;
}
```

In this .proto file, the service FileUploadService has a method UploadFile, which accepts a stream of FileChunk and returns an UploadStatus.

- **2. Generating Client and Server Code**

Post proto file creation, the next step is the generation of client and server code using the Protocol Compiler (protoc). In Python, the command looks like:

```
$ protoc -I=. --python_out=. --grpc_python_out=. fileupload.proto
```

Executing this command yields the necessary Python modules to begin implementing client and server logic.

- **3. Implementing the Server**

On the server side, the implementation of the streaming logic involves aggregating data received from the client stream and sending a summary response.

Below is a Python server implementation:

5.3. CLIENT STREAMING RPCS

```python
import grpc
from concurrent import futures
import fileupload_pb2
import fileupload_pb2_grpc

class FileUploadServiceServicer(fileupload_pb2_grpc.FileUploadServiceServicer):
    def UploadFile(self, request_iterator, context):
        total_chunks = 0
        for file_chunk in request_iterator:
            print(f"Received chunk {file_chunk.chunk_number} for file {file_chunk.filename}")
            total_chunks += 1
            # Process each chunk (e.g., save to disk)

        return fileupload_pb2.UploadStatus(message='File uploaded successfully',
            success=True)
def serve():
    server = grpc.server(futures.ThreadPoolExecutor(max_workers=10))
    fileupload_pb2_grpc.add_FileUploadServiceServicer_to_server(
        FileUploadServiceServicer(), server)
    server.add_insecure_port('[::]:50051')
    server.start()
    server.wait_for_termination()

if __name__ == '__main__':
    serve()
```

The server above processes each FileChunk delivered in the client stream, logs them, and counts the total number of chunks before sending a response indicating success.

- **4. Implementing the Client**

Client-side code involves setting up a stream to send data continually to the server.

A Python client implementation might look like:

```python
import grpc
import fileupload_pb2
import fileupload_pb2_grpc

def generate_file_chunks(filename):
    chunk_number = 0
    with open(filename, 'rb') as f:
        while chunk := f.read(1024):
            chunk_number += 1
            yield fileupload_pb2.FileChunk(filename=filename, data=chunk,
                chunk_number=chunk_number)

def run():
    with grpc.insecure_channel('localhost:50051') as channel:
```

CHAPTER 5. GRPC IN ACTION: IMPLEMENTING UNARY AND STREAMING APIS

```
    stub = fileupload_pb2_grpc.FileUploadServiceStub(channel)
    response = stub.UploadFile(generate_file_chunks('example.txt'))
  print("Upload finished:", response.message)
if __name__ == '__main__':
  run()
```

In this client example, a generator function generate_file_chunks reads a file and yields FileChunk objects to the streaming RPC method UploadFile. Each file chunk is sent independently, and once all have been sent, the server returns an UploadStatus.

- ### 5. Communication Process and Benefits

Client streaming RPCs capitalize on gRPC's capability to send data in parts over a single HTTP/2 connection, minimizing packet overhead and maintaining connection efficiency for numerous requests and a single response.

Core benefits of this pattern include:

- **Lower Latency**: Unlike having multiple separate requests, data is streamed steadily over one enduring connection.

- **Efficient Resource Usage**: Both client and server manage fewer connections, reducing resource strain.

- **Reduced Complexity**: Bandwidth and processing can be managed more flexibly, batch processing is enabled.

- ### 6. Error Handling in Client Streaming RPCs

Handling errors effectively ensures robust communication, even if parts of the stream encounter issues. Common strategies involve:

- **Graceful Stream Termination**: If an error occurs in the middle of streaming data, closing the stream allows both parties to free resources appropriately.

- **Detailed Error Responses**: Use gRPC codes to indicate issues, supplemented with explanatory messages.

5.3. CLIENT STREAMING RPCS

Implementing error handling on the server:

```
from grpc import StatusCode

class FileUploadServiceServicer(fileupload_pb2_grpc.FileUploadServiceServicer):
    def UploadFile(self, request_iterator, context):
        for file_chunk in request_iterator:
            if not file_chunk.data:
                context.abort(StatusCode.INVALID_ARGUMENT, "Chunk data
                    missing.")
        # Process and conclude normally
        return fileupload_pb2.UploadStatus(message='File uploaded successfully',
            success=True)
```

Proper exceptions in client-side logic capture and handle such aborts:

```
try:
    response = stub.UploadFile(generate_file_chunks('example.txt'))
except grpc.RpcError as e:
    if e.code() == grpc.StatusCode.INVALID_ARGUMENT:
        print("Error during upload:", e.details())
```

- **7. Testing Client Streaming RPCs**

Testing for client streaming RPCs necessitates evaluating scenarios like partial uploads, handling incorrect data, and completing successful streams. The following test uses *unittest* in Python:

```
import unittest
from unittest.mock import Mock
import grpc
import fileupload_pb2
import fileupload_pb2_grpc

class TestFileUploadService(unittest.TestCase):

    def setUp(self):
        self.service = fileupload_pb2_grpc.FileUploadServiceServicer()
        self.context = Mock()

    def test_upload_file_success(self):
        def mock_chunk_iterator():
            for i in range(5):
                yield fileupload_pb2.FileChunk(filename='test.txt', data=b'data',
                    chunk_number=i+1)

        response = self.service.UploadFile(mock_chunk_iterator(), self.context)
        self.assertTrue(response.success)
        self.assertEqual(response.message, 'File uploaded successfully')

    def test_upload_file_missing_data(self):
        def mock_chunk_iterator():
            yield fileupload_pb2.FileChunk(filename='test.txt', data=b'',
                chunk_number=1)
```

CHAPTER 5. GRPC IN ACTION: IMPLEMENTING UNARY AND STREAMING APIS

```
        with self.assertRaises(grpc.RpcError) as e:
            self.service.UploadFile(mock_chunk_iterator(), self.context)
        self.assertEqual(e.exception.code(), grpc.StatusCode.INVALID_ARGUMENT)
if __name__ == '__main__':
    unittest.main()
```

The test suite verifies the correct handling of both successful uploads and errors stemming from missing data.

- **8. Securing Client Streaming RPCs**

For scenarios needing reinforced security, employing TLS or SSL ensures data integrity and confidentiality across the streaming channel.

Adapting the server to use TLS includes:

```
def serve_secure():
    server = grpc.server(futures.ThreadPoolExecutor(max_workers=10))
    with open('server.key', 'rb') as f:
        private_key = f.read()
    with open('server.pem', 'rb') as f:
        cert_chain = f.read()
    server_credentials = grpc.ssl_server_credentials(((private_key, cert_chain),))

    fileupload_pb2_grpc.add_FileUploadServiceServicer_to_server(
        FileUploadServiceServicer(), server)
    server.add_secure_port('[::]:50051', server_credentials)
    server.start()
    server.wait_for_termination()
```

This setup necessitates that the client also uses matching TLS credentials to route requests securely.

- **9. Deployment and Scalability**

Deploying client streaming services demands that they be prepared for high-throughput, bursting client conversations. This can be accomplished by orchestrating services using containerization solutions like Docker and Kubernetes to automate scalability and maintain service quality.

Additionally, Azure DevOps or Jenkins can facilitate Continuous Integration and Deployment (CI/CD) pipelines to ensure frequent updates do not interrupt client service, allowing rapid iterations and seamless feature rollouts.

By leveraging these environments, engineers can rapidly enlarge capacity, manage workloads dynamically, and automate failover processes.

- **10. Observability and Debugging**

Integrating observability features into client streaming RPCs sheds light on performance bottlenecks, latency issues, and error tracking. Such integration allows engineers to trace RPC calls, measure latencies, and analyze data flow.

Applying logging interceptors allows for tracing client streams programmatically:

```
class StreamingLoggingInterceptor(grpc.ServerInterceptor):
    def intercept_service(self, continuation, handler_call_details):
        method = handler_call_details.method
        print(f"Client streaming method {method} invoked.")
        return continuation(handler_call_details)
```

Furthermore, coupling gRPC services with open-source telemetry tools such as OpenTelemetry, Prometheus, or Jaeger provides deep insights into complex pipeline operations and bottleneck identification.

Ultimately, understanding how to implement client streaming RPCs effectively results in secured, scalable, and high-performing services capable of handling large batches of client data while maintaining impeccably low latency and robust error handling. These qualities underscore the power of gRPC in building modern, resilient applications that are adaptable and responsive in dynamic environments. The insights offered within these implementations emphasize the significant benefits client streaming RPCs provide, ensuring they are a staple in software development for distributed systems.

5.4 Bidirectional Streaming RPCs

Bidirectional streaming RPCs in gRPC offer a sophisticated communication pattern where both client and server establish a stream to send and receive a series of messages asynchronously. This pattern allows for a continuous and dynamic interaction, resembling real-time conversations or data exchange scenarios such as chat applications, distributed logging systems, and collaborative tools. Understanding and implementing bidirectional streaming RPCs unlock the potential to develop highly interactive and efficient networked applications.

- **Defining the Protocol Buffers**

The implementation starts with the definition of services and associated messages in an appropriate .proto file. For bidirectional streaming, the service method returns a stream of messages while also accepting a stream of messages.

Consider this proto file for a chat application:

```
syntax = "proto3";

package chat;

service ChatService {
  rpc Chat (stream ChatMessage) returns (stream ChatResponse) {}
}

message ChatMessage {
  string user = 1;
  string message = 2;
}

message ChatResponse {
  string user = 1;
  string message = 2;
}
```

In this proto file, the Chat method in ChatService facilitates bidirectional streaming communication, receiving a stream of ChatMessage and returning a stream of ChatResponse.

- **Generating Client and Server Code**

With the proto file prepared, the next step involves generating the required client and server code using the Protocol Compiler (protoc). For Python, the command is typically:

```
$ protoc -I=. --python_out=. --grpc_python_out=. chat.proto
```

This command outputs Python modules that are used to implement the server and client logic.

- **Implementing the Server**

5.4. BIDIRECTIONAL STREAMING RPCS

The server-side implementation should handle bidirectional streaming by concurrently processing incoming and outgoing message streams. Below is an example Python server implementation:

```python
import grpc
from concurrent import futures
import chat_pb2
import chat_pb2_grpc

class ChatServiceServicer(chat_pb2_grpc.ChatServiceServicer):
    def Chat(self, request_iterator, context):
        for chat_message in request_iterator:
            print(f"Received message from {chat_message.user}: {chat_message.message}")
            response = chat_pb2.ChatResponse(user=chat_message.user, message="Acknowledged: " + chat_message.message)
            yield response

def serve():
    server = grpc.server(futures.ThreadPoolExecutor(max_workers=10))
    chat_pb2_grpc.add_ChatServiceServicer_to_server(ChatServiceServicer(), server)
    server.add_insecure_port('[::]:50051')
    server.start()
    server.wait_for_termination()

if __name__ == '__main__':
    serve()
```

The above server processes each ChatMessage from the client, logs it, and responds with a corresponding ChatResponse.

- **Implementing the Client**

On the client side, implementation involves creating a stream to continuously send data to and receive data from the server.

Below is a client implementation in Python:

```python
import grpc
import chat_pb2
import chat_pb2_grpc

def generate_chat_messages():
    while True:
        user = input("Enter your username: ")
        message = input("Enter your message: ")
        yield chat_pb2.ChatMessage(user=user, message=message)

def run():
    with grpc.insecure_channel('localhost:50051') as channel:
        stub = chat_pb2_grpc.ChatServiceStub(channel)
        responses = stub.Chat(generate_chat_messages())
```

147

```
        try:
            for response in responses:
                print(f"Reply from {response.user}: {response.message}")
        except grpc.RpcError as e:
            print(f"RPC failed: {e}")
if __name__ == '__main__':
    run()
```

This client example involves a generator function generate_chat_messages that continuously reads user input to generate ChatMessage objects, sending them to the server via a bidirectional stream.

- **Communication Process and Benefits**

Bidirectional streaming effectively uses persistent connections over HTTP/2, ensuring continuous data flow between client and server without the overhead of establishing and tearing down connections continuously.

Key advantages include:

- **Real-Time Interaction**: Low-latency and highly responsive communication similar to WebSockets, providing dynamic interaction patterns.

- **Efficient Resource Usage**: Fewer connections mean less overhead and better efficiency.

- **Asynchronous Communication**: Both peers can independently read from and write to the stream, enhancing flexibility.

- **Error Handling in Bidirectional Streaming RPCs**

Error handling within bidirectional streaming RPCs requires careful management to ensure that streams are gracefully closed in case of errors, so that resources are released smoothly on both sides.

Potential strategies include:

- **Stream Termination**: Both client and server should properly handle stream completion and partial transmission errors.

5.4. BIDIRECTIONAL STREAMING RPCS

- **Granular Error Codes**: gRPC status codes like UNIMPLEMENTED or OUT_OF_RESOURCE help specify error contexts.

On the server, implementation might look like:

```
class ChatServiceServicer(chat_pb2_grpc.ChatServiceServicer):
    def Chat(self, request_iterator, context):
        for chat_message in request_iterator:
            if not chat_message.message.strip():
                context.abort(grpc.StatusCode.INVALID_ARGUMENT, "Message
                    cannot be empty.")
            yield chat_pb2.ChatResponse(user=chat_message.user, message="Ack: " +
                chat_message.message)
```

On encountering an invalid message, the server terminates the stream using context.abort() with a suitable error code.

Client logic should also capture such exceptions and handle retries or notifications gracefully:

```
try:
    responses = stub.Chat(generate_chat_messages())
    for response in responses:
        print("Received:", response.message)
except grpc.RpcError as e:
    if e.code() == grpc.StatusCode.INVALID_ARGUMENT:
        print("Invalid input!")
```

- **Testing Bidirectional Streaming RPCs**

Testing bidirectional streams involves verifying scenarios where both parties can asynchronously send and receive messages, and interactions are correctly logged, acknowledged, and error conditions are appropriately handled.

The following test illustrates using unittest in Python:

```
import unittest
from unittest.mock import Mock
import grpc
import chat_pb2
import chat_pb2_grpc

class TestChatService(unittest.TestCase):

    def setUp(self):
        self.service = chat_pb2_grpc.ChatServiceServicer()
        self.context = Mock()
```

CHAPTER 5. GRPC IN ACTION: IMPLEMENTING UNARY AND STREAMING APIS

```
def test_chat_success(self):
    def mock_message_iterator():
        yield chat_pb2.ChatMessage(user="Alice", message="Hello")
        yield chat_pb2.ChatMessage(user="Bob", message="Hi there!")

    responses = list(self.service.Chat(mock_message_iterator(), self.context))
    self.assertTrue(all(resp.message.startswith("Ack: ") for resp in responses))

def test_chat_empty_message(self):
    def mock_message_iterator():
        yield chat_pb2.ChatMessage(user="Alice", message="")

    with self.assertRaises(grpc.RpcError) as e:
        list(self.service.Chat(mock_message_iterator(), self.context))
    self.assertEqual(e.exception.code(), grpc.StatusCode.INVALID_ARGUMENT)

if __name__ == '__main__':
    unittest.main()
```

This test suite checks both successful interactions and error conditions, ensuring service robustness.

- **Securing Bidirectional Streaming RPCs**

As with other streaming patterns, securing bidirectional communication is critical. Applying TLS/SSL ensures data is encrypted, maintaining communications' confidentiality and integrity.

A secure server setup involves changes like so:

```
def serve_secure():
    server = grpc.server(futures.ThreadPoolExecutor(max_workers=10))
    with open('server.key', 'rb') as f:
        private_key = f.read()
    with open('server.pem', 'rb') as f:
        cert_chain = f.read()
    server_credentials = grpc.ssl_server_credentials(((private_key, cert_chain),))
    chat_pb2_grpc.add_ChatServiceServicer_to_server(ChatServiceServicer(), server)

    server.add_secure_port('[::]:50051', server_credentials)
    server.start()
    server.wait_for_termination()
```

The client needs parallel implementation to establish a secure gRPC channel.

- **Deployment and Scalability**

Deploying bidirectional streaming services requires careful planning

5.4. BIDIRECTIONAL STREAMING RPCS

to ensure performance scalability and resource optimization. Technologies like Docker and Kubernetes can orchestrate the rolling deployments and elasticity needed to dynamically adjust resources as client interactions intensify.

For upscaling, it's imperative to:

- **Load Balance**: gRPC built-in capabilities can direct client connections across a pool of back-end servers.
- **Service Meshes**: Implementing service meshes such as Istio helps manage traffic flows uniformly and securely across services.

Such frameworks facilitate high availability, fault tolerance, and seamless recovery from node failures.

- **Monitoring and Debugging**

Observability is necessary for efficiently diagnosing issues in bidirectional streaming. Real-time logging, monitoring, and tracing enhance the understanding of stream behaviors under production conditions.

Establish logging via interceptors:

```
class ChatLoggingInterceptor(grpc.ServerInterceptor):
    def intercept_service(self, continuation, handler_call_details):
        method_name = handler_call_details.method
        print(f"Bidirectional streaming method {method_name} called.")
        return continuation(handler_call_details)
```

Incorporating tracing instruments like OpenTelemetry improves analyzing specific call performance, latency, or error distribution across distributed services.

Mastering bidirectional streaming RPCs enables the development of robust, dynamic applications that thrive in modern interactive network environments. This detailed understanding and implementation ensure that real-time, low-latency communication needs are met with reliability and security, extending gRPC's utility across a multitude of applications in distributed systems. Through careful adherence to these best practices and methodologies, the power and versatility of bidirectional streaming RPCs can be fully harnessed.

5.5 Handling Streaming Errors

In the domain of gRPC, streaming APIs introduce a suite of challenges unique to the nature of continuous data flows between clients and servers. Effective handling of streaming errors is crucial for maintaining robust communication channels that can endure and recover from disruptions. Streaming errors can arise from various origins including network instability, client and server constraints, faulty logic, or unexpected operational conditions.

This section explores strategies, techniques, and best practices for effectively managing and mitigating errors in gRPC streaming models, both unidirectional and bidirectional.

- **1. Understanding Error Types in Streaming RPCs**

Errors in streaming RPCs can be broadly categorized as:

- Network-Level Errors: Issues such as connection loss, high latency, or packet loss due to unstable networks.
- Application-Level Errors: Problems arising from logic defects, resource constraints, or unexpected input data.
- Resource Constraints: Errors due to exhausted compute or memory resources, potentially leading to timeouts or terminations.
- Protocol Errors: Invalid message format or protocol violations leading to aborted streaming.

Each of these errors affects the gRPC streaming lifecycle differently, necessitating tailored strategies for detection and recovery.

- **2. gRPC Error Handling Mechanisms**

gRPC's architecture encompasses mechanisms to facilitate effective error handling:

- Status Codes: gRPC defines an extensive set of status codes to convey error types, such as UNAVAILABLE, RESOURCE_EXHAUSTED, or INTERNAL.

5.5. HANDLING STREAMING ERRORS

- Context Objects: On the server side, context objects provide methods like abort() to propagate errors with specific status codes.
- Deadline and Cancellation: Both clients and servers can specify deadlines or cancel streams that exceed their utility or trigger errors.

- **3. Implementing Error Propagation**

When a server encounters an error during stream processing, it is essential to communicate this back to the client effectively. Consider a Python server managing a bidirectional streaming chat:

```
import grpc
import chat_pb2
import chat_pb2_grpc

class ChatService(chat_pb2_grpc.ChatServiceServicer):
    def Chat(self, request_iterator, context):
        try:
            for chat_message in request_iterator:
                if len(chat_message.message) > 256:
                    context.abort(grpc.StatusCode.INVALID_ARGUMENT, "Message too long.")
                yield chat_pb2.ChatResponse(user="Server", message="Got your message.")
        except Exception as e:
            context.abort(grpc.StatusCode.INTERNAL, str(e))

def serve():
    server = grpc.server(futures.ThreadPoolExecutor(max_workers=5))
    chat_pb2_grpc.add_ChatServiceServicer_to_server(ChatService(), server)
    server.add_insecure_port('[::]:50051')
    server.start()
    server.wait_for_termination()
```

The server employs context.abort() to halt the stream with a clear error status if the message exceeds a permissible length, thus safeguarding against protocol violations.

- **4. Client-Side Error Management**

The client application must be programmed to handle these errors responsibly, recovering or alerting users gracefully.

```
import grpc
```

```
import chat_pb2
import chat_pb2_grpc

def run():
    with grpc.insecure_channel('localhost:50051') as channel:
        stub = chat_pb2_grpc.ChatServiceStub(channel)
        try:
            responses = stub.Chat(iter([chat_pb2.ChatMessage(user="Alice", message
                ="Hello" * 100)]))
            for response in responses:
                print("Server:", response.message)
        except grpc.RpcError as e:
            print(f"Streaming error: {e.code()} - {e.details()}")

if __name__ == '__main__':
    run()
```

Upon receiving an error, the client logs the status code and message, providing users with clear feedback or retry mechanisms as appropriate.

- **5. Establishing Timeout and Retry Policies**

Timeouts and retries are key techniques to handle transient errors such as temporary network failures or lossy connections:

- Client-Side Timeouts: Clients can set deadlines post which a stream should be abandoned, managing resource commitments.

- Exponential Backoff: Implement retry strategies with increasing delays to avoid overwhelming the server.

$$\text{Backoff Time} = \text{base time} \times 2^{\text{retry count}}$$

Integrating these strategies into the client involves configuring channel options and logic to control retry behaviors smartly.

- **6. Monitoring and Observability Tools for Error Detection**

Real-time monitoring can significantly aid in spotting error patterns and localized issues. Using tracing and logging aids root cause diagnosis:

5.5. HANDLING STREAMING ERRORS

- Logging Interceptors: Captures and logs process flows and errors, annotated with metadata for deeper diagnostic.

- Distributed Tracing: Tools such as OpenTelemetry trace errors across service call graphs, unearthing latent chokepoints.

Example logging interceptor:

```
class LoggingInterceptor(grpc.ServerInterceptor):
    def intercept_service(self, continuation, handler_call_details):
        method_name = handler_call_details.method
        context = handler_call_details.invocation_metadata
        print(f"Incoming call: {method_name} with context: {context}")
        return continuation(handler_call_details)
```

Deploying these observability tools aids in proactive error management, ensuring issues are addressed before they escalate.

- **7. Employing Health Checks and Circuit Breakers**

Incorporating health check endpoints along with circuit breaker patterns can preempt service overloads or failures:

- Health Checks: Expose endpoints that respond to service health, while orchestrators like Kubernetes react by adjusting deployments.

- Circuit Breakers: Detect failing services to cease additional load requests, allowing recovery before resumption.

The grpc-health-probe utility can be integrated into deployment scripts to facilitate health reporting.

- **8. Security Considerations in Error Handling**

Errors must be handled without leaking sensitive information. Mindful design ensures error responses do not divulge internal states or configurations:

- Minimal Information in Errors: Limit exposed data in error details, focusing on clarification rather than operational insights.

- Secure Logging: Mask sensitive information when logging errors to prevent leakage risks.

Developers should assess logs for exposure risks, applying filters or masks as needed.

- **9. Protocol Versioning and Backward Compatibility**

Version mismatches can induce errors when clients or servers lack protocol compatibility:

- Version Headers: Incorporate version information into request headers for validation.
- Graceful Downgrade: Implement handlers for unexpected protocol versions, using downgraded capabilities when necessary.

Such strategies avert failures stemming from evolutionary protocol discrepancies.

- **10. Leveraging Community and Tooling Support**

Communities and ecosystem tools provide invaluable support for managing streaming errors:

- Open Source Libraries: Utilize external libraries offering wrappers for enhanced error handling beyond default gRPC features.
- Community Forums and GitHub: Engage with developer communities for collective insights into error patterns and resolutions.

The continued evolution of tools, libraries, and shared knowledge elevates error handling to an art, iteratively improving modernization efforts.

By mastering the multifaceted landscape of streaming error management within gRPC, stakeholders can uphold communication reliability and integrity. Employing a blend of programmatic strategies, design practices, and tooling enhances robustness, ensuring systems are resilient against diverse error scenarios while aligning with users' expectations and organizational goals. This knowledge empowers developers to fortify their applications, enabling enduring and expansive service offerings across distributed architectures.

5.6 Optimizing Streaming Performance

Optimizing performance in gRPC streaming applications is a crucial task that ensures efficient use of resources, low latency, and an excellent user experience. Given the continuous data flow in streaming RPCs, various factors can significantly affect performance, such as network conditions, data serialization, message size, and resource management. This section provides detailed insights into strategies for optimizing streaming performance, focusing on enhancing throughput, reducing latency, and optimizing resource utilization.

- **1. Understanding Streaming Performance Metrics**

To begin with optimization, it's crucial to understand the key performance metrics involved in streaming:

- **Throughput**: The amount of data transmitted over a period. Optimizing throughput involves maximizing the volume of data processed and transmitted in a streaming session.

- **Latency**: The delay before a transfer of data begins following an instruction for its transfer. Reducing latency involves minimizing this delay to ensure responsive streaming.

- **Bandwidth Utilization**: Efficient use of available bandwidth is essential for optimizing performance, minimizing wasted transmission capacity.

By profiling these metrics in your application, you can identify potential bottlenecks and areas for improvement.

- **2. Efficient Data Serialization and Compression**

The choice of data serialization format and compression strategy directly impacts streaming efficiency:

- **Protocol Buffers Compression**: gRPC uses Protocol Buffers by default, which are faster and smaller than other serialization formats like XML or JSON. Configuring compression algorithms such as gzip or Brotli can significantly reduce message sizes, especially for text or highly redundant data.

```
compression_options = grpc.Compression.Gzip

channel = grpc.insecure_channel(
    'localhost:50051',
    options=[
        ('grpc.max_send_message_length', 1024 * 1024 * 2), # 2 MiB
        ('grpc.default_compression_algorithm', compression_options)
    ]
)
```

- **Data Chunking**: For large datasets, breaking them into smaller chunks allows for faster processing and more manageable transmission rates.

```
def generate_chunks(data_source):
    chunk_size = 1024 # bytes
    for start in range(0, len(data_source), chunk_size):
        yield data_source[start:start + chunk_size]
```

Efficient serialization and compression help in optimizing the data flow by reducing overhead and improving packet delivery rates.

- **3. Adjusting Message Size and Window Limits**

Messaging limits influence performance greatly:

- **Batched Messages**: Combining small messages into batches diminishes processing overhead and improves network efficiency.

```
batched_data = [message_a, message_b, message_c]
stub.SendBatchedMessages(chat_pb2.MessageBatch(messages=batched_data))
```

5.6. OPTIMIZING STREAMING PERFORMANCE

- **Windows and Flow Control**: Effective buffer window management prevents network congestion. HTTP/2 implements flow control at multiple levels to regulate sending rates between clients and servers.

Use gRPC options to configure window settings:

```
options = [
    ('grpc.http2.write_buffer_size', 128 * 1024), # write buffer
    ('grpc.http2.receive_buffer_size', 128 * 1024) # receive buffer
]
channel = grpc.insecure_channel('localhost:50051', options=options)
```

Effective management of these settings ensures smoother data flow and prevents backlog pileups in the network buffers.

- **4. Network Optimizations and Load Balancing**

Network resources profoundly impact streaming performance:

- **Load Balancing**: Efficient distribution of client requests across multiple servers can lead to better throughput and resiliency. gRPC supports client-side load balancing strategies such as round-robin and pick-first policies.

Enable this with custom configurations:

```
resolver_policy = [('grpc.lb_policy_name', 'round_robin')]
channel = grpc.insecure_channel('myservice:50051', options=resolver_policy)
```

- **Optimizing Network Routes**: Reduced hop count and caching may lower latency and jitter. Employ Content Delivery Networks (CDN) to bring resources closer to end-users for quicker access.

- **5. Leveraging Asynchronous Programming Models**

Adopting asynchronous patterns aids in non-blocking data flows:

- **AsyncIO in Python**: By leveraging asyncio, one can handle IO-bound operations more efficiently, freeing up threads for other tasks.

Here is an example with asyncio in a client:

```python
import asyncio
import grpc
import chat_pb2
import chat_pb2_grpc

async def run():
    async with grpc.aio.insecure_channel('localhost:50051') as channel:
        stub = chat_pb2_grpc.ChatServiceStub(channel)
        response = await stub.Chat(chat_pb2.ChatMessage(user="Alice", message="
            Hello World"))
        print("Received:", response.message)

asyncio.run(run())
```

The use of asynchronous operations significantly increases the application's throughput and responsiveness, especially important in high-scale scenarios.

- **6. Hardware Utilization and Deployment Environment**

Hardware capabilities are central to performance optimization:

- **Vertical Scaling**: Scaling resources such as CPU, memory, and network interfaces on the individual node improves performance, especially where computational intensity is high.

- **Horizontal Scaling**: Increasing the number of nodes handling workloads via orchestrators like Kubernetes augments both reliability and processing power.

Effective monitoring tools and deployment environments ensure that hardware utilizations are maximized, identifying scaling bottlenecks early.

- **7. Monitoring and Profiling for Performance Planning**

Continuous monitoring and profiling can guide performance optimization:

- **Profiling Tools**: Instruments like cProfile, Py-Spy, and gRPC built-in forge are vital to analyzing code execution paths, resource consumption, and latency sources.

5.6. OPTIMIZING STREAMING PERFORMANCE

Example of using cProfile in application:

```
python -m cProfile -o output.pstats my_grpc_service.py
```

Analyze with visualization tools like gprof2dot to generate call graphs.

- **Real-Time Monitoring**: Implement Prometheus or Grafana for tracking active metrics, offering dashboards to visualize traffic, latency, and error trends.

- **8. Security Optimization**

Security principles often intersect with performance:

- **TLS Optimization**: While crucial for data protection, TLS incurs computational overhead. Optimizing certificate and key usage reduces handshake delays.

- **Data Minimization**: Transmit minimal data necessary, avoiding the overhead of encrypting and decrypting excess payloads.

Secure and efficient configurations simultaneously satisfy both security policies and performance goals, streamlining resource consumption.

- **9. Case Study: Optimizing a Real-Time Streaming Service**

A practical example involves optimizing a live analytics feed receiving millions of events per second. Key measures were:

- **Efficient Batching**: Enabling micro-batching within the service reduced stress on compute nodes while maintaining near-real-time analytics.

- **Load Distribution**: Balancing heavy client connections using round-robin strategies efficiently utilized network resources and minimized single-point bottlenecks.

- **Asynchronous Processing**: Adopting asyncio methodologies ensured that processing was distributed efficiently across compute resources without queue bottlenecks.

With a single architecture tuning and profile assessment, the service realized a 50% reduction in average latency, handling a fivefold increase in data flow with no additional resource outlay.

- ## 10. Conclusion and Continued Iteration

Optimization is a continual process involving iterative refinement and evaluation as application demands evolve. By employing precise measurements, strategic configurations, and keen understanding of the gRPC ecosystem, applications can consistently deliver high-performance, low-latency streams that align with organizational goals and user expectations.

Comprehensive understanding and application of these optimization strategies not only bolster performance but also enhance the overall resilience and adaptability of the streaming infrastructure, laying a robust foundation for future scalability and innovation. Developers and architects can thus ensure their systems are ready to meet both current demands and future opportunities in a rapidly transforming technological landscape. Through ongoing engagement with emerging technologies and community insights, performance optimization remains at the forefront of designing next-generation streaming solutions.

Chapter 6

Error Handling and Debugging in gRPC

This chapter focuses on the critical aspects of error handling and debugging within gRPC applications. It explains the gRPC status codes and their role in managing errors effectively. Readers will learn how to implement robust error handling strategies on both the client and server sides, utilizing debugging tools and techniques for diagnosing issues. The chapter also delves into handling deadlines and timeouts to prevent resource exhaustion. Additionally, it covers the use of interceptors for global error management and offers insights into testing error scenarios to ensure application reliability.

6.1 Understanding gRPC Status Codes

gRPC, or Google Remote Procedure Call, is a high-performance hybrid RPC framework that can function in a variety of environments. At the core of its design, gRPC utilizes HTTP/2 for transport, protocol buffers as the interface description language, and a range of utilities that enable efficient, robust client-server interactions. An essential aspect of these interactions involves handling errors gracefully, which is where gRPC status codes play a fundamental role. This section provides an in-depth examination of these codes, elucidating their purpose, classification, and relation to widely known HTTP status codes.

gRPC Status Code	Description
OK	The operation completed successfully without any errors.
CANCELLED	The operation was cancelled, typically originating from the client's request.
UNKNOWN	Unknown error status; often used as a fallback for unexpected issues not covered by other status codes.
INVALID_ARGUMENT	The client specified an invalid argument; the server could not process the request.
DEADLINE_EXCEEDED	The deadline for the operation was exceeded before completion. May also occur on the server side.
NOT_FOUND	Requested entity (e.g., a file or database entry) was not found.
ALREADY_EXISTS	The entity the client attempted to create already exists.
PERMISSION_DENIED	The caller does not have permission to execute the specified operation.
RESOURCE_EXHAUSTED	Some resource needed to complete the operation is exhausted.
FAILED_PRECONDITION	The operation was rejected due to a failed system precondition.
ABORTED	The operation was aborted, typically due to a concurrency issue such as a sequencer conflict.
OUT_OF_RANGE	An operation attempted to access data outside its valid range.
UNIMPLEMENTED	Operation is not implemented or not supported in this service.
INTERNAL	Internal server error has occurred. This is a non-recoverable issue from the client's perspective.
UNAVAILABLE	The service is currently unavailable. This status may be returned when the server is overloaded.
DATA_LOSS	Unrecoverable data loss or corruption.
UNAUTHENTICATED	The request does not have valid authentication credentials for the operation.

The gRPC status codes are integral to providing meaningful feedback in distributed systems. They serve not only as a mechanism for error reporting but also as guiding principles for designing a robust interaction model between client and server. This understanding is solidified by the detailed enumeration above, which elicits how each status code aligns with specific failure scenarios or informational messages.

6.1. UNDERSTANDING GRPC STATUS CODES

- Mapping to HTTP Status Codes

Understanding how gRPC status codes relate to HTTP status codes is essential for engineers migrating or dealing with applications interfacing traditional HTTP services. Although HTTP/2 underpins gRPC as a transport protocol, gRPC status codes are distinct and point to more granular operational insights specific to RPC operations.

For example, a gRPC status code, such as INVALID_ARGUMENT, loosely correlates with the HTTP 400 Bad Request code, signaling a client-side error. However, gRPC provides less ambiguous and more operation-specific feedback. Similarly, the UNAVAILABLE status finds its counterpart in HTTP 503 Service Unavailable, indicating server-side network conditions or overloads.

To provide a practical perspective on how these mappings work, consider the following enhanced code example that handles gRPC status codes in the context of a Python gRPC client application:

```
import grpc
from my_protos import my_proto_pb2, my_proto_pb2_grpc

def make_request():
    with grpc.insecure_channel('localhost:50051') as channel:
        stub = my_proto_pb2_grpc.MyServiceStub(channel)
        try:
            # Attempt to call the RPC method
            response = stub.MyMethod(my_proto_pb2.MyRequest(name='Example'))
            print("Response received:", response.message)
        except grpc.RpcError as rpc_error:
            status_code = rpc_error.code()
            if status_code == grpc.StatusCode.INVALID_ARGUMENT:
                print("Invalid argument provided")
            elif status_code == grpc.StatusCode.UNAVAILABLE:
                print("Service is currently unavailable")
            elif status_code == grpc.StatusCode.DEADLINE_EXCEEDED:
                print("Deadline has been exceeded")
            else:
                print(f"An error occurred: {rpc_error.details()}")

make_request()
```

In this example, each gRPC status code is matched with a specific error handling block. This mechanism allows a granular response to each potential error scenario. It not only informs the client application about the nature of the issue but also provides richer details for implementing appropriate mitigation strategies.

- Detailed Examination of Status Codes

RESOURCE_EXHAUSTED and DEADLINE_EXCEEDED are two status codes that warrant a deeper dive due to their frequent occurrence in scalable system architectures.

RESOURCE_EXHAUSTED: This status often emerges when network, memory, or processing resources are saturated. In distributed systems design, encountering exhaustion is critical for scaling applications. Proper backpressure and load-shedding mechanisms can mitigate such errors. A common approach involves implementing retry logic with exponentially backing off latent delays. Additionally, employing horizontal scaling strategies can help distribute loads effectively.

```
Operation failed: Resource exhausted. Retrying operation...
```

DEADLINE_EXCEEDED: This code is chiefly related to latency and timeout management. Time-sensitive gRPC operations must establish appropriate deadlines to avoid indefinite waits, ultimately subjecting the server or network to strain. Deadline-related issues necessitate precise tuning based on empirical measurements and latency expectations.

```
Operation failed: Deadline exceeded.
```

In practice, handling deadlines and delineating retry policies require precise client-side orchestration, primarily through gRPC client API configurations. For illustration:

```
with grpc.insecure_channel('localhost:50051') as channel:
    stub = my_proto_pb2_grpc.MyServiceStub(channel)
    response = stub.MyMethod(my_proto_pb2.MyRequest(name='Example'), timeout
        =10)
```

The above code sets a ten-second deadline for execution, enforcing limits on the client side and preventing system degradation due to excessive wait times.

- Use Cases and Consequences

In enterprise contexts, each gRPC status code represents not just an error condition but also an opportunity for iterative improvement and alignment with service level agreements (SLAs). For instance, the frequent occurrence of UNAVAILABLE may imply indicative trends concerning service overcommitment or network outliers, meriting deeper infrastructural analysis and enhancement.

Similarly, instances of INVALID_ARGUMENT may beckon upstream process auditing—ensuring client data compliance with expected server contracts, possibly needing interface contract refinements.

Furthermore, a systematic approach toward analyzing these status codes through centralized logging and monitoring tools allows operational teams to extract insights into system health and user interaction patterns. Integrating gRPC status codes with modern observability frameworks like Prometheus for monitoring and Grafana for visualization enables real-time error tracking and trend analysis, aiding in preemptive identification of anomalies.

For monitoring error prevalence and impact:

```
from prometheus_client import start_http_server, Summary

REQUEST_TIME = Summary('request_processing_seconds', 'Time spent processing request')

@REQUEST_TIME.time()
def make_request():
    # Function execution code as defined previously
    pass

if __name__ == '__main__':
    start_http_server(8000)
    make_request()
```

This setup captures the latency metrics, helping stakeholders understand delay concentrations, shouldered across gRPC operations.

In synthesis, understanding gRPC status codes transcends mere error handling. It becomes an empowering framework to refine system designs, enhance performance, and shape robust client-server paradigms. Each code insightfully reflects operational health, guiding practitioners toward better practices, informed adaptations, and insightful diagnostics conducive to high-quality distributed systems engineering.

6.2 Implementing Error Handling in gRPC

In distributed systems, error handling is a cornerstone for effective application management, indispensable not only in identifying and managing faults but also in ensuring resilience and scalability. In gRPC, implementing robust error handling mechanisms is critical, considering the diverse range of applications where gRPC is deployed, including microservices architectures, mobile applications, and IoT devices. This section explores gRPC error handling strategies for both client and server applications, offering insights into efficient error management techniques, practical coding examples, and best practices to enhance overall system robustness.

6.2.1 The Necessity of Structured Error Handling

Given the asynchronous and highly distributed nature of gRPC, errors can arise due to numerous factors, such as network issues, timeout exceedances, resource limitations, and incorrect client inputs. To address these effectively, engineered solutions must involve both defensive programming on the client side and resilient error reporting and management on the server side. Enhancing error handling involves understanding error types, predicting potential failure points, and designing appropriate responses that ensure system stability and user transparency.

```
import grpc
from my_service import service_pb2, service_pb2_grpc

def handle_errors():
    with grpc.insecure_channel('localhost:50051') as channel:
        stub = service_pb2_grpc.MyServiceStub(channel)
        try:
            response = stub.MyMethod(service_pb2.MyRequest(name='Test'))
            print("Response received: ", response.message)
        except grpc.RpcError as rpc_error:
            print("RPC Failed with status: ", rpc_error.code())
            print("Details: ", rpc_error.details())
```

In this basic setup, the client intercepts and prints errors that occur during an RPC call. While straightforward, implementing a streamlined error management logic enables further robust error practices, especially by incorporating retry logic, exponential backoff, context-based cancellation, and advanced error reporting mechanisms.

6.2.2 Client-Side Error Handling

As the entry point for error handling logic, the client must efficiently handle various error scenarios, relying on predefined conditions to manage differing levels of service anomalies. This includes, but is not limited to, network failures, server unavailability, incorrect request formation, and failure to authenticate requests.

Implementing Retry Logic

To mitigate transient errors, implementing retry logic is often necessary. This involves setting up custom rules defining failure thresholds and retry intervals. A common pattern in retry logic includes exponential backoff, which intends to space out retry attempts, reducing load during high failure rates and allowing recovery time.

```
import time
import grpc
from retrying import retry
from my_service import service_pb2, service_pb2_grpc

@retry(stop_max_attempt_number=5, wait_exponential_multiplier=1000,
       wait_exponential_max=10000)
def call_my_method_with_retry(stub):
    response = stub.MyMethod(service_pb2.MyRequest(name='Example'))
    return response

def retry_sample(client_channel):
    stub = service_pb2_grpc.MyServiceStub(client_channel)
    try:
        response = call_my_method_with_retry(stub)
        print("Response:", response.data)
    except grpc.RpcError as rpc_error:
        print("Failed after multiple retries:", rpc_error.details())

if __name__ == '__main__':
    with grpc.insecure_channel('localhost:50051') as channel:
        retry_sample(channel)
```

In this illustrative pythonic implementation, the retrying library decorates the call_my_method_with_retry function to apply retry attempts with exponential backoff logic. The exponential parameters ensure increasing intervals up to the defined maximum.

Context Propagation for Handling Cancellations

By using contexts in gRPC, clients can send cancellation signals to facilitate clean resource cleanup and unblock awaiting threads when errors like network timeouts occur.

```
def call_with_timeout(channel, timeout_seconds):
    stub = service_pb2_grpc.MyServiceStub(channel)
    request = service_pb2.MyRequest(name='TimeoutTest')

    try:
        response = stub.MyMethod(request, timeout=timeout_seconds)
        print("Received response:", response.message)
    except grpc.RpcError as rpc_error:
        if rpc_error.code() == grpc.StatusCode.CANCELLED:
            print("Request was cancelled")
        else:
            print("RPC error occurred:", rpc_error.details())

# Sample usage
with grpc.insecure_channel('localhost:50051') as channel:
    call_with_timeout(channel, 3)
```

This design pattern provides avenues for handling client-requested cancellations through the exploitation of the context object for propagating timeout constraints.

6.2.3 Server-Side Error Handling

Server-side implementations have a complementary responsibility in error management through error reporting, exception management, and failure notifications tailored to inform clients about operational statuses or constraints that lead to RPC execution failures.

Error Propagation and Exception Scenarios

On the server side, explicitly handling and translating exceptions to gRPC status codes ensures clients receive coherent error messages aligning with RPC protocol expectations.

```
import grpc
```

6.2. IMPLEMENTING ERROR HANDLING IN GRPC

```python
from concurrent import futures
import my_service.service_pb2 as service_pb2
import my_service.service_pb2_grpc as service_pb2_grpc

class MyService(service_pb2_grpc.MyServiceServicer):
    def MyMethod(self, request, context):
        if request.name == '':
            context.set_code(grpc.StatusCode.INVALID_ARGUMENT)
            context.set_details('Name must not be empty.')
            return service_pb2.MyResponse()
        try:
            # Perform some operations...
            return service_pb2.MyResponse(message='Hello, ' + request.name)
        except Exception as e:
            context.set_code(grpc.StatusCode.INTERNAL)
            context.set_details(f'Internal error: {str(e)}')
            return service_pb2.MyResponse()

def serve():
    server = grpc.server(futures.ThreadPoolExecutor(max_workers=10))
    service_pb2_grpc.add_MyServiceServicer_to_server(MyService(), server)
    server.add_insecure_port('[::]:50051')
    server.start()
    server.wait_for_termination()

if __name__ == '__main__':
    serve()
```

Here, using context for setting status codes and descriptions allows method MyMethod to define server-specific business logic errors, codifying them into semantically meaningful gRPC responses.

6.2.4 Advanced Error Handling Strategies

Beyond basic exception handling, integrating comprehensive error management infrastructures and adopting industry-ready solutions paves the way for resilient application execution and servicing.

Centralized Logging and Monitoring

A vital component of deploying production-level gRPC applications involves an efficient logging strategy capturing errors, system health metrics, and transaction traces. Sophisticated systems leverage ELK (Elasticsearch, Logstash, Kibana) or cloud-native logging solutions such as Google Cloud Logging and AWS CloudWatch to manage and scrutinize service logs.

Python's logging library amends gRPC applications with rich logging features as below:

```python
import logging

logging.basicConfig(level=logging.INFO, format='%(asctime)s - %(levelname)s - %(
    message)s')

def log_example():
    try:
        # Assume this triggers an operation which may fail
        response = risky_operation()
        logging.info("Operation succeeded")
    except Exception as e:
        logging.error(f"Operation failed: {e}")

# Integration into gRPC logic
with grpc.insecure_channel('localhost:50051') as channel:
    log_example()
```

Comprehensive logging provides a blend of real-time monitoring and retrospective analysis capabilities, helping diagnose and attribute causation in failure scenarios.

Global Retry and Timeout Policies

Strategically employing global retrials through interceptors or middleware assures error handling is not manually repeated across source files but implemented cohesively for modular acts of resilience.

```python
import grpc
from grpc_interceptor import ClientCallDetails, Interceptor

class RetryInterceptor(Interceptor):
    def intercept(self, method, request_or_iterator, call_details):
        response = None
        for _ in range(3):  # 3 retry attempts
            try:
                response = method(request_or_iterator, call_details)
                break
            except grpc.RpcError as rpc_error:
                if rpc_error.code() not in (grpc.StatusCode.UNAVAILABLE, grpc.
                        StatusCode.DEADLINE_EXCEEDED):
                    raise
                else:
                    logging.warning("Retrying method due to error: %s", rpc_error)
        return response or "Maximum retries reached"

# Channel with interceptor
channel = grpc.intercept_channel(
    grpc.insecure_channel('localhost:50051'),
    RetryInterceptor()
```

This interceptor design pattern aligns global retry logics, allowing service interactions to self-heal incrementally without explicitly altering service implementations.

6.2.5 Conclusion

Robust error handling in gRPC forms the backbone of dependable distributed application delivery. By marrying precise delve into client-side strategies with profound server-side insights, developers can leverage comprehensive frameworks suitable for handling sophisticated error scenarios and extensive load conditions. In embracing structured error mechanisms employing retries, context management, logging, and global error policies, engineers craft robust system architectures equipped to address modern application challenges in face of uncertainty and scale. By doing so, they ensure sustained reliability, enhanced user experience, and the longevity of software solutions deployed across diverse service environments characteristic of the gRPC ecosystem. Through diligent assessment and adaptation of error handling systems, applications strive not only for perfection but inevitable excellence.

6.3 Debugging gRPC Applications

Debugging in the context of gRPC applications presents a unique set of challenges and opportunities. As a communications framework designed for high-performance and cross-platform interoperability, gRPC applications benefit from streamlined protocols, efficient data serialization, and robust transport security. Yet, these same features can complicate the debugging process, obscuring visibility into communication flows and complicating error diagnosis. In this section, we delve into the strategies and tools available for effectively debugging gRPC applications, offering a comprehensive guide to diagnosing network anomalies, service misconfigurations, and performance bottlenecks, all crucial for sustaining reliable operations.

The Intricacies of Debugging gRPC

A major challenge in debugging gRPC applications is the intrinsic opacity brought about by HTTP/2 and protocol buffer serialization, which aims at optimizing transport rather than providing human readability. With binary rather than textual data exchanges, in-depth protocol inspections require focused tooling and a structured approach. Coupled with distributed architecture models, pinpointing faults may entail transcending network boundaries and correlating logs across microservices.

Thus, debugging gRPC applications necessitates a dual approach encompassing both dynamic and static analysis: identifying faults dynamically through execution trails—using logs, traces, and interactive debugging—along with static analysis via code reviews and configurations audits.

Diagnostic Tools for gRPC

Logging

Effective logging remains the cornerstone of any debugging process, offering real-time insights into operational behavior and error scopes. For gRPC applications, logging should extend beyond basic error capturing to encompass metadata details, method invocation specifics, and RPC latency metrics.

Python's standard logging library can be extended into gRPC methods to capture vital statistics and errors.

```
import logging
from concurrent import futures
import grpc
from my_protos import my_service_pb2, my_service_pb2_grpc

logging.basicConfig(filename='my_service.log', level=logging.DEBUG,
            format='%(asctime)s - %(levelname)s - %(message)s')

class MyService(my_service_pb2_grpc.MyServiceServicer):
    def MyMethod(self, request, context):
        logging.info("Received request: %s", request)
        try:
```

6.3. DEBUGGING GRPC APPLICATIONS

```
            # Perform operation
            result = perform_operation(request)
            return my_service_pb2.MyResponse(message=result)
        except Exception as e:
            logging.error("Exception occurred: %s", e)
            raise e

def serve():
    server = grpc.server(futures.ThreadPoolExecutor(max_workers=10))
    my_service_pb2_grpc.add_MyServiceServicer_to_server(MyService(), server)
    server.add_insecure_port('[::]:50051')
    server.start()
    server.wait_for_termination()

serve()
```

This configuration captures requests, responses, and any exceptions, aiding in both audit trails and rapid failure diagnosis. Adopting formats that include timestamps and log levels enhances log comprehensibility, while centralized logging systems like ELK (Elasticsearch, Logstash, and Kibana) or cloud-native alternatives bolster analysis and alerting capabilities.

Tracing

Tracing provides a broader observability into the flow of requests as they traverse through distributed components. Systems like OpenTracing or Jaeger capture and visualize traces efficiently, particularly for multi-service operations where identifying bottleneck points or faulty connections is crucial.

Tracing inherently involves instrumenting applications to log trace points at crucial interaction junctures, feeding into an aggregation system for comprehensive visualization.

```
from jaeger_client import Config
import grpc
from my_protos import my_service_pb2, my_service_pb2_grpc
from opentracing_instrumentation.client_interceptors import TracingInterceptor

def setup_tracer(service_name='my_service'):
    config = Config(
        config={'sampler': {'type': 'const', 'param': 1}, 'logging': True},
        service_name=service_name
    )
    return config.initialize_tracer()

def make_traced_call(channel):
```

CHAPTER 6. ERROR HANDLING AND DEBUGGING IN GRPC

```
tracer = setup_tracer()
try:
    stub = my_service_pb2_grpc.MyServiceStub(channel)
    response = stub.MyMethod(my_service_pb2.MyRequest(name='TraceMe'))
    return response.message
finally:
    tracer.close()

if __name__ == '__main__':
    channel = grpc.insecure_channel('localhost:50051')
    intercepted_channel = grpc.intercept_channel(channel, TracingInterceptor())
    print(make_traced_call(intercepted_channel))
```

This integration captures and retains trace spans, enriching gRPC performance insights and spanning analysis across RPC boundaries, supporting root-cause analysis for latency hits and failures.

Interactive Debugging

Interactive debugging, although traditionally confined to local development, remains indispensable for understanding gRPC control flows, especially when verifying logic correctness or investigating unforeseen behaviors. Tools like Python's pdb can iterate breakpoints, inspect closures, and evaluate expression scopes to debug server or client logic.

```
import pdb
import grpc
from my_protos import my_service_pb2, my_service_pb2_grpc

def mock_operation():
    with grpc.insecure_channel('localhost:50051') as channel:
        stub = my_service_pb2_grpc.MyServiceStub(channel)
        response = stub.MyMethod(my_service_pb2.MyRequest(name='Debug'))
        return response.message

if __name__ == '__main__':
    # Set a breakpoint
    pdb.set_trace()
    print("Returned message: ", mock_operation())
```

By setting breakpoints through pdb, you can examine state conditions during execution, facilitating the discovery of logical discrepancies without leaving the development interface.

176

Configuration and Network Analysis

Configuring and troubleshooting network intricacies – critical to efficient gRPC tasking – often demands investigation of underlying HTTP/2 settings, authentication credentials, and RPC method definitions.

Configuration Checks

Configuration audits ensure correctness in environment variables, accurate service descriptors, and consistent endpoint declarations. Spotting configuration mismatches frequently resolves issues involving incorrect credential use, service availability problems, and data serialization errors.

For instance, wrong method descriptors or mismatched service definitions can lead to misdirected requests or unimplemented method errors. Examining proto files and matching client-generated stubs against server implementations can resolve these.

Network Monitoring and Packet Inspection

Network monitoring unveils potential transport-level issues, such as network partitioning, congestion, or segment drops, impacting overall application availability. Using network analysis tools, such as Wireshark, allows for inspection of HTTP/2 frames and certificate exchanges, uncovering issues related to SSL handshakes or improper payload configurations.

Simultaneously, integrating application-level metrics using platforms like Prometheus facilitates time-series insights into network behavior, correlating client-server throughput with error conditions or performance anomalies.

```
from prometheus_client import Summary, Counter, Gauge, start_http_server
import grpc
import my_protos.my_service_pb2 as service_pb2
import my_protos.my_service_pb2_grpc as service_pb2_grpc

REQUEST_TIME = Summary('request_processing_seconds', 'Time spent processing
    request')
ERROR_COUNTER = Counter('request_errors_total', 'Total request processing
    errors')
```

```
ACTIVE_REQUESTS = Gauge('active_requests_total', 'Total number of active
    requests')

def serve():
    server = grpc.server(futures.ThreadPoolExecutor(max_workers=10))
    service_pb2_grpc.add_MyServiceServicer_to_server(MyService(), server)
    ACTIVE_REQUESTS.inc()

    server.add_insecure_port('[::]:50051')
    server.start()
    start_http_server(8000)
    server.wait_for_termination()

class MyService(service_pb2_grpc.MyServiceServicer):
    @REQUEST_TIME.time()
    def MyMethod(self, request, context):
        logging.info("Processing request")
        try:
            # Process request here
            return service_pb2.MyResponse(message='Processed')
        except Exception as e:
            logging.error("Error processing request")
            ERROR_COUNTER.inc()
            context.set_code(grpc.StatusCode.INTERNAL)
            context.set_details('Internal server error')
            raise e

serve()
```

This setup provides metrics observability critical to diagnosing throughput and error trends, potentially triggering alerts to operational teams in response to predefined conditions.

Systematic Debugging Workflow

Establishing a Baseline

Establishing a baseline involves defining observable metrics and operational logs under normal circumstances. This yardstick allows you to contrast subsequent logs and metrics to identify aberrations accurately.

Incremental Logging and Observability Enhancements

Especially in production scenarios, adding more comprehensive logging is often resisted due to performance detriments; selectively implementing fine-grained logging during suspicious conditions through feature flags or dynamic log level switching minimizes this overhead and focuses on capturing problem-centric data.

Reproduce and Isolate Conditions

The replication of error scenarios in controlled environments enables isolation of contextual parameters contributing to failures. Reproducing conditions - configuring similar load scenarios or using mock services - allows for precise testing and verification of discovered fixes.

Measure, Tweak, and Validate Performance Metrics

Performance tuning follows diagnostic identification, aiming at not only error resolution but enhanced operational efficiency. Changes are validated against performance baselines, measuring improvements or regressions introduced by any refined configurations or logic alterations.

Conclusion

Debugging gRPC applications is inherently multifaceted, touching on various systemic aspects from network configurations to runtime executions. By leveraging structured logging, tracing, and modern debugging techniques, developers can comprehensively diagnose issues, propose corrective strategies, and enhance application resilience. Integrating metrics monitoring and adopting systematic workflows delineates clearer paths for ensuring service reliability, while interactive debugging aids in unraveling inherent complexities. Amid the challenges, the adoption of a rich mix of tools, combined with a principled approach, enables developers to maintain robust gRPC applications, elucidating operational insights and driving toward continuous optimizations and improved service delivery.

6.4 Handling Deadlines and Timeouts

In gRPC, managing deadlines and timeouts is critical to ensuring efficient resource allocation and robust application performance. Deadlines and timeouts control the permissible duration for remote procedure calls, preventing resources from being tied indefinitely to slow or unresponsive operations. This functionality is vital in creating responsive systems that adhere to latency requirements and offer consistent service availability under varied load conditions. This section explores the mechanisms, implementation strategies, and best practices for effectively handling deadlines and timeouts within gRPC-based applications.

Understanding Deadlines and Timeouts in gRPC

Deadlines and timeouts in gRPC are closely related concepts used to manage the lifespan of an RPC. A *deadline* is a specific point in time by which the operation must complete, while a *timeout* is the duration within which the call must finish. Handling these in gRPC involves setting appropriate constraints on both client-initiated calls and server-expected execution times, thus maintaining service integrity and enhancing user experiences by returning timely feedback or alerts when operations do not complete as anticipated.

When properly utilized, these features help prevent unintended resource consumption, ensuring that RPCs do not linger indefinitely. This is especially pertinent in large-scale distributed systems where network conditions might fluctuate, or diverse service latencies prevail.

Client-Side Deadline and Timeout Management

On the client side, setting deadlines involves specifying the maximum permissible time for an RPC to complete. If this deadline is exceeded, gRPC automatically terminates the call and notifies the application through an error with the DEADLINE_EXCEEDED status code. It is the client's responsibility to define these deadlines based on application needs, service-level agreements (SLAs), or empirical performance data.

```
import grpc
from my_service import service_pb2, service_pb2_grpc
```

6.4. HANDLING DEADLINES AND TIMEOUTS

```
def call_with_deadline():
    with grpc.insecure_channel('localhost:50051') as channel:
        stub = service_pb2_grpc.MyServiceStub(channel)
        try:
            # Setting a call deadline of 5 seconds
            response = stub.MyMethod(service_pb2.MyRequest(name='DeadlineTest'),
                    timeout=5)
            print("Response received: ", response.message)
        except grpc.RpcError as rpc_error:
            if rpc_error.code() == grpc.StatusCode.DEADLINE_EXCEEDED:
                print("Deadline exceeded while trying to contact the server.")
            else:
                print("RPC error: ", rpc_error.details())

call_with_deadline()
```

Here, the client dictates a 5-second deadline for the server response, ensuring operations beyond this period trigger a DEADLINE_EXCEEDED status, thus preventing unnecessary waiting and resource blocking.

Server-Side Deadline Awareness

The server, while executing an RPC, is aware of the client's specified deadlines. Through the gRPC context object, the server can retrieve this deadline and potentially adjust its processing strategy accordingly. If the server identifies imminent deadline breaches, it may choose to pre-emptively abort processing to free resources.

```
import time
import grpc
from concurrent import futures
from my_service import service_pb2, service_pb2_grpc

class MyService(service_pb2_grpc.MyServiceServicer):
    def MyMethod(self, request, context):
        # Display the deadline
        deadline_timestamp = context.time_remaining()
        print(f"Time remaining: {deadline_timestamp} seconds")

        # Simulate a long processing time
        time.sleep(10)  # Sleep time exceeding likely deadlines

        # If we reach here, we assume an error would have notified the client
        return service_pb2.MyResponse(message="This response may not reach the
                client")

def serve():
    server = grpc.server(futures.ThreadPoolExecutor(max_workers=10))
    service_pb2_grpc.add_MyServiceServicer_to_server(MyService(), server)
    server.add_insecure_port('[::]:50051')
    server.start()
    server.wait_for_termination()
```

```
serve()
```

This example illustrates how a server might use the context object to detect remaining time and ensure efficient resource utilization by tailoring its workload based on available time.

Best Practices for Configuring Deadlines and Timeouts

Defining appropriate deadline values should consider factors such as network latency variability, resource availability, and user expectations for response times. Developers should adopt a data-driven approach, leveraging historical response times to inform suitable timeout configurations, balancing between allowing sufficient server processing time and ensuring timely client feedback.

- **Empirical Measurement**: Use real-world performance and latency metrics to guide deadline settings for various RPCs, optimizing measures for specific service paths or operations.

- **Consistent SLA Definitions**: Align deadlines with your service-level agreement expectations, communicating these SLA constraints between system components.

- **Graceful Degradation and Retry Strategies**: When deadlines lead to call failures, integrate retry logic (employing mechanisms such as exponential backoff) to mitigate transient faults while managing system load effectively.

- **Dynamic Adjustments and Monitoring**: Utilize real-time monitoring to adjust timeout configurations dynamically based on current system loads and observed latencies. Tools like Prometheus can provide live metrics indicating when deadlines are frequently exceeded, prompting adjustments.

- **Client and Server Compatibility**: Ensure that client-side deadline configurations are understood by and compatible with server-side logic, promoting proper load handling and avoiding automated timeouts misinterpreted as errors.

Advanced Techniques for Deadline Management

6.4. HANDLING DEADLINES AND TIMEOUTS

Cancelation Propagation

In scenarios where a client cancels a request due to a deadline exceeding, the cancellation should ideally propagate across all associated operations, preventing unnecessary processing and conserving resources.

```
from concurrent import futures
import grpc
from my_service import service_pb2, service_pb2_grpc
import threading

class MyService(service_pb2_grpc.MyServiceServicer):
    def MyMethod(self, request, context):
        def long_running_task():
            try:
                for i in range(1, 10):
                    time.sleep(1)
                    print(f"Running task {i}")
                    # Check if cancelation was triggered
                    if context.is_active() == False:
                        print("Canceled")
                        return
                return service_pb2.MyResponse(message="Completed Task")
            except Exception as e:
                print("Exception: ", e)

        thread = threading.Thread(target=long_running_task)
        thread.start()
        thread.join() # Ensure clean shutdown

def serve():
    server = grpc.server(futures.ThreadPoolExecutor(max_workers=10))
    service_pb2_grpc.add_MyServiceServicer_to_server(MyService(), server)
    server.add_insecure_port('[::]:50051')
    server.start()
    server.wait_for_termination()

serve()
```

The concept showcased involves threading where server tasks respecting context cancellation state prevent workload processing after a deadline-triggered cancellation.

Optimizing for Retry-able Operations

Given transient network faults, it's critical that applications offer retry capabilities for operations not reaching completion due to shortfall against deadline constraints. Retries must be carefully crafted not to overwhelm the system, often using retry policies with backoff strategies.

```
import grpc
from retrying import retry
from my_service import service_pb2, service_pb2_grpc

# Define retry with exponential backoff
@retry(stop_max_attempt_number=5, wait_exponential_multiplier=2000,
    wait_exponential_max=10000)
def call_remote_procedure_with_retry(stub, request):
    return stub.MyMethod(request, timeout=3)

def execute_with_retry():
    with grpc.insecure_channel('localhost:50051') as channel:
        stub = service_pb2_grpc.MyServiceStub(channel)
        request = service_pb2.MyRequest(name='RetryTest')
        try:
            response = call_remote_procedure_with_retry(stub, request)
            print("Received response: ", response.message)
        except grpc.RpcError as e:
            print("Failed after retries: ", e.details())

execute_with_retry()
```

This example deploys retries, allowing the application to navigate through transient errors more efficiently leveraging exponential back-off strategies.

Conclusion

Proper application of deadlines and timeouts in gRPC reinforces the capability of distributed systems to serve users consistently under variable network and server load conditions. By implementing these controls, developers can ensure operations are not only within expected response times but also contribute to reducing costs and improving user satisfaction by efficiently utilizing system resources. Setting realistic deadline and timeout values, examining empirical data, and constantly iterating on configurations, form intelligent service strategies ensuring sustained operational proficiency. As we innovate in increasingly complex service environments, gRPC's robust handling of deadlines and the supportive tooling framework offers stable ground for deploying scalable, high-performing, and user-centric applications. Through meticulous calibration and responsive design, these mechanisms unlock the pathway to delivering perceptively reliable and proactive digital experiences.

6.5 Using Interceptors for Error Management

Interceptors in gRPC provide a powerful mechanism for implementing cross-cutting concerns, such as error management, logging, authentication, and monitoring. They function as middleware, offering hooks in the request-response lifecycle where specific logic can be executed transparently across multiple service methods. In this section, we focus on employing interceptors for error handling and management, detailing their implementation, configuration, and use cases within gRPC applications. This discussion will also encompass strategies to leverage interceptors for enhancing error visibility, transforming errors consistently, and neatly managing fault propagation.

- The Role of Interceptors in gRPC

Interceptors can be thought of as filters that wrap around gRPC calls. They operate at either the client or server side, allowing operations such as pre-processing of outgoing requests, handling incoming responses, or providing consistent error transformations and logging. By centralizing these operations, interceptors reduce code redundancy and simplify common logic application across various service methods.

gRPC classifies interceptors into two primary types:

- Unary Interceptors: These work with standard unary RPCs where each request receives a direct response.
- Stream Interceptors: These handle streaming RPCs allowing for complex sequencing of data or states across method invocations.

In the domain of error management, interceptors streamline the capture, manipulation, and propagation of error states, providing coherent mechanisms for dealing with faults on a global service level.

- Implementing Client Interceptors

Client-side interceptors operate as wrappers around method calls, frequently employed to augment request origination with attributes like authentication tokens or centralized error handling.

```python
import grpc
from grpc_interceptor import ClientCallDetails, ClientInterceptor

class ErrorHandlingInterceptor(ClientInterceptor):
    def intercept(self, method, request_or_iterator, call_details):
        try:
            response = method(request_or_iterator, call_details)
            return response
        except grpc.RpcError as rpc_error:
            self.handle_error(rpc_error)
            raise # Re-raise the exception after logging or additional handling

    def handle_error(self, rpc_error):
        # Standardized error message or logging
        print(f"RPC failed with status code: {rpc_error.code()}. Details: {rpc_error.
            details()}")

def make_request_with_interceptor():
    intercept_channel = grpc.intercept_channel(
        grpc.insecure_channel('localhost:50051'),
        ErrorHandlingInterceptor()
    )
    stub = my_service_pb2_grpc.MyServiceStub(intercept_channel)
    try:
        result = stub.MyMethod(my_service_pb2.MyRequest(name='Example'))
        print("Received response:", result.message)
    except grpc.RpcError as e:
        print("Operation failed with interception.")

make_request_with_interceptor()
```

This interceptor captures the RpcError raised during method execution, logs standardized information about the failure, and optionally performs transformations or retries based on custom logic.

- Implementing Server-Side Interceptors

Server-side interceptors handle errors post-processing an incoming request. They play a pivotal role in error propagation, enabling servers to adopt uniform error-reporting mechanisms to clients and ensuring exceptions translate into meaningful gRPC status codes.

```python
import grpc
from concurrent import futures
from grpc_interceptor import ServerInterceptor

class GlobalErrorHandlingInterceptor(ServerInterceptor):
    def intercept_service(self, continuation, handler_call_details):
        try:
            return continuation(handler_call_details)
        except Exception as ex:
            print(f"Handling exception globally: {str(ex)}")
```

6.5. USING INTERCEPTORS FOR ERROR MANAGEMENT

```
            raise grpc.RpcError(grpc.StatusCode.INTERNAL, "Internal server error
                occurred")
def serve():
    server = grpc.server(
        futures.ThreadPoolExecutor(max_workers=10),
        interceptors=[GlobalErrorHandlingInterceptor()]
    )
    my_service_pb2_grpc.add_MyServiceServicer_to_server(MyService(), server)
    server.add_insecure_port('[::]:50051')
    server.start()
    server.wait_for_termination()

serve()
```

The server interceptor in this example provides a catch-all mechanism to handle unforeseen exceptions, converting such occurrences into a structured RpcError that is communicated to the client.

- Synchronizing Error States Across Interceptors

Interceptors facilitate interaction between client and server states, ensuring error generation and handling procedures remain consistent across the communication spectrum. By employing log and metric tools within interceptors, developers gain detailed insight into error metrics and fault trends.

For example, integrating with a metrics collection framework can translate interceptor results into Prometheus metrics, providing real-time insights into service behavior:

```
from prometheus_client import Counter

# Define Prometheus metrics
REQUEST_FAILURES = Counter('request_failures_total', 'Total number of request
    failures due to errors')

class MetricsInterceptor(ServerInterceptor):
    def intercept_service(self, continuation, handler_call_details):
        try:
            # Proceed with the normal flow
            return continuation(handler_call_details)
        except grpc.RpcError as rpc_error:
            if rpc_error.code() != grpc.StatusCode.OK:
                REQUEST_FAILURES.inc()
            raise

# Implementation in server setup
server = grpc.server(
    futures.ThreadPoolExecutor(max_workers=10),
    interceptors=[MetricsInterceptor(), GlobalErrorHandlingInterceptor()]
```

This setup accumulates failure counts, enriching monitoring capabilities and offering data essential for diagnosing service reliability concerns.

- Error Propagation and Transformation

Consistent error propagation ensures that error handling and messages remain predictable, allowing developers to react programmatically to detected states. Well-defined error transformations within interceptors add another layer of robustness by mapping exceptions to standardized error messages or alternate gRPC statuses when necessary.

Even complex error processes, such as translating domain-specific exceptions to service responses, benefit from interceptor management, driving developers to:

- Formulate a uniform error vocabulary: Define a subset of gRPC status codes pertinent to common domain failures.

- Ensure clarity: Leverage standardized error details providing concise, meaningful client-side messages.

- Implement structured transformation logic: For instance, beyond mapping JSON-deserialized error metadata, pinpointing root causes, and provisionally suggesting resolutions.

- Multi-Layered Interceptor Strategies

Adopting layered interceptor approaches that cascade error transformations across tiers—encompassing network level, application logic, and business rule processing—provides sophisticated error modeling and promotes modular growth. Logic that nests within intermediate interceptor layers may encapsulate scenarios such as specialized financial tax aggregation validation, market access compliance restrictions, or other domain-centered intricacies.

- Advanced Retry Mechanisms via Interceptors

6.5. USING INTERCEPTORS FOR ERROR MANAGEMENT

Sophisticated retry logics are empowered by interceptors—apt for applications adhering to eventual consistency models. When configured judiciously and aligned with business operational models, interceptors offer self-healing capabilities foundational for handling transient faults. Interceptors, by embodying retry conditions, encapsulate holistic backoff strategies consistently, reducing individual method burden:

```python
import time

class RetryInterceptor(ClientInterceptor):
    def intercept(self, method, request_or_iterator, call_details):
        for attempt in range(3):
            try:
                return method(request_or_iterator, call_details)
            except grpc.RpcError as rpc_error:
                if self.is_retryable(rpc_error):
                    time.sleep(2 ** attempt)  # Exponential backoff
                    continue
                raise
        raise grpc.RpcError(grpc.StatusCode.UNAVAILABLE, "Request failed after retries")

    def is_retryable(self, rpc_error):
        return rpc_error.code() in {grpc.StatusCode.UNAVAILABLE, grpc.StatusCode.DEADLINE_EXCEEDED}

# Usage within client-side communication
channel = grpc.intercept_channel(
    grpc.insecure_channel('localhost:50051'),
    RetryInterceptor()
)
```

- Conclusion

Interceptors present a unique vantage point for managing and unifying error handling mechanisms within gRPC applications, minimizing redundancy and encouraging scalable designs. By abstracting error processing logic, they simplify integrations across diverse service portfolios and ensure coherent, predictable fault management. Adopting interceptors broadens observability and supports proactive adjustments, cultivating introspective systems that elucidate failure trends while accommodating evolving service needs. Through meticulous and strategic application, interceptors emerge as indispensable allies, driving advancements in error resilience, fault tolerance, and robust service design integral to managing complex multilayered architectures indicative of contemporary digital ecosystems.

6.6 Testing gRPC Error Scenarios

In the development of robust gRPC applications, thorough testing of error scenarios is a fundamental requirement. Robust error testing ensures that an application can gracefully handle failures, providing useful feedback and appropriate resolution strategies to maintain a high level of service reliability and user satisfaction. This section delves into various techniques and methodologies for effectively testing gRPC error scenarios, offering insights into the setup and execution of test cases aimed at simulating diverse error conditions. By covering multiple error domains, including network failures, improper input handling, and server-side exceptions, this discussion provides a comprehensive guide for implementing and managing test strategies in gRPC environments.

Importance of Error Scenario Testing

Testing error scenarios is crucial for several reasons:

- Resilience: Helps ensure systems can maintain functionality under adverse conditions or react appropriately to system anomalies.
- Security: Avoids information leakage through improper error messages.
- User Experience: Ensures users receive useful feedback, even when errors occur.
- System Reliability: Allows for timely error detection and prevention mechanisms by anticipating possible failure modes.

Setting Up Test Environments

Establishing a testbed for simulating gRPC error conditions requires a microservices infrastructure where service dependencies, network characteristics, and failure interactions are modeled. Using local services or staging environments with realistic configurations allows for dynamic scenario management.

6.6. TESTING GRPC ERROR SCENARIOS

Utilizing Python's unittest or pytest frameworks provides a structured, systematic approach to executing test suites indicating potential vulnerabilities or inefficiencies in the gRPC service layer.

Base Test Structure

The basic structure of a test can be established as follows:

```
import grpc
import unittest
from my_service import service_pb2, service_pb2_grpc

class TestMyService(unittest.TestCase):

    def setUp(self):
        self.channel = grpc.insecure_channel('localhost:50051')
        self.stub = service_pb2_grpc.MyServiceStub(self.channel)

    def tearDown(self):
        self.channel.close()

    def test_invalid_input(self):
        request = service_pb2.MyRequest(name="*InvalidChars")
        with self.assertRaises(grpc.RpcError) as context:
            self.stub.MyMethod(request)
        self.assertEqual(context.exception.code(), grpc.StatusCode.INVALID_ARGUMENT)

if __name__ == '__main__':
    unittest.main()
```

In this setup, unittest orchestrates connection lifecycle management and applies assertions, verifying service responses match with anticipated error conditions.

Specific gRPC Error Scenario Simulations

Network Failures

Network failures are common real-world scenarios where gRPC clients might experience timeouts, DNS lookup failures, or server unavailability.

```
import grpc
import unittest
from my_service import service_pb2, service_pb2_grpc
import socket
```

CHAPTER 6. ERROR HANDLING AND DEBUGGING IN GRPC

```
class TestNetworkFailures(unittest.TestCase):

    def test_timeout_error(self):
        channel = grpc.insecure_channel('non_existent_server:9999')
        stub = service_pb2_grpc.MyServiceStub(channel)
        with self.assertRaises(grpc.RpcError) as context:
            _ = stub.MyMethod(service_pb2.MyRequest())
        self.assertIn(context.exception.code(), (grpc.StatusCode.UNAVAILABLE, grpc.
            StatusCode.DEADLINE_EXCEEDED))

if __name__ == '__main__':
    unittest.main()
```

This setup utilizes a non-existent server domain to trigger network-induced failure reflections, aligned with timeout or unavailability codes.

Server-Side Exceptions

Server-side exceptions should be anticipated during testing to confirm exceptions translate into RpcError responses adequately.

```
class TestServerErrorHandling(unittest.TestCase):

    def test_unexpected_server_exception(self):
        request = service_pb2.MyRequest(name="trigger_exception")
        with self.assertRaises(grpc.RpcError) as context:
            self.stub.MyMethod(request)
        self.assertEqual(context.exception.code(), grpc.StatusCode.INTERNAL)
        self.assertEqual(context.exception.details(), "Internal server error occurred")

if __name__ == '__main__':
    unittest.main()
```

This example validates that unforeseen server exceptions transform into structured gRPC status responses, conveying the occurrence and nature of the server-side disruption.

Input Validations

Input cases where improper data violates service expectations must be explicitly tested for graceful error management, ensuring data integrity and service security.

```
class TestInputValidation(unittest.TestCase):
```

6.6. TESTING GRPC ERROR SCENARIOS

```
def setUp(self):
    self.channel = grpc.insecure_channel('localhost:50051')
    self.stub = service_pb2_grpc.MyServiceStub(self.channel)

def test_invalid_data(self):
    invalid_request = service_pb2.MyRequest(name="<>Invalid")
    with self.assertRaises(grpc.RpcError) as context:
        self.stub.MyMethod(invalid_request)
    self.assertEqual(context.exception.code(), grpc.StatusCode.
        INVALID_ARGUMENT)
    self.assertEqual(context.exception.details(), "Invalid name format")

if __name__ == '__main__':
    unittest.main()
```

In this test, malformed inputs are deliberately sent to confirm the service's robustness in rejecting undesirable data formats with clear INVALID_ARGUMENT messages.

Advanced Testing Techniques

Mocking and Simulation

Utilizing mocking libraries, such as unittest.mock, allows for simulating component interactions outside standard gRPC execution paths. Mocking external service dependencies facilitates error scenario exploration without affecting real-world service operations.

```
from unittest.mock import MagicMock, patch

class TestWithMocking(unittest.TestCase):

    @patch('my_service.service_pb2_grpc.MyServiceServicer.MyMethod')
    def test_service_with_mock(self, mock_my_method):
        mock_my_method.side_effect = grpc.RpcError(grpc.StatusCode.INTERNAL, "
            Injected Error Message")
        response = self.stub.MyMethod(service_pb2.MyRequest(name="Mock"))
        self.assertFalse(response)

if __name__ == '__main__':
    unittest.main()
```

The example demonstrates typed behavior simulation, vital for preemptively identifying error-causing interactions between integrated components via mocks.

Load and Stress Testing

Testing gRPC services under load and stress conditions reveals potential pitfalls with request handling efficiency, resource exhaustion, or race conditions, offering insights into the limits and capacities of the service infrastructure.

Load testing frameworks, such as locust or grpc-bench, facilitate gauging performance and uncovering bottlenecks through varying levels of concurrency:

```
locust -f gRPC_test_file.py --host grpc://localhost
```

This command invokes designated load specification files, offering a Python-native approach to configure and execute load tests against gRPC endpoints, informing optimizations for scaling needs.

Conclusion

Thoroughly testing error scenarios in gRPC applications is integral to ensuring resilient operations and a high caliber of service delivery. By aligning with systematic testing principles—involving simulated network failures, server disruptions, input validations, and performance-related tests—developers establish a reliable foundation for identifying and addressing potential vulnerabilities. Strategic error testing not only empowers robustness against anticipated failures but also enriches insights into inherent complexities, driving refinements in system designs. Proactive measures elevate service continuity, offering predictability and clarity in operations, thus underscoring the role of comprehensive testing in maintaining the overarching integrity and success of gRPC deployments. As developers continue to harness these techniques effectively, they safeguard architecture resilience in the face of evolving demands and challenges intrinsic to the distributed computing paradigm.

Chapter 7

gRPC Security and Authentication

This chapter addresses the security and authentication mechanisms available in gRPC to safeguard communications. It examines how transport layer security is implemented using TLS to encrypt data in transit. Various authentication methods, including token-based and mutual TLS, are explored to ensure secure access control. The integration of OAuth2 and JSON Web Tokens (JWT) is discussed to enhance authentication procedures. Additionally, the chapter covers strategies for implementing role-based access control and methods for encrypting data within gRPC messages to bolster privacy and security measures.

7.1 Overview of gRPC Security

gRPC, an open-source Remote Procedure Call (RPC) framework, facilitates the development of distributed systems and microservices by enabling client-server applications to communicate seamlessly. An integral component of any such communication protocol is security.

The gRPC framework implements a comprehensive security model that aligns with industry standards to protect data in transit and ensure authenticity, integrity, and confidentiality.

The gRPC security model is fundamentally built upon principles that underline modern cybersecurity approaches: securing data against unauthorized access, authenticating user identities, and maintaining data integrity. This is achieved through encryption, authentication, and authorization mechanisms, making gRPC competitive with other communication protocols such as REST.

gRPC supports both HTTP/2 and ProtoBuf, which together facilitate efficient and robust communication. HTTP/2 improves performance and resource utilization with features such as multiplexing, header compression, and request prioritization. However, the focus of this section is the security dimension that gRPC provides, especially drawing contrasts and parallels with traditional HTTP/1.x security protocols.

Core Security Principles in gRPC

The core security principles central to gRPC include confidentiality, integrity, and authenticity. These principles aim to prevent unauthorized data access, ensure that data is not tampered with during transmission, and verify the identities of communicating parties. These principles are enforced primarily through Transport Layer Security (TLS), but gRPC also supports custom security solutions tailored via interceptors in the application layer.

Confidentiality is achieved through encryption protocols. Data being transmitted is encrypted to prevent eavesdropping by unauthorized entities. TLS plays a pivotal role in this aspect by encrypting the communication channel.

Integrity ensures that any data received is exactly as it was sent, without any unauthorized modifications during transit. This is achieved by cryptographic mechanisms that validate the data integrity, such as Message Authentication Codes (MACs) or Integrity Checks.

Authenticity is focused on verifying the identity of the parties involved in the communication. This is predominantly handled through certificates and various authentication mechanisms. Client and server certificates serve as proof of identity.

```
syntax = "proto3";
```

```
service DataService {
    rpc SendData(DataRequest) returns (DataResponse) {}
}
message DataRequest {
    string data = 1;
}
message DataResponse {
    bool success = 1;
}
```

The service definition above represents a simple service in gRPC that would require a secure channel to send and receive data securely. Applying security constraints to this service involves configuring its communication over TLS.

Transport Security and TLS

Transport Layer Security (TLS), the successor to Secure Sockets Layer (SSL), is a critical component of gRPC's security model, ensuring data confidentiality, integrity, and authenticity. TLS employs robust cryptographic techniques to encrypt data transmission channels between gRPC clients and servers. With HTTPS/2 as the transport protocol, gRPC inherently operates over a secure communication channel.

TLS provides several key security benefits:

- *Encrypted Communication*: By encrypting data in transit, TLS prevents eavesdroppers from reading sensitive information.

- *Data Integrity*: Via cryptographic checksums, TLS ensures that data has not been altered in transit.

- *Mutual Authentication*: TLS can authenticate both parties, ensuring the client and server are communicating with intended counterparts.

TLS configuration in gRPC services is facilitated through certificate management. Certificates must be issued by a trusted Certificate Authority (CA), and they exist in a chain of trust leading back to a recognized root authority.

```
package main
```

```go
import (
    "log"
    "net"
    "google.golang.org/grpc"
    "google.golang.org/grpc/credentials"
    pb "example.com/mypackage/protobuf"
)

func main() {
    // Load server's certificate and key
    certFile := "server-cert.pem"
    keyFile := "server-key.pem"
    creds, err := credentials.NewServerTLSFromFile(certFile, keyFile)
    if err != nil {
        log.Fatalf("failed to create credentials: %v", err)
    }

    // Create a listener on TCP port
    lis, err := net.Listen("tcp", ":50051")
    if err != nil {
        log.Fatalf("failed to listen: %v", err)
    }

    // Create a new gRPC server
    s := grpc.NewServer(grpc.Creds(creds))

    // Register gRPC service
    pb.RegisterDataServiceServer(s, &server{})
    log.Printf("server listening at %v", lis.Addr())
    if err := s.Serve(lis); err != nil {
        log.Fatalf("failed to serve: %v", err)
    }
}
```

The configuration above demonstrates how to initialize a gRPC server with TLS credentials in Go. This setup ensures that any data exchanged between the client and server is encrypted and authenticated against tampering or impersonation attempts.

Client Authentication in gRPC

gRPC supports several client authentication mechanisms, including mutual TLS (mTLS) and token-based authentication. OAuth2 and JWT are commonly used in token-based scenarios. These methods permit greater flexibility and integration capabilities within the broader security infrastructure of an organization.

Mutual TLS extends the regular TLS model by requiring both the client and the server to present valid certificates. This ensures authentication for both parties, significantly enhancing the security model.

For token-based authentication, OAuth2 provides a comprehensive framework by which access credentials are delegated through tokens rather than exposing sensitive data or credentials. This is particularly useful in microservice architectures, where services need to communicate securely without repeating credential validation processes.

Security Threats and Mitigations

When implementing gRPC security, one must consider possible attack vectors. Common threats include man-in-the-middle attacks, replay attacks, and more intricate scenarios involving malicious node impersonation.

- *Man-in-the-Middle (MitM) Attacks*: These are addressed by using TLS to ensure encrypted channels, where the attacker cannot decipher the data.

- *Replay Attacks*: These involve intercepting and replaying valid data transmissions. Solutions involve using nonce or timestamps to restrict the validity period of requests.

- *Impersonation*: Occurs when an attacker masquerades as a legitimate client or server. Countered effectively with mTLS where certificates ensure authenticity.

Incorporating best practices in certificate management plays a vital role in maintaining a secure gRPC infrastructure. Regular updates and rotation of certificates, stringent access control to certificate stores, and ensuring proper certificate revocation lists (CRLs) are pivotal in fortifying security further.

Conclusion on gRPC Security Model

The security model in gRPC delves deeply into the use of TLS for transport security, offering a robust framework to authenticate participants, encrypt communications, and protect the integrity of data exchanges. The flexibility of gRPC allows for varied authentication mechanisms, accommodating diverse security needs across different architectures and use cases. By implementing these security protocols, gRPC ensures that service-to-service communications remain both reliable and secure, setting a benchmark for modern RPC frameworks in the age of microservices and distributed systems.

Server listening on secure channel with credentials.
All communication is encrypted and authenticated.

The message above signifies a successful secure communication session, indicative of a well-configured gRPC service framework.

7.2 Transport Security with TLS

Transport Layer Security (TLS) is the cornerstone for securing communications over network protocols, including gRPC. TLS offers critical functionalities such as encryption, integrity verification, and peer authentication, ensuring that data transmitted between clients and servers remains confidential and untampered. This section delves into the mechanisms of TLS, its integration within gRPC, and how it surpasses traditional protocol security measures.

TLS operates over the HTTP/2 protocol, which natively supports multiplexing and improved latency features essential for the operation of gRPC. These enhancements afford gRPC efficiencies that are not only performance-based but also security-centric.

Understanding TLS Protocol Operations

TLS, a successor to SSL, ensures secure communications through a combination of symmetric and asymmetric cryptography. During a TLS handshake, a client and server establish a secure connection by negotiating encryption parameters. This includes:

- *Version Negotiation*: Establishing the highest version of TLS supported by both parties.

- *Cipher Suites*: Choosing a preferred set of cryptographic algorithms to secure data.

- *Peer Authentication*: Verifying identities of the parties using digital certificates.

- *Session Key Agreement*: Establishing a shared secret (often via Diffie-Hellman process) that encrypts the communication channel.

This negotiation phase is critical as it sets parameters for all subsequent communications.

```
ClientHello
  Version: TLS 1.2
  Cipher Suites: [TLS_ECDHE_RSA_WITH_AES_128_GCM_SHA256, ...]
  Server Name: www.example.com

ServerHello
  Version: TLS 1.2
  Cipher Suite: TLS_ECDHE_RSA_WITH_AES_128_GCM_SHA256

Certificate
  Subject: CN=www.example.com
  Issuer: CN=Root CA

ServerHelloDone

ClientKeyExchange
ChangeCipherSpec
Finished
```

In the snippet above, you observe the process of a client initiating a handshake. The server responds with a selected cipher suite and demonstrates identity through a digital certificate.

TLS Certificates and Authentication

Authentication is a critical component supported through X.509 certificates. These certificates, issued by trusted certificate authorities, contain a public key and data verifying the identity of the certificate holder. Certificates establish trust by creating a chain from a "leaf" certificate back to a trusted root certificate.

Mutual TLS (mTLS) offers additional security by mandating that both client and server authenticate each other. mTLS eliminates risks associated with rogue servers or unauthorized clients by binding the authentication process to valid certificates.

Here's a Go implementation for setting up gRPC with mTLS, ensuring that only authenticated clients connect to the server:

```
package main

import (
  "crypto/tls"
  "crypto/x509"
  "log"
  "google.golang.org/grpc"
  "google.golang.org/grpc/credentials"
  "io/ioutil"
```

```go
)
func main() {
    cert, err := tls.LoadX509KeyPair("server-cert.pem", "server-key.pem")
    if err != nil {
        log.Fatalf("failed to load server key pair: %v", err)
    }

    caCert, err := ioutil.ReadFile("ca-cert.pem")
    if err != nil {
        log.Fatalf("failed to read CA cert: %v", err)
    }

    caCertPool := x509.NewCertPool()
    if !caCertPool.AppendCertsFromPEM(caCert) {
        log.Fatalf("failed to add CA cert to pool")
    }

    // Setup tls.Config with mutual TLS
    tlsConfig := &tls.Config{
        Certificates: []tls.Certificate{cert},
        ClientAuth:   tls.RequireAndVerifyClientCert,
        ClientCAs:    caCertPool,
    }

    opts := []grpc.ServerOption{grpc.Creds(credentials.NewTLS(tlsConfig))}
    server := grpc.NewServer(opts...)

    log.Println("Server started on port 50051 with mTLS")
}
```

The Go code establishes a secure gRPC server through mTLS, ensuring mutual authentication using certificates. The server requires all connecting clients to present valid certificates trusted by the CA.

Establishing Secure Channels

Once the TLS handshake completes, a secure channel is established with both parties holding a shared session key. Any data sent over this channel is encrypted using symmetric encryption algorithms defined in the negotiated cipher suite. This ensures both high performance and security.

gRPC clients typically connect to servers employing TLS by setting up TLS credentials. Below demonstrates client TLS setup in Go, ensuring data confidentiality:

```go
import (
    "google.golang.org/grpc"
    "google.golang.org/grpc/credentials"
)

func main() {
```

7.2. TRANSPORT SECURITY WITH TLS

```
creds, err := credentials.NewClientTLSFromFile("server-cert.pem", "")
if err != nil {
    log.Fatalf("failed to load TLS credentials: %v", err)
}

conn, err := grpc.Dial("localhost:50051", grpc.WithTransportCredentials(creds))
if err != nil {
    log.Fatalf("failed to connect: %v", err)
}
defer conn.Close()

log.Println("Connected to server with TLS")
}
```

The client setup involves creating transport credentials from a server certificate and using these credentials when dialing the server, ensuring a TLS encrypted connection.

TLS Versions and Cipher Suites

TLS has evolved over time, moving from older, less secure versions to newer, more robust versions. It is advisable to enable only the latest stable TLS versions in gRPC deployments to guard against vulnerabilities. Configuration of cipher suites is equally crucial to guarantee a balance between performance and security.

Administrators should configure services to prefer strong cipher suites, such as those with AES-GCM for encryption and SHA-256 or stronger for hashing. They should disable weak algorithms commonly exploited in security attacks, like those using RC4 or MD5.

Real-world Challenges and Best Practices

Deployment of TLS in real-world environments brings challenges, including:

- *Certificate Management*: Managing the lifecycle of certificates, including renewal and revocation, can be complex.
- *Server Scalability*: High-volume deployments may need efficient load balancing with consistent SSL session management.
- *Performance Impacts*: TLS handshake introduces latency due to computational overhead, which can be reduced using session resumption techniques.

To mitigate such challenges, implementing automated tools for monitoring certificates and employing hardware security modules (HSMs) for key management are advisable. Regularly reviewing and updating TLS configurations ensures alignment with current security standards.

Ultimately, TLS within gRPC guarantees robust, real-time security measures essential for modern distributed systems. Its dynamic nature allows organizations to meet their evolving security needs while preserving communication integrity and confidentiality across their application infrastructure.

The rigorous application of these security principles makes TLS not just the backbone of gRPC's security model, but a critical component in securing microservices and enabling trustworthy service communications in dynamic, large-scale environments.

7.3 Authentication Mechanisms

Authentication mechanisms in gRPC establish trusted communication channels by verifying the identity of clients and servers. This validation process is essential for access control, ensuring that only legitimate entities can interact with services. gRPC offers multiple authentication techniques, providing flexibility to meet various security requirements across diverse systems.

The primary forms of authentication in gRPC include basic authentication, token-based authentication using OAuth2 or JWT, and mutual TLS (mTLS). The choice of mechanism hinges on factors such as system architecture, scalability requirements, cryptographic security needs, and ease of integration into existing security frameworks.

Basic Authentication

Basic authentication involves transmitting client credentials, typically a username and password, with each request. It is one of the simplest forms of authentication but comes with security trade-offs. To improve security, basic authentication must be used over a secure TLS channel to protect credentials from being intercepted.

The use of interceptors in gRPC can facilitate the implementation of basic authentication by intercepting RPC calls and validating the credentials before processing the request:

7.3. AUTHENTICATION MECHANISMS

```go
package main

import (
    "context"
    "google.golang.org/grpc"
    "google.golang.org/grpc/metadata"
    "log"
    "net/http"
)

func authInterceptor(ctx context.Context) (context.Context, error) {
    md, ok := metadata.FromIncomingContext(ctx)
    if !ok {
        return nil, grpc.Errorf(http.StatusUnauthorized, "No metadata found")
    }

    var (
        username string
        password string
    )

    if auth, ok := md["authorization"]; ok && len(auth) > 0 {
        userPass := parseBasicAuth(auth[0])
        username = userPass[0]
        password = userPass[1]

        if !validUser(username, password) {
            return nil, grpc.Errorf(http.StatusUnauthorized, "Invalid username or
                password")
        }
    }
    return ctx, nil
}

func validUser(username, password string) bool {
    return username == "validUser" && password == "ValidPassword"
}

func parseBasicAuth(authHeader string) []string {
    // Parsing logic for Basic Auth
    return []string{"validUser", "ValidPassword"} // simplified
}

func main() {
    server := grpc.NewServer(grpc.UnaryInterceptor(authInterceptor))
    log.Println("Starting server with basic authentication")
    // register services and other details...
}
```

The above Go example demonstrates a basic authentication mechanism by employing a unary interceptor that checks authorization metadata in incoming requests. It verifies credentials against a defined username and password pair.

Token-Based Authentication

Token-based authentication provides a more secure, scalable method of verifying identities using tokens. Two prevalent token formats used in gRPC are OAuth 2.0 tokens and JSON Web Tokens (JWT). These tokens are self-contained, meaning they encapsulate all the necessary information to verify the identity and permissions of the requesting entity.

OAuth 2.0 operates on an authorization grant-type basis, typically involving a client application obtaining an access token from the authorization server. This token is then presented to the gRPC server for access to resources. OAuth 2.0 tokens are time-limited, adding a layer of security by ensuring tokens expire and are not perpetually valid.

To implement OAuth 2.0, gRPC services rely on interceptors to validate tokens passed with service requests:

```python
import grpc
from oauth2client.contrib import gce

def oauth2_interceptor(call, context):
    metadata = dict(context.invocation_metadata())
    token = metadata.get('authorization', None)

    if token is None:
        context.abort(grpc.StatusCode.UNAUTHENTICATED, "Missing token")

    # Validate token here using an OAuth2 library or service
    valid_token = validate_oauth2_token(token)

    if not valid_token:
        context.abort(grpc.StatusCode.UNAUTHENTICATED, "Invalid token")

    return call.request

def validate_oauth2_token(token):
    # Example OAuth2 token validation logic
    # Use an OAuth2 library or token introspection service
    return token == "valid-token"

class AuthUnaryInterceptor(grpc.ServerInterceptor):
    def intercept_service(self, continuation, handler_call_details):
        return oauth2_interceptor

# Server setup
server = grpc.server(futures.ThreadPoolExecutor())
server.add_insecure_port('[::]:50051')
server.start()
```

The code snippet above showcases how to extract and validate OAuth2 access tokens in a Python gRPC server through interceptor logic. This example skeleton is simplistic; actual implementations would require

7.3. AUTHENTICATION MECHANISMS

more extensive token validation against an authorization server.

JSON Web Tokens (JWT) provide another alternative, offering a compact, URL-safe means of representing claims. JWTs consist of three parts: a header, payload, and signature. The payload encompasses user data, while the signature ensures integrity and authenticity.

JWT implementation in gRPC may be configured as follows:

```
import io.grpc.*;

public class JwtAuthInterceptor implements ServerInterceptor {

    @Override
    public <ReqT, RespT> ServerCall.Listener<ReqT> interceptCall(
            ServerCall<ReqT, RespT> call, Metadata headers, ServerCallHandler<
                ReqT, RespT> next) {

        String jwt = headers.get("authorization");

        if (jwt == null || !isValidJwt(jwt)) {
            call.close(Status.UNAUTHENTICATED.withDescription("Invalid JWT"),
                headers);
            return new ServerCall.Listener<ReqT>() {};
        }

        return next.startCall(call, headers);
    }

    private boolean isValidJwt(String jwt) {
        // JWT validation logic
        return jwt.equals("eyExampleValidJWTToken"); // Placeholder
    }

    public static void main(String[] args) {
        Server server = ServerBuilder.forPort(50051)
                .addService(ServerInterceptors.intercept(new MyService(), new
                    JwtAuthInterceptor()))
                .build().start();

        Runtime.getRuntime().addShutdownHook(new Thread(server::shutdown));
    }
}
```

This example Java code introduces a basic JWT validation mechanism. In production systems, JWT validation would typically involve decoding, verifying its signature, checking claims like aud, iss, sub, and assessing expiration.

Mutual TLS (mTLS)

Mutual TLS (mTLS) extends standard TLS by requiring both client and server to present certificates, creating a dual-authentication scenario.

mTLS is especially beneficial in environments involving machine-to-machine communication, such as microservices architectures, where establishing confidence in service identities is critical.

Implementing mTLS in gRPC involves configuring both server and client to request and present valid certificates:

```go
package main

import (
    "crypto/tls"
    "crypto/x509"
    "fmt"
    "google.golang.org/grpc"
    "google.golang.org/grpc/credentials"
    "io/ioutil"
)

func main() {
    // Load client certificate
    cert, err := tls.LoadX509KeyPair("client-cert.pem", "client-key.pem")
    if err != nil {
        log.Fatalf("failed to load client key pair: %v", err)
    }

    // Load CA certificate
    caCert, err := ioutil.ReadFile("ca-cert.pem")
    if err != nil {
        log.Fatalf("failed to read CA cert: %v", err)
    }

    caCertPool := x509.NewCertPool()
    if !caCertPool.AppendCertsFromPEM(caCert) {
        log.Fatalf("failed to add CA cert to pool")
    }

    tlsConfig := &tls.Config{
        Certificates: []tls.Certificate{cert},
        RootCAs:      caCertPool,
    }

    creds := credentials.NewTLS(tlsConfig)

    conn, err := grpc.Dial("localhost:50051", grpc.WithTransportCredentials(creds))
    if err != nil {
        log.Fatalf("failed to connect: %v", err)
    }
    defer conn.Close()

    fmt.Println("Connected to server using mTLS")
}
```

This Go client demonstrates configuring mutual TLS. The client loads its certificate and root CA's certificate as part of establishing a secure and authenticated connection with a gRPC server.

Choosing the Right Authentication Mechanism

Selecting the appropriate authentication mechanism involves understanding the security requirements and operational constraints of the system. For internal service-to-service communications, mutual TLS may be ideal due to its robust security features. In contrast, client-facing applications might benefit from token-based solutions, which easily integrate with existing OAuth2 or OpenID Connect infrastructure.

Organizations must also consider factors like:

- *Scalability*: Token-based systems like OAuth2 can better handle large numbers of clients with minimal overhead.

- *Interoperability*: Standards-based methods (e.g., OAuth2, JWT) are more likely to integrate with heterogeneous systems.

- *Complexity*: Simpler mechanisms (e.g., basic auth) might suffice for small, internal applications with extra security assurances through TLS.

Ultimately, a sound approach may involve layering different methods and implementing them contextually based on access levels, data sensitivity, and network security.

The nuanced implementation of authentication mechanisms ensures that gRPC can be both a versatile and secure framework, catering not only to traditional requirements but also accommodating emerging needs in rapidly evolving technical landscapes.

7.4 Using OAuth2 and JWT

Integrating OAuth2 and JSON Web Tokens (JWT) with gRPC services is a powerful approach for ensuring secure authentication and authorization. This section explores how OAuth2 and JWT can be utilized in gRPC to establish secure, scalable, and standards-compliant authentication mechanisms. We will examine how these technologies work in concert to validate client identities and manage access to gRPC endpoints.

OAuth2 is a widely adopted, open standard for access delegation, commonly used to grant authorization to third-party services without exposing user credentials. It separates the authorization process by introducing token-based access, which can be efficiently integrated with gRPC.

JWTs, on the other hand, are compact, self-contained tokens often used for encoding claims to be transferred between two parties. JWTs can be used within OAuth2 frameworks, conveying authorized user information and permissions in a secure manner. They offer benefits such as statelessness and the ability to include rich, signed claims, making them highly suitable for modern distributed applications.

Overview of OAuth2 in gRPC

OAuth2 operates on four key roles: the resource owner, the client, the resource server, and the authorization server. The protocol involves multiple flows, or grant types, each serving different use cases, including authorization code, implicit, client credentials, and resource owner password credentials.

For securing gRPC APIs, the Authorization Code Flow is commonly used due to its enhanced security. This flow involves three steps: the client directs the resource owner (user) to an authorization server, the user grants access, and the server issues an access token.

An OAuth2 token provides controlled access to the resource server (gRPC service), representing the permissions granted by the resource owner. The use of these tokens requires server-side token validation to authorize requests.

```
import grpc
from concurrent import futures
from yourapp_pb2 import YourResponse
from yourapp_pb2_grpc import YourAppServicer, add_YourAppServicer_to_server

class AuthInterceptor(grpc.ServerInterceptor):
    def intercept_service(self, continuation, handler_call_details):
        metadata = dict(handler_call_details.invocation_metadata)
        token = metadata.get('authorization')

        if not token or not validate_oauth2_token(token):
            context.abort(grpc.StatusCode.UNAUTHENTICATED, "Invalid or missing token")
```

7.4. USING OAUTH2 AND JWT

```
        return continuation(handler_call_details)
def validate_oauth2_token(access_token):
    # Validate the OAuth2 token with the OAuth2 provider function here
    # i.e., token introspection endpoint or relying on locally cached info
    return access_token == "this-is-a-valid-access-token"

class MyService(YourAppServicer):
    def YourRPCMethod(self, request, context):
        return YourResponse(message="Access Granted")

def serve():
    server = grpc.server(futures.ThreadPoolExecutor(), interceptors=(AuthInterceptor
        (),))
    add_YourAppServicer_to_server(MyService(), server)
    server.add_insecure_port('[::]:50051')
    server.start()
    server.wait_for_termination()

if __name__ == '__main__':
    serve()
```

This code illustrates how a Python gRPC server can validate OAuth2 tokens by implementing a server interceptor that checks for a token's presence and validity. The validation function confirms token authenticity, either through direct inspection or by checking with an OAuth2 provider's endpoint, enhancing security.

JWT Structure and Practical Implementation

JWTs are structured in three main parts: a header, a payload, and a signature, each encoded in Base64URL. The header specifies the signing algorithm, the payload comprises claims about an entity and additional data, and the signature validates the token's integrity and authenticity.

Claims can be registered, public, or private. Common registered claims include 'iss' (issuer), 'exp' (expiration), 'sub' (subject), and 'aud' (audience).

JWTs can guarantee statelessness in distributed systems since the payload contains all necessary data to authorize requests. This enables easy scaling without sharing state information among instances.

The following Java snippet demonstrates validating JSON Web Tokens in a gRPC service:

```
import io.jsonwebtoken.Claims;
import io.jsonwebtoken.Jwts;
import io.jsonwebtoken.SignatureException;
```

```java
import io.grpc.*;

public class JwtServerInterceptor implements ServerInterceptor {

    private static final String SECRET_KEY = "your-256-bit-secret";

    @Override
    public <ReqT, RespT> ServerCall.Listener<ReqT> interceptCall(
            ServerCall<ReqT, RespT> call, Metadata headers, ServerCallHandler<
                ReqT, RespT> next) {

        String jwt = headers.get(Metadata.Key.of("authorization", Metadata.
            ASCII_STRING_MARSHALLER));

        if (jwt == null || !validateJwt(jwt)) {
            call.close(Status.UNAUTHENTICATED.withDescription("Invalid JWT"),
                headers);
            return new ServerCall.Listener<ReqT>() {};
        }

        return next.startCall(call, headers);
    }

    private boolean validateJwt(String jwt) {
        try {
            Claims claims = Jwts.parser()
                .setSigningKey(SECRET_KEY.getBytes())
                .parseClaimsJws(jwt)
                .getBody();

            // Ensure custom claim validation if necessary
            return true;
        } catch (SignatureException e) {
            return false;
        }
    }

    public static void main(String[] args) {
        Server server = ServerBuilder.forPort(50051)
                .intercept(new JwtServerInterceptor())
                .addService(new YourService())
                .build()
                .start();

        Runtime.getRuntime().addShutdownHook(new Thread(server::shutdown));
    }
}
```

The Java example demonstrates JWT validation within a gRPC server interceptor. A JWT parser decodes tokens, extracting and verifying claims against a secret key to ensure data integrity and authorization.

Adopting OAuth2 and JWT in gRPC Architectures

Implementing OAuth2 and JWT necessitates thoughtful integration within gRPC architectures to streamline both development and operations:

- *Security by Design*: Implement defenses against token forgery and misuse by adopting modern cryptographic techniques and securing secret keys.
- *Efficient Token Handling*: Cache tokens or introspection responses to reduce latency in real-time validations.
- *Scalable Infrastructures*: Decompose roles like authorization server and resource servers for improved load balancing, easily handling increased authentication requests.
- *Token Rotation Policies*: Implement mechanisms for token rotation and expiration checks to refresh long-lived tokens without compromising security.
- *Audit and Logging*: Log authorization events and data consistently to quickly identify potential breaches or anomalies.

The convergence of OAuth2 and JWT in gRPC achieves a high level of interoperability and separation of concerns, qualities that are pivotal in loosely-coupled microservice ecosystems. In such contexts, where services interact with numerous clients and each other, using OAuth2 with JWTs elevates security while simplifying the complexity of managing identities and permissions across diverse tech stacks.

Despite the seamless benefits offered, balancing security rigor with user experience and system resources is crucial. Especially in high-transaction environments or where sensitive data is exchanged, sufficiently thorough planning and diligence during the secure API design phase can offset risks, ensuring that only authorized entities efficiently access gRPC services.

The insights gained here can act as a blueprint for robust systems, adopting OAuth2 and JWTs to fortify server communication in evolving network frameworks. Through these tokens' efficient delegation and well-considered application, developers can enhance both security and performance in equal measure, achieving modern authentication goals.

7.5 Role-Based Access Control

Role-Based Access Control (RBAC) is a model for restricting system access to authorized users based on their roles within an organization. By assigning permissions to roles rather than individual users, RBAC facilitates efficient and scalable management of permissions and resources within distributed systems like gRPC services. This section explores implementing RBAC within gRPC, detailing its importance, functional concepts, implementation strategies, and best practices in secure service design.

RBAC is characterized by its abstraction of permissions, assigning them to roles rather than individuals. A user's actions within a system are determined by their assigned role(s), streamlining authorization management. This facilitates easier policy updates and ensures consistency across large user bases.

Core Concepts of RBAC

RBAC is built upon several core concepts crucial to its effective implementation:

- *Roles*: Defined based on job functions or duties within an organization, roles are the central element in RBAC. Examples include roles like "admin," "editor," or "viewer."

- *Permissions*: These are rights granted to roles to perform specific actions on resources, such as read, write, or delete operations.

- *Users*: Individuals who are assigned to one or more roles, receiving permissions by virtue of their membership in those roles.

- *Sessions*: These represent a user's active application context, allowing a user to assume roles during their use of a system.

Implementing RBAC in gRPC

In gRPC, RBAC can be implemented by incorporating interceptors to enforce access controls based on user roles. The interceptor, a layer that sits between the client and the server, checks a user's roles prior to processing an RPC call, allowing or denying access based on predefined policies.

7.5. ROLE-BASED ACCESS CONTROL

Below is an example of a simple RBAC implementation setup in a gRPC server using Go, where user roles are evaluated during request handling:

```go
package main

import (
    "context"
    "google.golang.org/grpc"
    "google.golang.org/grpc/metadata"
    "log"
    "net"
    "errors"
)

type role string

const (
    Admin role = "admin"
    Editor role = "editor"
    Viewer role = "viewer"
)

var rolePermissions = map[role][]string{
    Admin: {"create", "read", "update", "delete"},
    Editor: {"create", "read", "update"},
    Viewer: {"read"},
}

func hasPermission(userRole role, action string) bool {
    for _, perm := range rolePermissions[userRole] {
        if perm == action {
            return true
        }
    }
    return false
}

func roleAuthorizationInterceptor(ctx context.Context) (context.Context, error) {
    md, ok := metadata.FromIncomingContext(ctx)
    if !ok {
        return nil, grpc.Errorf(grpc.Code(errors.New("no metadata")), "No metadata found")
    }

    userRole, ok := md["role"]
    if !ok || len(userRole) == 0 {
        return nil, errors.New("missing role information")
    }

    action, ok := md["action"]
    if !ok || len(action) == 0 {
        return nil, errors.New("missing action information")
    }

    if hasPermission(role(userRole[0]), action[0]) {
```

215

```
        return ctx, nil
    }
    return nil, errors.New("unauthorized action")
}
func main() {
    lis, err := net.Listen("tcp", ":50051")
    if err != nil {
        log.Fatalf("failed to listen: %v", err)
    }

    s := grpc.NewServer(grpc.ChainUnaryInterceptor(
        func(ctx context.Context) (context.Context, error) {
            return roleAuthorizationInterceptor(ctx)
        },
    ))

    log.Println("Starting gRPC server with RBAC")
    if err := s.Serve(lis); err != nil {
        log.Fatalf("failed to serve: %v", err)
    }
}
```

The above code sets up a basic RBAC system in a gRPC server where actions like "create" and "read" are tied to specific user roles using metadata to carry role and action information. It demonstrates a simple permission model where users are granted access based on their roles.

Advantages of RBAC in Distributed Systems

Implementing RBAC in gRPC offers numerous advantages within distributed systems:

- *Scalability*: As organizations grow, managing permissions via roles rather than individuals greatly simplifies administrative tasks, enabling seamless scalability.

- *Security*: By consistently applying roles to users, organizations reduce security risks and enforce uniform access policies across services.

- *Role Consistency*: Roles create a clear structure for operations, establishing a uniform approach across departments and functions, enhancing compliance with regulations and standards.

- *Ease of Management*: Changes in user roles are easily managed without directly altering underlying permission sets, reducing administrative effort.

Challenges in Implementing RBAC

Despite its benefits, implementing RBAC in practical scenarios involves overcoming multiple challenges:

- *Role Explosion*: As systems become more complex, defining overly granular roles can lead to an overwhelming number of distinct role definitions.

- *Dynamic Access Needs*: Adapting roles to dynamic and sometimes unpredictable access requirements can be difficult.

- *Role Mismanagement*: Incorrect role assignments can inadvertently grant users excessive or inadequate permissions, leading to potential security issues.

To address these challenges, organizations should consider role hierarchy design. Role hierarchies inherit permissions from parent roles, reducing duplication and allowing manageable complexity.

Here is an example illustrating a basic role hierarchy in a gRPC environment:

```python
class RBAC:
    def __init__(self):
        self.roles = {
            'admin': set(['create', 'read', 'update', 'delete']),
            'editor': set(['create', 'read', 'update']),
            'viewer': set(['read']),
        }

        self.hierarchy = {
            'admin': ['editor', 'viewer'],
            'editor': ['viewer'],
            'viewer': []
        }

    def has_permission(self, role, action):
        permissions = self.roles.get(role)
        if permissions and action in permissions:
            return True

        for parent_role in self.hierarchy.get(role, []):
            if self.has_permission(parent_role, action):
                return True
        return False

rbac = RBAC()
```

```
def authorization_interceptor():
    def auth_interceptor(call, context):
        metadata = dict(context.invocation_metadata())
        role = metadata.get("role")
        action = metadata.get("action")

        if role is None or action is None:
            context.abort(grpc.StatusCode.UNAUTHENTICATED, "Missing role or
                action")

        if not rbac.has_permission(role, action):
            context.abort(grpc.StatusCode.PERMISSION_DENIED, "Unauthorized")
        return call
    return auth_interceptor

# Server setup and usage
```

The Python code demonstrates concepts of role hierarchies, allowing higher roles to inherit permissions from lower ones. This practice reduces complexities by enabling membership inheritance.

Best Practices in RBAC Implementation for gRPC

- *Define Clear Roles*: Ensure roles accurately reflect job functions without overlap, avoiding redundancy.

- *Implement Role Auditing*: Regularly audit roles and permissions to verify and validate adherence to policies and compliance.

- *Leverage Automation*: Utilize tools and scripts to automate role assignments, reduce chances of human errors, and increase efficiency.

- *Employ Role Minimization*: Use the principle of least privilege to ensure users have only necessary access, minimizing exposure to sensitive operations.

- *Documentation and Policy Review*: Maintain comprehensive documentation on role descriptions and update policies regularly to reflect changes accurately.

In summary, RBAC streamlines regime permissions across gRPC services, providing a scalable and effective solution in dynamic environments characterized by multiple users and roles. By embracing role hierarchies, maintaining clarity, and implementing best practices, organizations can effectively harness the power of RBAC, ensuring secure, uniform, and efficient access control across their distributed systems. This enhances not only security but operational coherence, fostering environments where services interact seamlessly while respecting access boundaries.

7.6 Securing Data with Encryption

Securing data with encryption is a fundamental aspect of protecting information confidentiality and integrity within gRPC communications. While Transport Layer Security (TLS) provides encryption for data in transit, certain scenarios necessitate encrypting data at rest or within the payloads of gRPC messages to ensure an additional layer of security. This section delves into the principles of encryption, techniques for securing data within gRPC, and the integration of encryption strategies for comprehensive data protection.

Understanding Encryption Principles

Encryption is the process of converting data into a form that is unreadable to unauthorized users, ensuring that only parties with the appropriate cryptographic keys can access the original information. There are two primary types of encryption: symmetric and asymmetric.

- *Symmetric Encryption*: A single key is used for both encryption and decryption. This key must be securely shared and kept confidential. Symmetric algorithms, such as AES (Advanced Encryption Standard), provide fast and efficient encryption, ideal for encrypting large amounts of data.

- *Asymmetric Encryption*: Comprises a pair of keys—public and private. The public key encrypts data, while the private key decrypts it. Asymmetric encryption, typically used for secure key exchange and digital signatures, includes algorithms like RSA (Rivest-Shamir-Adleman).

Data Encryption in gRPC

Within gRPC, encryption at the application layer involves encrypting the contents of messages before transmission. This approach is often utilized when additional confidentiality is required beyond transport security, such as in regulatory environments or when handling sensitive customer data.

To encrypt gRPC payloads, symmetric encryption is typically employed due to its speed and effectiveness. The following Go example illustrates encrypting and decrypting message data using AES encryption:

```go
package main

import (
    "crypto/aes"
    "crypto/cipher"
    "crypto/rand"
    "errors"
    "fmt"
    "io"
)

const key = "examplekey123456" // AES-128 key size must be 16 bytes long

func encrypt(data []byte) ([]byte, error) {
    block, err := aes.NewCipher([]byte(key))
    if err != nil {
        return nil, err
    }

    ciphertext := make([]byte, aes.BlockSize+len(data))
    iv := ciphertext[:aes.BlockSize]

    if _, err := io.ReadFull(rand.Reader, iv); err != nil {
        return nil, err
    }

    stream := cipher.NewCFBEncrypter(block, iv)
    stream.XORKeyStream(ciphertext[aes.BlockSize:], data)

    return ciphertext, nil
}

func decrypt(ciphertext []byte) ([]byte, error) {
    block, err := aes.NewCipher([]byte(key))
    if err != nil {
        return nil, err
    }

    if len(ciphertext) < aes.BlockSize {
        return nil, errors.New("ciphertext too short")
    }

    iv := ciphertext[:aes.BlockSize]
    ciphertext = ciphertext[aes.BlockSize:]

    stream := cipher.NewCFBDecrypter(block, iv)
    stream.XORKeyStream(ciphertext, ciphertext)
```

7.6. SECURING DATA WITH ENCRYPTION

```go
        return ciphertext, nil
}
func main() {
    message := "This is a secret message"
    fmt.Printf("Original message: %s\n", message)

    encrypted, err := encrypt([]byte(message))
    if err != nil {
        fmt.Printf("Error encrypting message: %v\n", err)
        return
    }

    fmt.Printf("Encrypted message: %x\n", encrypted)

    decrypted, err := decrypt(encrypted)
    if err != nil {
        fmt.Printf("Error decrypting message: %v\n", err)
        return
    }

    fmt.Printf("Decrypted message: %s\n", decrypted)
}
```

This Go program demonstrates AES encryption and decryption, where data is encrypted before being sent over the network, and decrypted upon receipt. The encryption key needs to be securely shared among trusted parties to prevent unauthorized access.

Integrating Encryption in gRPC Services

To effectively integrate encryption within gRPC services, developers need to handle key management, choose appropriate encryption strategies, and ensure that performance remains acceptable. Encryption could be applied at different levels:

- *Transport-Level Encryption*: Employs TLS to encrypt all data in transit, preventing interception during transmission. It is a standard requirement for securing gRPC services.

- *Payload Encryption*: Data within gRPC messages is encrypted before being serialized and transmitted, adding a layer of security within the application layer.

- *Field-Level Encryption*: Specific fields within gRPC messages are encrypted, protecting particularly sensitive information like Personally Identifiable Information (PII) or financial details.

Incorporating payload encryption within a gRPC service involves interceptors that handle encryption and decryption at the application level. A Python example illustrating payload encryption using gRPC interceptors is as follows:

```python
import grpc
from cryptography.fernet import Fernet
from concurrent import futures

class EncryptionInterceptor(grpc.ServerInterceptor):
    def __init__(self, key):
        self.cipher = Fernet(key)

    def encrypt(self, data):
        return self.cipher.encrypt(data)

    def decrypt(self, encrypted_data):
        return self.cipher.decrypt(encrypted_data)

    def intercept_service(self, continuation, handler_call_details):
        request = next(handler_call_details.invocation_metadata())
        encrypted_message = request.payload
        decrypted_message = self.decrypt(encrypted_message)

        response = continuation(handler_call_details)
        response.payload = self.encrypt(response.message)

        return response

def generate_key():
    return Fernet.generate_key()

def serve():
    key = generate_key()
    interceptor = EncryptionInterceptor(key)
    server = grpc.server(futures.ThreadPoolExecutor(), interceptors=(interceptor,))

    # Add service registration and server details
    server.add_insecure_port('[::]:50051')
    server.start()
    server.wait_for_termination()

if __name__ == '__main__':
    serve()
```

In the Python example above, the 'Fernet' symmetric encryption provided by the cryptography library is used to encrypt and decrypt gRPC messages. This example focuses on ensuring that messages remain encrypted during RPC calls, enhancing security for sensitive data transmission.

Challenges and Considerations in gRPC Encryption

7.6. SECURING DATA WITH ENCRYPTION

Applying encryption within gRPC requires a comprehensive understanding of cryptographic practices, including:

- *Key Management*: Managing encryption keys, including their generation, distribution, rotation, and storage, is pivotal for secure encryption. Keys should be kept confidential and accessible only to authorized entities.

- *Performance Impact*: Encryption adds computational overhead, which could impact service performance. Balancing security needs with efficiency is crucial when selecting encryption algorithms and approaches.

- *Compliance and Standards*: Considerations for regulatory compliance (e.g., GDPR, HIPAA) impact encryption strategies, requiring adherence to industry standards such as NIST-recommended techniques.

- *Scalability*: Ensuring that the encryption approach can scale alongside service demands, without compromising performance or security.

- *Interoperability*: Encryption techniques must integrate seamlessly with clients and services across various environments and languages, necessitating standardized protocols.

Best Practices for Ensuring Secure gRPC Communications

- *Enforce Multi-Layer Encryption*: Combine transport layer security with application-layer encryption for defense-in-depth, addressing potential risks across multiple vectors.

- *Regularly Rotate Keys*: Implement regular encryption key rotation to minimize the risk of key compromise and limit exposure in the event of key leaks.

- *Use Hardware Security Modules (HSMs)*: Leverage HSMs to manage and protect cryptographic keys against unauthorized access or leakage.

- *Encrypt Sensitive Data*: Prioritize encrypting sensitive information, ensuring compliance with regulations and safeguarding privacy.

- *Monitor and Audit*: Continuously monitor encrypted service interactions, audit logs for suspicious activities, and implement alert mechanisms to detect anomalous behavior swiftly.

Through rigorous application of these principles, gRPC empowers developers to secure data communications consistently, protecting organizations against data breaches and unauthorized access. Properly implemented encryption bolsters data privacy, confidentiality, and integrity, laying down a resilient foundation for modern distributed systems operating in ever-evolving threat landscapes. By melding established cryptographic practices with innovative, scalable gRPC architectures, organizations can secure their services to safeguard not only data but also their reputations and trust.

Chapter 8

Advanced gRPC Features and Techniques

This chapter explores advanced features and techniques in gRPC to enhance functionality and performance. It covers the use of custom metadata for passing additional information and demonstrates design patterns for implementing interceptors to address cross-cutting concerns. Readers will learn about sophisticated load balancing strategies and how to capitalize on HTTP/2 features like flow control and header compression. The chapter also discusses advanced asynchronous programming models and techniques for incorporating reflection and dynamic service discovery, providing a deeper understanding of how to leverage gRPC's full capabilities in complex applications.

CHAPTER 8. ADVANCED GRPC FEATURES AND TECHNIQUES

8.1 Custom Metadata in gRPC

gRPC, a high-performance RPC framework used widely for microservices communication, allows transmitting not only basic request and response data but also additional information through custom metadata. This capability is crucial for enhancing functionality, optimizing communication, and handling ancillary processes such as passing authentication tokens, session identifiers, or logging information between clients and servers. By thoroughly understanding the mechanisms and applications of custom metadata in gRPC, developers can exploit its potential to fine-tune the interactions within distributed systems.

Metadata in gRPC operates in parallel to the primary message payloads. It comprises key-value pairs that are appended to requests or responses. In gRPC, metadata can be used to carry additional, out-of-band data which might not directly correspond to the formal API request-response semantics but are necessary for correct, efficient processing. It is essential to understand how to implement this feature robustly and in accordance with best practices to ensure compatibility and maintainability across various components and systems.

Consider the scenario where a client needs to authenticate with a server. The client attaches an authentication token to each request as custom metadata. This process involves defining the appropriate metadata keys and ensuring security through practices such as using standardized keys and transmitting sensitive information securely. Below is an example illustrating the use of metadata in a gRPC client in Go:

```
package main

import (
  "context"
  "log"
  "os"

  "google.golang.org/grpc"
  "google.golang.org/grpc/metadata"
  pb "path/to/your/protobuf"
)

func main() {
  conn, err := grpc.Dial("localhost:50051", grpc.WithInsecure())
  if err != nil {
    log.Fatalf("did not connect: %v", err)
```

8.1. CUSTOM METADATA IN GRPC

```
}
defer conn.Close()

client := pb.NewYourServiceClient(conn)

md := metadata.New(map[string]string{
  "authorization": "Bearer " + os.Getenv("AUTH_TOKEN"),
  "client-id": "my-client-id-123",
})

ctx := metadata.NewOutgoingContext(context.Background(), md)

response, err := client.YourMethod(ctx, &pb.YourRequest{})
if err != nil {
  log.Fatalf("could not execute request: %v", err)
}

log.Printf("Response: %s", response.GetMessage())
}
```

In this example, metadata containing an authorization bearer token and a client ID is added to the context of a gRPC request. It is then sent alongside the gRPC message to the server. The metadata keys are standardized and align with common authentication frameworks like OAuth2, facilitating seamless integration with secure protocols.

The server-side handling of metadata is equally crucial. Metadata must be extracted, validated, and potentially sanitized before its information is used in processing the request. The following example shows how to access metadata in a gRPC server implemented in Go:

```
package main

import (
  "context"
  "log"
  "net"

  "google.golang.org/grpc"
  "google.golang.org/grpc/metadata"
  pb "path/to/your/protobuf"
)

type server struct {
  pb.UnimplementedYourServiceServer
}

func (s *server) YourMethod(ctx context.Context, req *pb.YourRequest) (*pb.
      YourResponse, error) {
  md, ok := metadata.FromIncomingContext(ctx)
  if !ok {
    return nil, grpc.Errorf(codes.InvalidArgument, "missing metadata")
  }
```

CHAPTER 8. ADVANCED GRPC FEATURES AND TECHNIQUES

```go
    authToken := md["authorization"]
    clientID := md["client-id"]

    // Validate the authorization token and client ID here

    log.Printf("Authorization: %s, Client ID: %s", authToken, clientID)

    // Proceed with normal handling of the request

    return &pb.YourResponse{Message: "Success"}, nil
}
func main() {
    lis, err := net.Listen("tcp", ":50051")
    if err != nil {
        log.Fatalf("failed to listen: %v", err)
    }

    s := grpc.NewServer()
    pb.RegisterYourServiceServer(s, &server{})

    if err := s.Serve(lis); err != nil {
        log.Fatalf("failed to serve: %v", err)
    }
}
```

When handling incoming messages, the server extracts metadata and performs necessary operations such as authentication checks. It is essential to verify the integrity and authenticity of any tokens or identifiers to prevent security vulnerabilities.

Implementing custom metadata requires meticulous consideration of potential security concerns, particularly related to data confidentiality and integrity. The use of encrypted transmission channels such as TLS/SSL is mandatory when transferring sensitive metadata like authentication tokens. Furthermore, the scope and format of metadata keys should be carefully defined. Using free-form keys can lead to namespace collisions or unintended interactions. Employing a prefix or hierarchical key structure, similar to namespace conventions in programming languages, helps in maintaining order and avoiding conflicts.

The versatility of custom metadata allows many additional applications beyond authentication. It can be utilized for implementing monitoring and diagnostics through tracing identifiers or transaction IDs that follow requests through various services. This visibility greatly aids in troubleshooting and optimizing distributed systems by providing insight into request paths and performance bottlenecks.

8.1. CUSTOM METADATA IN GRPC

The following Python example demonstrates adding and retrieving trace information using custom metadata, catering to enhanced observability in a gRPC service system:

```python
import grpc
from concurrent import futures
import your_service_pb2_grpc

class YourService(your_service_pb2_grpc.YourServiceServicer):

    def YourMethod(self, request, context):
        metadata = dict(context.invocation_metadata())
        trace_id = metadata.get('trace-id')

        # Log or process the trace_id for monitoring purposes
        print(f"Received request with trace id: {trace_id}")

        # Additional handling...

        return your_service_pb2.YourResponse(message='Success!')

def serve():
    server = grpc.server(futures.ThreadPoolExecutor(max_workers=10))
    your_service_pb2_grpc.add_YourServiceServicer_to_server(YourService(), server)
    server.add_insecure_port('[::]:50051')
    server.start()
    server.wait_for_termination()

if __name__ == '__main__':
    serve()
```

In this code snippet, a gRPC service in Python extracts a 'trace-id' from the incoming metadata, enabling the tracking of the request through different systems for logging or performance monitoring purposes. This application highlights the flexibility of custom metadata to support service observability without modifying business logic.

In complex systems, it is prudent to abstract metadata handling into layers or middleware components. This design separation assists in clean, manageable codebases where concerns like logging, authentication, and diagnostics are decoupled from core business logic. For instance, using interceptors in gRPC, developers can centralize metadata management tasks without polluting service implementations:

```go
func loggingInterceptor(
    ctx context.Context,
    req interface{},
    info *grpc.UnaryServerInfo,
    handler grpc.UnaryHandler,
) (resp interface{}, err error) {
    md, _ := metadata.FromIncomingContext(ctx)
    traceID := md["trace-id"]
```

```go
        log.Printf("Invocation of %s with trace-id: %s", info.FullMethod, traceID)

        // Call the handler to go on processing the request
        return handler(ctx, req)
    }
}
func main() {
    serverOptions := []grpc.ServerOption{
        grpc.UnaryInterceptor(loggingInterceptor),
    }

    grpcServer := grpc.NewServer(serverOptions...)
    // Register service handlers etc.

    if err := grpcServer.Serve(lis); err != nil {
        log.Fatalf("failed to serve: %v", err)
    }
}
```

This example demonstrates an interceptor in Go that logs metadata before proceeding with the request processing. Such abstraction allows additional processing (e.g., logging or authentication checks) to be managed consistently across all service methods, promoting the DRY (Don't Repeat Yourself) principle and enhancing maintainability.

These practices and examples illustrate the profound implications and versatility of custom metadata in gRPC, positioning developers to optimize inter-service communications and manage cross-cutting concerns effectively. Understanding and employing custom metadata adeptly can significantly enhance the robustness and capability of applications built on gRPC, particularly in complex distributed environments.

8.2 Interceptor Design Patterns

In the framework of gRPC, interceptors are a powerful feature that allows developers to insert custom logic, known as middleware, at different stages of the request-response lifecycle. They are instrumental in handling cross-cutting concerns such as logging, authentication, rate limiting, and monitoring without cluttering the business logic of service handlers. Interceptor design patterns provide structured approaches to implementing these functionalities, ensuring that they are reusable, maintainable, and easily manageable across different services.

8.2. INTERCEPTOR DESIGN PATTERNS

Interceptors function analogously to middleware in web frameworks. They can be categorized into two types: unary interceptors, which deal with single request-response RPCs, and streaming interceptors, which handle streaming RPCs. The distinct advantage of interceptors is their ability to modify the context of gRPC calls, allowing the addition of custom metadata or other forms of enrichment before and after a call is handled.

The interception mechanism in gRPC is encompassed by two principal components: UnaryServerInterceptor and StreamServerInterceptor. These components enable the implementation of middleware-like behavior that spans the different phases of a gRPC request-handling process.

A typical implementation of a unary interceptor involves defining a function that takes a context, request, server information, and a handler function as parameters. Within this function, pre-processing can be performed before invoking the actual handler, and post-processing can happen after the handler returns. To elucidate this concept, let us examine a basic unary interceptor for logging purposes:

```go
package main

import (
    "context"
    "fmt"
    "log"

    "google.golang.org/grpc"
)

// UnaryInterceptor logs each request and response along with method name.
func UnaryLoggingInterceptor(
    ctx context.Context,
    req interface{},
    info *grpc.UnaryServerInfo,
    handler grpc.UnaryHandler,
) (interface{}, error) {
    log.Printf("Unary call to method: %s", info.FullMethod)
    resp, err := handler(ctx, req)
    log.Printf("Response: %v", resp)
    return resp, err
}

func main() {
    serverOptions := []grpc.ServerOption{
        grpc.UnaryInterceptor(UnaryLoggingInterceptor),
    }

    grpcServer := grpc.NewServer(serverOptions...)
```

```
    // Register service handlers here

    fmt.Println("Server running with logging interceptor")
    if err := grpcServer.Serve(lis); err != nil {
        log.Fatalf("failed to serve: %v", err)
    }
}
```

In this example, the UnaryLoggingInterceptor intercepts each request and logs the method name before the call is processed. It also logs the response once the handler function returns. This design allows consistent and centralized logging, reducing code duplication across service handlers.

Interceptors become even more valuable in scenarios requiring complex logic or the orchestration of multiple cross-cutting concerns. For instance, consider an interceptor that handles authentication by validating tokens found in the metadata of incoming requests. This interceptor can be implemented to either allow the request to proceed or terminate it with an error if check fails:

```
package main

import (
    "context"
    "log"

    "google.golang.org/grpc"
    "google.golang.org/grpc/metadata"
    "google.golang.org/grpc/codes"
    "google.golang.org/grpc/status"
)

// UnaryAuthInterceptor validates the authentication token.
func UnaryAuthInterceptor(
    ctx context.Context,
    req interface{},
    info *grpc.UnaryServerInfo,
    handler grpc.UnaryHandler,
) (interface{}, error) {
    md, ok := metadata.FromIncomingContext(ctx)
    if !ok {
        return nil, status.Error(codes.Unauthenticated, "missing metadata")
    }

    authTokens := md["authorization"]
    if len(authTokens) == 0 {
        return nil, status.Error(codes.Unauthenticated, "authorization token is required")
    }

    if isValidToken(authTokens[0]) {
        // Proceed with the handler
```

8.2. INTERCEPTOR DESIGN PATTERNS

```go
    return handler(ctx, req)
  } else {
    return nil, status.Error(codes.Unauthenticated, "invalid authorization token")
  }
}

func isValidToken(token string) bool {
  // Token validation logic, e.g., JWT signature verification
  return token == "valid-token" // simplified for demonstration purposes
}

func main() {
  serverOptions := []grpc.ServerOption{
    grpc.UnaryInterceptor(UnaryAuthInterceptor),
  }

  grpcServer := grpc.NewServer(serverOptions...)
  // Register service handlers here

  log.Println("Server running with authentication interceptor")
  if err := grpcServer.Serve(lis); err != nil {
    log.Fatalf("failed to serve: %v", err)
  }
}
```

This example demonstrates an interceptor checking for the presence and validity of an authentication token in the incoming metadata. Depending on the token's validity, the interceptor either allows the request to proceed or stops it with an authentication error.

Stream interceptors are implemented similarly but must manage the nuances of gRPC's stream handling. A stream interceptor might control or monitor long-lived connections, ensuring stream integrity or adherence to specific protocols over more extended interactions. Stream pipes can be iterated over and modified, offering developers extensive control at each stage of the request processing pipeline.

To apply multiple interceptors, gRPC allows chaining them together. This is particularly useful for balancing various middleware functions like logging, authentication, and rate limiting. Consider the example below in Python where interceptors are chained to manage both logging and authentication:

```python
import grpc
from grpc import ServerInterceptor

class LoggingInterceptor(ServerInterceptor):
    def intercept_service(self, continuation, handler_call_details):
        print(f"Received call to: {handler_call_details.method}")
        return continuation(handler_call_details)
```

```python
class AuthInterceptor(ServerInterceptor):
    def intercept_service(self, continuation, handler_call_details):
        metadata = dict(handler_call_details.invocation_metadata)
        if 'authorization' not in metadata:
            raise grpc.RpcError(grpc.StatusCode.UNAUTHENTICATED, "Missing
                token")
        if metadata['authorization'] != 'valid-token':
            raise grpc.RpcError(grpc.StatusCode.UNAUTHENTICATED, "Invalid token
                ")

        return continuation(handler_call_details)

def serve():
    server = grpc.server(
        futures.ThreadPoolExecutor(max_workers=10),
        interceptors=[
            AuthInterceptor(),
            LoggingInterceptor(),
        ]
    )
    # Add service handlers to the server
    server.add_insecure_port('[::]:50051')
    server.start()
    server.wait_for_termination()

if __name__ == '__main__':
    serve()
```

Here, two interceptors are chained: a logging interceptor logs each call, and an authentication interceptor verifies authorization tokens. Their order is crucial, as it affects the sequence of operations performed. Chaining permits efficient and clean implementation of different policies applied to each request.

When designing interceptors, the developer should adhere to a set of best practices to ensure efficiency and reliability. Foremost among these is understanding the idempotent nature required for reliable middleware logic. The operations should be stateless between different calls, ensuring that repeat or retry attempts do not cause unintended side effects. This is especially pivotal in scenarios with potential retries due to network transient errors.

One must also consider the potential performance implications of interceptors. They introduce additional processing overhead, as they execute code before or after every request. Therefore, optimization and limiting the scope of processing within interceptors are critical. Monitoring and benchmarking may be necessary to avoid bottlenecks linked to interceptor execution.

Additionally, interceptors should be designed with the principle of separation of concerns in mind. Each interceptor should ideally encapsulate a single responsibility, such as logging, authentication, or monitoring. This modular approach aids in testing and facilitates potential updates or replacements of specific functionalities without widespread changes to interceptor logic.

By employing a strategic approach to designing and implementing interceptors in gRPC, developers can significantly enhance their application's modularity, security, and maintainability. This mechanism enables seamless integration of critical cross-cutting concerns while allowing clear separation from core business logic. The systematic application of these design patterns provides a robust foundation for managing interservice communication in modern distributed systems.

8.3 Load Balancing Strategies

Load balancing is a critical component for achieving scalability and availability in distributed systems. Within the realm of gRPC, load balancing ensures that client requests are efficiently distributed across multiple server instances. Effective load balancing minimizes response time, maximizes throughput, and improves system resilience by preventing any single server from becoming a bottleneck.

In gRPC, load balancing can be implemented at various layers: at the client-side, the server-side, or through external load balancing infrastructure. Each approach has its own set of strategies, implications, and performance characteristics. Understanding these strategies helps developers design systems that are capable of meeting the demands of modern applications, which typically require highly available and scalable architectures.

- **Client-Side Load Balancing**

    Client-side load balancing involves distributing requests among servers directly from the client without intermediary load balancers. In this paradigm, the client is aware of multiple server instances and chooses the appropriate server for each request.

Client-side load balancing is advantageous due to reduced latency and network overhead, as the decision-making process occurs directly within the client, bypassing additional network hops.

To implement client-side load balancing in gRPC, clients need to maintain an up-to-date list of available server addresses. This can be achieved using service discovery mechanisms in conjunction with a load balancing policy. Popular client-side load balancing policies include round-robin, least connections, and hash-based approaches:

- **Round-Robin:** This is a straightforward and widely-used method where each server receives an equal number of requests, distributed cyclically. Round-robin is easily implemented and effective in scenarios where all server nodes are assumed to have equal capacity and performance characteristics.

- **Least Connections:** This strategy involves dynamically monitoring the number of active connections each server is handling and directing new requests to the server with the fewest connections. Least connections is beneficial for utilizing server resources efficiently, particularly when server loads vary over time.

- **Hash-Based Load Balancing:** In hash-based load balancing, a hash function is applied to some characteristic of the request (such as a user ID) to determine the server assignment. This method ensures request stickiness, where specific clients consistently communicate with the same server, facilitating cache coherence and minimized session-based overhead.

Consider the following example showcasing a basic client-side load balancer using the round-robin strategy in a gRPC setup:

```
package main

import (
    "context"
    "log"
    "time"

    "google.golang.org/grpc"
```

8.3. LOAD BALANCING STRATEGIES

```go
    pb "path/to/your/protobuf"
)

func main() {
    servers := []string{"localhost:50051", "localhost:50052", "localhost:50053"}
    nextServerIdx := 0

    // Basic round-robin load balancer
    for {
        conn, err := grpc.Dial(servers[nextServerIdx], grpc.WithInsecure())
        if err != nil {
            log.Fatalf("did not connect: %v", err)
        }
        defer conn.Close()

        client := pb.NewYourServiceClient(conn)

        response, err := client.YourMethod(context.Background(), &pb.YourRequest{})
        if err != nil {
            log.Fatalf("could not execute request: %v", err)
        }

        log.Printf("Response from server [%s]: %s", servers[nextServerIdx], response.GetMessage())

        nextServerIdx = (nextServerIdx + 1) % len(servers)

        time.Sleep(time.Second)
    }
}
```

In this basic load balancer implementation, the client iterates over a list of server addresses in a round-robin manner. This approach works well for simple applications but may need enhancement with more sophisticated service discovery and health check mechanisms in production environments.

- **Server-Side Load Balancing**

  Server-side load balancing involves an intermediary load balancer that controls the distribution of requests to backend servers. Unlike client-side techniques, server-side load balancing abstracts the decision-making from the client, which communicates through a single endpoint. This abstraction offers simplicity to the client configuration and better encapsulation of the load balancing logic.

  Server-side load balancers often support more complex algorithms and can adapt in real time based on server health and request patterns. Technologies such as Envoy, HAProxy, and NG-INX are commonly used server-side load balancing solutions that seamlessly integrate with gRPC services.

- **Weighted Round-Robin:** An improvement over simple round-robin, where servers are assigned weights proportional to their capacity. The load balancer uses these weights to distribute requests accordingly, ensuring that more capable servers handle a larger share of traffic.
- **Priority-Based Routing:** This entails defining priorities for server instances, directing critical requests to high-priority servers. Such strategies are valuable in multi-cluster setups where certain regions or server types need precedence.
- **Randomized Load Balancing:** Employing random selection to scatter requests across servers can be valuable in environments with ever-changing server states, preventing overutilization of ostensibly optimal servers.

Server-side solutions benefit from centralized control over traffic distribution and the ability to incorporate health checks, rate limiting, and more sophisticated algorithms. However, they introduce additional network hops, potentially increasing latency and creating a single point of failure unless configured in highly available clusters.

Consider an Envoy configuration file as an example of server-side load balancing to distribute gRPC traffic:

```
static_resources:
  listeners:
  - name: listener_0
    address:
      socket_address:
        address: 0.0.0.0
        port_value: 80
    filter_chains:
    - filters:
      - name: envoy.filters.network.http_connection_manager
        config:
          codec_type: AUTO
          stat_prefix: ingress_http
          route_config:
            name: local_route
            virtual_hosts:
            - name: backend
```

8.3. LOAD BALANCING STRATEGIES

```
              domains: ["*"]
              routes:
              - match: { prefix: "/" }
                route:
                  cluster: local_service_grpc
          http_filters:
          - name: envoy.filters.http.router

    clusters:
    - name: local_service_grpc
      connect_timeout: 0.25s
      type: STATIC
      lb_policy: ROUND_ROBIN
      load_assignment:
        cluster_name: local_service_grpc
        endpoints:
        - lb_endpoints:
          - endpoint:
              address:
                socket_address:
                  address: localhost
                  port_value: 50051
          - endpoint:
              address:
                socket_address:
                  address: localhost
                  port_value: 50052
```

In this YAML configuration for Envoy, gRPC traffic is load balanced across two backend servers using a round-robin policy. Envoy's robust feature set permits extensive customization and supports different load balancing strategies, health checking, TLS termination, and traffic routing.

- **External Load Balancing Infrastructure**

  For large-scale applications with stringent performance and reliability requirements, external load balancing infrastructure may be employed. Solutions such as cloud-native load balancers (e.g., Google Cloud Load Balancer, AWS Elastic Load Balancing) offer advanced features including auto-scaling, global load balancing, and integration with service discovery.

  External load balancers decouple business logic from the application, allowing developers to leverage managed services with built-in reliability and availability. They offer additional controls, such as automatic failover, regional traffic distribution, and service mesh integration, providing a fully-managed abstraction to traffic management that is both scalable and resilient.

- **Advanced Load Balancing Considerations**

  The integration of load balancing strategies requires careful consideration of various system aspects. It is critical to clearly define objectives such as latency, throughput, fault tolerance, and resource utilization when choosing a load balancing strategy. Considerations include:

  - **Health Checks:** Integral to maintaining high availability, health checks ensure that requests are only routed to healthy servers. Server-side load balancers and external infrastructure typically include sophisticated health monitoring tools to detect and route around faulty instances.

  - **Session Persistence:** Certain applications necessitate that client requests are consistently routed to the same server. Load balancing must account for this persistence requirement using strategies like IP hashing or cookie-based session tracking.

  - **Scalability and Elasticity:** Load balancers should dynamically adjust to varying traffic loads, scaling server instances as needed. Auto-scaling and scaling policies should be well-configured in cloud environments to accommodate sudden changes in traffic.

  - **Latency and Failover Handling:** Minimizing latency while ensuring efficient failover capabilities demands geographically distributed servers and routing mechanisms that support nearby server selection and seamless failover transitions.

With these considerations in mind, developers are positioned to exploit gRPC's capabilities, implementing load balancing strategies that effectively optimize distributed systems for peak performance and reliability. Understanding the nuances of different load balancing techniques, along with practical implementation insights, ensures that applications not only scale effectively but also maintain excellent operational standards.

8.4 gRPC with HTTP/2 Features

gRPC leverages HTTP/2, a modern version of the HTTP protocol that introduces significant advancements over its predecessor, HTTP/1.1. HTTP/2 offers features like multiplexing, header compression, and flow control, which are instrumental for boosting the performance, efficiency, and scalability of gRPC applications. Understanding how these features work and their integration with gRPC is key to fully utilizing the potential of gRPC in building robust, efficient distributed systems.

Multiplexing

Multiplexing in HTTP/2 allows multiple streams (or requests) to be sent over a single connection simultaneously. Unlike HTTP/1.1, which requires separate connections for parallel requests or suffers from head-of-line blocking, HTTP/2's multiplexing ensures that individual streams are independent. This independence significantly reduces latency and increases throughput as multiple RPC calls can coexist on the same connection without interference.

gRPC inherently benefits from HTTP/2's multiplexing during both unary and streaming RPCs. Multiplexing optimizes network utilization by maintaining a single connection for transferring data, allowing for efficient use of resources.

Let us explore an example where a gRPC client makes multiple parallel RPC calls to demonstrate the efficiency gained from HTTP/2 multiplexing:

```
package main

import (
  "context"
  "log"
  "sync"

  "google.golang.org/grpc"
  pb "path/to/your/protobuf"
)

func makeConcurrentCalls(client pb.YourServiceClient, wg *sync.WaitGroup, id int) {
  defer wg.Done()
  response, err := client.YourMethod(context.Background(), &pb.YourRequest{Id:
      int32(id)})
  if err != nil {
    log.Printf("Error calling YourMethod: %v", err)
    return
```

```
    }
    log.Printf("Response for request %d: %s", id, response.GetMessage())
}

func main() {
    conn, err := grpc.Dial("your.grpc.server:50051", grpc.WithInsecure())
    if err != nil {
        log.Fatalf("did not connect: %v", err)
    }
    defer conn.Close()

    client := pb.NewYourServiceClient(conn)

    var wg sync.WaitGroup
    for i := 0; i < 10; i++ {
        wg.Add(1)
        go makeConcurrentCalls(client, &wg, i)
    }
    wg.Wait()
}
```

In this Go example, 10 simultaneous RPC calls are executed in goroutines. HTTP/2 multiplexing efficiently handles these concurrent requests over a single connection, reducing overall latency and allowing faster processing times.

Header Compression

Another pivotal feature of HTTP/2 is header compression, using the HPACK compression format, designed specifically to minimize overhead. Traditional HTTP headers can be verbose. In environments where numerous requests are sent rapidly, such as in a gRPC context, repeated transmission of large headers would severely impact performance. HPACK resolves this by compressing and efficiently encoding headers, dramatically decreasing header size and transmission time.

Header compression proves invaluable for gRPC applications that inherently involve frequent communication requiring the repeated transmission of metadata. This feature also reduces bandwidth usage, making applications more responsive.

Consider an application scenario involving frequent gRPC method calls where each call carries substantial metadata. Leveraging header compression, the large size of metadata is mitigated, allowing more efficient communication across networks:

```
import grpc
import time
from concurrent import futures
```

8.4. GRPC WITH HTTP/2 FEATURES

```python
import your_service_pb2
import your_service_pb2_grpc

def run():
    with grpc.insecure_channel('your.grpc.server:50051') as channel:
        stub = your_service_pb2_grpc.YourServiceStub(channel)

        def make_request(id):
            metadata = [('key', 'value' * 20)] # Large metadata to be compressed
            response = stub.YourMethod(your_service_pb2.YourRequest(id=id),
                metadata=metadata)
            print(f"Response for {id}: {response}")

        with futures.ThreadPoolExecutor(max_workers=10) as executor:
            for i in range(10):
                executor.submit(make_request, i)
if __name__ == '__main__':
    run()
```

This Python program demonstrates gRPC calls with substantial repeated metadata, compressed by the HPACK algorithm, significantly reducing the size and overhead compared to transmitting raw headers.

Flow Control

Flow control in HTTP/2 allows the regulation of data flow between sender and receiver based on the available resources. This feature prevents the sender from overwhelming the receiver with data, thus optimizing resource usage and ensuring smooth throughput even under different network conditions.

Flow control uses window size mechanisms to allow the receiver to signal how much data it can process, facilitating optimal bandwidth usage and avoiding congestion. This adaptability is crucial for achieving stable and predictable performance in gRPC applications dealing with large data volumes or sustaining long-lived streams.

Let's take the example of a server-side streamed gRPC service employing flow control to manage data flow:

```go
package main

import (
  "log"
  "net"

  "google.golang.org/grpc"
  "google.golang.org/grpc/metadata"
  pb "path/to/your/protobuf"
)
```

```go
type server struct {
  pb.UnimplementedYourServiceServer
}

func (s *server) YourStreamingMethod(req *pb.YourRequest, stream pb.
    YourService_YourStreamingMethodServer) error {
  md := metadata.New(map[string]string{
    "stream-metadata-key": "stream-metadata-value",
  })
  stream.SetHeader(md)

  for i := 0; i <= 10; i++ {
    if err := stream.Send(&pb.YourResponse{Message: "Response Message"}) ; err !=
        nil {
      return err
    }
  }

  return nil
}

func main() {
  lis, err := net.Listen("tcp", ":50051")
  if err != nil {
    log.Fatalf("failed to listen: %v", err)
  }

  s := grpc.NewServer()
  pb.RegisterYourServiceServer(s, &server{})

  log.Println("Server is running...")
  if err := s.Serve(lis); err != nil {
    log.Fatalf("failed to serve: %v", err)
  }
}
```

This Go server example uses a server-side stream to send multiple responses to a single client request. The HTTP/2 flow control capabilities regulate the transmission to match the client's ingestion capacity without flooding its resources.

Prioritization and Dependencies

Though less commonly leveraged directly in gRPC due to its high-level abstraction, HTTP/2 introduces mechanisms for stream prioritization and dependencies. Prioritization provides the ability to relay more critical data streams over less important ones, while dependencies help build complex hierarchies among streams.

These features, despite their complexity, are beneficial for applications where varying service quality is necessary, such as video streaming

8.4. GRPC WITH HTTP/2 FEATURES

or interactive services demanding low-latency delivery for prioritized streams.

Integrating HTTP/2 Features in gRPC Workflows

System architects designing gRPC-based systems must focus on thoroughly integrating HTTP/2 features. This involves:

- **Optimizing Existing Infrastructure:** Assessing how existing infrastructure and network conditions might benefit from the multiplexing, compression, and flow control provided by HTTP/2 to reduce latencies and improve throughput.

- **Designing Flexible Frameworks:** Architecting systems capable of dynamically scaling and distributing workloads effectively across multiplexed channels with efficient header management to utilize bandwidth judiciously.

- **Enhancing Security:** While HTTP/2 enhances performance, its security configurations must be rigorously managed to mitigate risks such as man-in-the-middle attacks and enhance data confidentiality.

- **Profiling and Benchmarking:** Continuously profiling system performance to identify potential bottlenecks introduced by protocol usage and configuring flow control parameters to balance data transmission with processing capacities.

gRPC's integration with HTTP/2 is a paradigm shift tailored for contemporary high-demand, data-driven environments. By leveraging HTTP/2's innovative enhancements, developers can not only maintain but significantly amplify their applications' performance, leading to faster, more resilient, and highly scalable distributed solutions. As infrastructure evolves, incorporating HTTP/2's full capability set becomes increasingly essential for competitive and future-proof service architectures.

8.5 Asynchronous Programming Models

Asynchronous programming models lie at the heart of developing highly responsive and scalable applications. In the context of gRPC, leveraging asynchronous communication can significantly boost performance by allowing operations to proceed concurrently instead of sequentially waiting for each to complete. This is particularly vital when managing thousands of simultaneous client requests or when interfacing with I/O-bound or long-duration processes.

The primary motivation for adopting asynchronous programming models is to enhance an application's ability to efficiently utilize system resources, particularly CPU and I/O. When employed properly, these models can minimize latency, optimize throughput, and improve resource utilization across networks and computing infrastructure.

Fundamental Asynchronous Programming Concepts

In asynchronous programming, function calls are non-blocking, meaning operations initiate and execute while allowing the calling thread to proceed without waiting for the operation's completion. The completion is typically handled through callbacks, promises, or future constructs designed to register completion handlers once a result is available.

Key benefits of asynchronous programming include:

- **Concurrency:** Allows multiple operations to execute in overlapping timeframes, improving application responsiveness and overall throughput.

- **Resource Management:** Reduces idle times for CPU and other critical resources by overlapping I/O and computation tasks, which is crucial for systems processing multiple workload streams.

- **Scalability:** Facilitates scaling horizontally as asynchronous models often offer better performance under increasing loads due to efficient resource usage.

Asynchronous Patterns in gRPC

8.5. ASYNCHRONOUS PROGRAMMING MODELS

gRPC fully supports asynchronous programming models across various languages, offering non-blocking APIs to maximize performance in client-server interactions. These asynchronous models provide considerable flexibility, catering to different programming styles and application requirements.

Callbacks

A traditional approach to asynchronous operations, callbacks are functions passed as arguments and invoked when an asynchronous task completes. While straightforward to implement, the heavy use of callbacks can lead to callback hell, where nested callback sequences become complex and challenging to manage.

Consider the following example using gRPC in Python, illustrating a basic asynchronous client using callbacks:

```python
import grpc
import your_service_pb2
import your_service_pb2_grpc

def response_callback(future):
    try:
        response = future.result()
        print(f"Received response: {response.message}")
    except grpc.RpcError as e:
        print(f"RPC failed: {e.status()}")

def main():
    with grpc.insecure_channel('your.grpc.server:50051') as channel:
        stub = your_service_pb2_grpc.YourServiceStub(channel)
        future = stub.YourMethod.future(your_service_pb2.YourRequest(name='Test')
        )
        future.add_done_callback(response_callback)

if __name__ == '__main__':
    main()
```

This example demonstrates a gRPC client making a request using an asynchronous API. The 'future' object allows the specification of a callback to be invoked on operation completion, thereby facilitating non-blocking processing within the application.

Promises and Futures

To improve upon traditional callback models, modern programming paradigms use promises and futures to capture the eventual result of asynchronous operations. Futures are placeholders for results not yet available, allowing code execution to continue while monitoring for task completion.

In Java, gRPC offers an extensive futures-based API. Consider this Java example:

```java
import io.grpc.ManagedChannel;
import io.grpc.ManagedChannelBuilder;
import com.example.grpc.YourServiceGrpc;
import com.example.grpc.YourServiceOuterClass.YourRequest;
import com.example.grpc.YourServiceOuterClass.YourResponse;

import java.util.concurrent.ExecutionException;

public class AsyncClient {

    public static void main(String[] args) {
        ManagedChannel channel = ManagedChannelBuilder.forAddress("localhost",
            50051)
            .usePlaintext()
            .build();

        YourServiceGrpc.YourServiceFutureStub stub = YourServiceGrpc.
            newFutureStub(channel);

        YourRequest request = YourRequest.newBuilder().setName("Test").build();

        try {
            YourResponse response = stub.yourMethod(request).get();
            System.out.println("Response received: " + response.getMessage());
        } catch (InterruptedException | ExecutionException e) {
            e.printStackTrace();
        } finally {
            channel.shutdown();
        }
    }
}
```

Here, 'FutureStub' allows non-blocking RPC calls. The 'get()' method is employed to obtain the result; however, it will block if the result is not yet ready.

Reactive Streams

The reactive programming paradigm embraces handling data as streams rather than discrete signals. Reactive streams enable processing sequences of data asynchronously, reacting to the availability of new data. This model is particularly fit for processing streams with large volumes of data or events efficiently. In practice, reactive frameworks like RxJava or Reactor are used with gRPC for rich asynchronous programming models.

Java's gRPC reactive API can leverage Reactor:

8.5. ASYNCHRONOUS PROGRAMMING MODELS

```java
import io.grpc.ManagedChannel;
import io.grpc.ManagedChannelBuilder;
import reactor.core.publisher.Mono;

import com.example.grpc.YourServiceGrpc;
import com.example.grpc.YourServiceOuterClass.YourRequest;
import com.example.grpc.YourServiceOuterClass.YourResponse;

public class ReactiveClient {

    public static void main(String[] args) {
        ManagedChannel channel = ManagedChannelBuilder.forAddress("localhost",
            50051)
                .usePlaintext()
                .build();

        YourServiceReactiveStub stub = YourServiceGrpc.newReactiveStub(channel);

        YourRequest request = YourRequest.newBuilder().setName("Test").build();

        Mono<YourResponse> responseMono = stub.yourMethod(ReactorPublisher.
            create(request));

        responseMono.subscribe(response -> {
            System.out.println("Response received: " + response.getMessage());
        }, error -> {
            System.err.println("Error occurred: " + error.getMessage());
        });
    }
}
```

This client subscribes to a reactive stream, handling responses asynchronously as they arrive, which elegantly handles both success and failure states.

Implementing Asynchronous Servers

Just as clients benefit from asynchrony, gRPC servers can also be configured to handle requests asynchronously, ensuring efficient resource use and reducing request wait times, even under heavy load.

Let's analyze a simple example in Go where an asynchronous server processes calls:

```go
package main

import (
  "context"
  "log"
  "net"
  "time"

  "google.golang.org/grpc"
```

CHAPTER 8. ADVANCED GRPC FEATURES AND TECHNIQUES

```go
  pb "path/to/your/protobuf"
)

type server struct {
  pb.UnimplementedYourServiceServer
}

func (s *server) YourMethod(ctx context.Context, req *pb.YourRequest) (*pb.
     YourResponse, error) {
  done := make(chan *pb.YourResponse)

  go func() {
    // Perform complex operation asynchronously
    time.Sleep(2 * time.Second)
    done <- &pb.YourResponse{Message: "Hello " + req.Name}
  }()

  select {
  case res := <-done:
    return res, nil
  case <-ctx.Done():
    return nil, ctx.Err()
  }
}

func main() {
  lis, err := net.Listen("tcp", ":50051")
  if err != nil {
    log.Fatalf("failed to listen: %v", err)
  }
  grpcServer := grpc.NewServer()
  pb.RegisterYourServiceServer(grpcServer, &server{})

  log.Println("Server is running...")
  if err := grpcServer.Serve(lis); err != nil {
    log.Fatalf("failed to serve: %v", err)
  }
}
```

The server employs goroutines to handle each request asynchronously, freeing the main thread to handle new connections. This approach maximizes throughput and system resource utilization.

Considerations for Asynchronous Programming Models

When implementing asynchronous models, developers must navigate potential complexities and pitfalls:

- **Error Handling:** Asynchronous programming introduces deferred error handling, complicating debugging processes. Accurate and comprehensive error handling mechanisms are essential to ensure robust applications.

- **State Management:** Managing state across asynchronous calls can be challenging, especially when sharing state between callback or thread interactions. Employing thread-safe data structures or leveraging inherent language constructs for state synchronization, such as goroutines or locks, can mitigate concurrency issues.

- **Resource Management:** Excessive spawning of threads or over-subscribing to resources such as file handles or memory can incur performance degradation. It is critical to control concurrency levels through pooling mechanisms and efficient resource allocation strategies.

- **Performance Profiling:** Continuous profiling and testing are paramount to identify and rectify bottlenecks. Monitoring and optimizing performance attributes, such as latency and throughput, ensures the application meets established quality-of-service targets.

Ultimately, asynchronous programming unlocks substantial performance and scalability improvements for gRPC applications. By deftly applying asynchronous constructs like callbacks, futures, promises, and reactive streams, developers can craft highly efficient and responsive systems able to meet the demands of dynamic and evolving operational environments.

8.6 Reflection and Dynamic Service Discovery

In complex distributed systems, service discovery and reflection are fundamental for achieving seamless communication between dynamically changing services. gRPC supports these concepts through built-in reflection mechanisms and integration capabilities with service discovery frameworks. Understanding and integrating these features effectively into a microservices architecture can lead to significant improvements in adaptability, scalability, and ease of maintenance.

Reflection in gRPC facilitates dynamic inspection of services, allowing clients to query server metadata and capabilities at runtime. This capability eliminates the need for predefined service information, enabling tools to automatically detect and understand services, which is particularly useful for interactive client generation, development tools, and dynamic service interfacing.

Enabling Reflection on a gRPC Server

To enable reflection, integrate the reflection library into the server codebase. This setup typically involves importing the reflection package and registering it with your gRPC server:

Here's how to enable reflection in a Go-based gRPC server:

```
package main

import (
  "log"
  "net"

  "google.golang.org/grpc"
  "google.golang.org/grpc/reflection"
  pb "path/to/your/protobuf"
)

type server struct {
  pb.UnimplementedYourServiceServer
}

func (s *server) YourMethod(req *pb.YourRequest, stream pb.
    YourService_YourMethodServer) error {
  // Service method implementation
  return nil
}

func main() {
  lis, err := net.Listen("tcp", ":50051")
  if err != nil {
    log.Fatalf("failed to listen: %v", err)
  }

  s := grpc.NewServer()
  pb.RegisterYourServiceServer(s, &server{})

  // Enable reflection
  reflection.Register(s)

  log.Println("Server is running with reflection enabled...")
  if err := s.Serve(lis); err != nil {
    log.Fatalf("failed to serve: %v", err)
  }
}
```

With reflection enabled, clients can dynamically interrogate the server

8.6. REFLECTION AND DYNAMIC SERVICE DISCOVERY

to discover available services and methods. This feature simplifies the development of client-side tools and utilities that can auto-generate client stubs or offer exploratory capabilities.

Using gRPC Reflection for Client Discovery

Clients, including command-line tools like grpcurl, can leverage reflection to browse server capabilities without prior knowledge of the service interface. Consider the following example utilizing grpcurl to inspect a reflected service:

```
grpcurl -plaintext localhost:50051 list
```

This command lists all gRPC services running on a particular server utilizing reflection. Similarly, one can enact more profound inspections:

```
grpcurl -plaintext localhost:50051 describe your.service.Name
```

Such commands identify methods, parameter, and result types, providing insightful runtime exploration of gRPC servers.

Security Considerations for Reflection

While reflection offers significant convenience, it introduces potential security risks, particularly in exposing service metadata over networks. It is crucial to employ best practices such as:

- **Access Controls:** Implement authentication and authorization to regulate access to reflection services. This restricts exposed metadata only to authorized entities.
- **Encrypted Channels:** Use SSL/TLS to secure communications, ensuring reflection queries and responses are protected from interception.

Dynamic service discovery allows clients to locate instances of services in large, dynamic environments, like those defined by microservices architectures. Service discovery mitigates the complexities involved in maintaining hardcoded service endpoints, offering flexibility towards scaling operations tied to deployment frequency and server availability.

Service discovery involves registering services with centralized components—often registries or service meshes—which maintain service metadata and provide client lookup facilities. Prominent service discovery frameworks widely adopted in conjunction with gRPC include:

- **Consul:** A strong key-value store for managing service registration and discovery across distributed nodes.
- **etcd:** A distributed reliable key-value store for distributed settings.
- **Zookeeper:** A centralised service for maintaining configuration information, naming, providing distributed synchronization, and providing group services.

Implementing Service Discovery with Consul

Implementing Consul for service discovery often involves configuring both server registration and client-side discovery. The following is an example of registering services with Consul using a gRPC application in Go:

Service Registration

```
package main

import (
  "log"
  "fmt"
  "os"
  "net"

  "github.com/hashicorp/consul/api"
  "google.golang.org/grpc"
  pb "path/to/your/protobuf"
)

func registerServiceWithConsul() {
  config := api.DefaultConfig()
  consulClient, err := api.NewClient(config)
  if err != nil {
    log.Fatalf("failed to create consul client: %v", err)
  }

  registration := new(api.AgentServiceRegistration)
  registration.ID = "yourService-1"
  registration.Name = "yourService"
  registration.Port = 50051
```

8.6. REFLECTION AND DYNAMIC SERVICE DISCOVERY

```
    registration.Tags = []string{"your-gRPC-service"}

    consulClient.Agent().ServiceRegister(registration)
    fmt.Println("Service successfully registered with Consul!")
}

type server struct {
    pb.UnimplementedYourServiceServer
}

func main() {
    lis, err := net.Listen("tcp", ":50051")
    if err != nil {
        log.Fatalf("failed to listen: %v", err)
    }

    s := grpc.NewServer()
    pb.RegisterYourServiceServer(s, &server{})

    registerServiceWithConsul()

    log.Println("Server is running...")
    if err := s.Serve(lis); err != nil {
        log.Fatalf("failed to serve: %v", err)
    }
}
```

Here, the service registers itself with a Consul agent using service ID, name, and tags to facilitate easier discovery and load balancing.

Service Discovery

For client-side implementation, the discovery process involves querying Consul to retrieve service information. Using the retrieved metadata, clients can dynamically connect to available endpoints.

Load Balancing with Service Discovery

In combination with service discovery, load balancing addresses scaling and fault tolerance by distributing incoming service requests evenly across available instances. gRPC clients can dynamically adjust to shifting endpoint states facilitated by discovery mechanisms, maintaining system balance and minimizing downtime.

Integrating service discovery with load balancing involves:

- **Service Catalog Querying:** Clients consistently query registries for updates on service states, leveraging this data to perform client-side balancing.

- **Health Checking:** Employing health checks to confirm instance availability and performance, ensuring efficient resource utilization.

Service Mesh Integration

Service mesh architectures, such as Istio and Linkerd, offer more comprehensive discovery mechanisms by abstracting discovery, observability, and security configuration layers away from the control of individual services. gRPC integrates seamlessly with these meshes, enhancing service capabilities through enhanced tracing, load balancing, and observability.

Istio, for instance, provides dynamic discovery compatible with gRPC through sidecar proxies configuring service interaction policies and capturing telemetry data.

Design Considerations

Developers must carefully consider deployment strategies, security configurations, and scalability needs while implementing reflection and dynamic service discovery. Key aspects include:

- **Scalability and Performance:** Ensuring discovery mechanisms can scale without introducing latency or performance overhead.

- **Security and Compliance:** Implement robust security policies safeguarding sensitive metadata and controlling access to discovery registries.

- **Monitoring and Tracing:** Services should be monitored for infrastructure insights, employing tracing to diagnose latency or communication issues.

Utilizing reflection and dynamic service discovery empowers gRPC applications with significant flexibility and adaptability, central to thriving in complex microservice-driven environments. Embracing these capabilities facilitates streamlined client-server interfacing, proactive service management, and ultimately, robust application design and deployment.

Chapter 9

gRPC for Microservices and Distributed Systems

This chapter examines the application of gRPC within microservices and distributed systems. It discusses how gRPC facilitates efficient communication between microservices and explores integration with service discovery tools like Consul and etcd. The chapter outlines strategies for failure management and retry policies, while addressing the challenges of load balancing in distributed environments. Techniques for implementing distributed tracing and monitoring are also covered, alongside leveraging gRPC's streaming capabilities for real-time data transfer. Readers will gain insights into optimizing gRPC for decentralized architectures, enhancing both reliability and performance.

9.1 Integrating gRPC with Microservices

In microservices architecture, the challenge of ensuring seamless communication between services is paramount. gRPC, an open-source Remote Procedure Call (RPC) framework developed by Google, has emerged as a powerful tool to address this challenge. It employs HTTP/2 for transport, offers language-agnostic interfaces, and utilizes Protocol Buffers (protobuf) for efficient data serialization, making it well-suited for microservices.

gRPC's unique advantages over traditional HTTP REST communication include improved performance through binary serialization and multiplexing requests over a single TCP connection. Furthermore, it inherently supports service definitions through Protocol Buffers, enabling strong type checking and streamlined service-to-service communication.

The integration of gRPC within a microservices ecosystem involves multiple considerations, ranging from service definition and implementation to handling asynchronous communication and interfacing with non-gRPC components. This section delves into these various aspects, emphasizing practical implementation and best practices.

First, consider the process of defining a gRPC service. One begins by writing a .proto file that specifies the service interface, including service methods and their request and response message types. Below is an example of a simple gRPC service definition in Protocol Buffers:

```
syntax = "proto3";

package ecommerce;

service OrderService {
  rpc CreateOrder(OrderRequest) returns (OrderResponse);
  rpc GetOrder(OrderId) returns (OrderDetails);
}

message OrderRequest {
  string product_id = 1;
  int32 quantity = 2;
  string customer_id = 3;
}

message OrderResponse {
  string order_id = 1;
  string status = 2;
}
```

9.1. INTEGRATING GRPC WITH MICROSERVICES

```
message OrderId {
  string order_id = 1;
}
message OrderDetails {
  string order_id = 1;
  string product_id = 2;
  int32 quantity = 3;
  string customer_id = 4;
  string status = 5;
  string delivery_date = 6;
}
```

In this example, an OrderService is defined with two RPC methods: CreateOrder and GetOrder. These methods utilize OrderRequest, OrderResponse, OrderId, and OrderDetails messages to exchange information across services.

Once the .proto file is defined, the next step is to generate client and server code for the desired programming languages using the protoc compiler. This facilitates language interoperability. For instance, running the following command generates Java and Python code:

```
protoc --java_out=./src --plugin=protoc-gen-grpc-java --grpc-java_out=./src
    OrderService.proto
protoc --python_out=./src --plugin=protoc-gen-grpc-python --grpc-python_out=./src
    OrderService.proto
```

These generated code snippets act as the foundation for implementing the service's logic and integrating it with business processes.

The server-side implementation of a gRPC service involves extending a base class generated by protoc and implementing the service methods. An example using Java might appear as follows:

```java
import io.grpc.Server;
import io.grpc.ServerBuilder;
import io.grpc.stub.StreamObserver;
import ecommerce.OrderServiceGrpc;
import ecommerce.OrderServiceOuterClass.*;

public class OrderServiceImplementation extends OrderServiceGrpc.
    OrderServiceImplBase {

  @Override
  public void createOrder(OrderRequest request, StreamObserver<OrderResponse>
      responseObserver) {
    String orderId = "order123"; // Example order ID generation logic
    OrderResponse response = OrderResponse.newBuilder()
        .setOrderId(orderId)
```

```
        .setStatus("CONFIRMED")
        .build();

    responseObserver.onNext(response);
    responseObserver.onCompleted();
}

@Override
public void getOrder(OrderId request, StreamObserver<OrderDetails>
    responseObserver) {
  OrderDetails details = OrderDetails.newBuilder()
        .setOrderId(request.getOrderId())
        .setProductId("prod456")
        .setQuantity(3)
        .setCustomerId("cust789")
        .setStatus("DELIVERED")
        .setDeliveryDate("2023-10-12")
        .build();

    responseObserver.onNext(details);
    responseObserver.onCompleted();
}

public static void main(String[] args) throws Exception {
  Server server = ServerBuilder.forPort(50051)
        .addService(new OrderServiceImplementation())
        .build()
        .start();

    System.out.println("Server started, listening on 50051");
    server.awaitTermination();
  }
}
```

This Java implementation of the OrderService defines the logic for two RPC methods, addressing how the server processes incoming requests, generates a response, and completes the RPC call using a StreamObserver.

On the client side, the gRPC stub generated by protoc allows seamless communication with the server. Here is a Python example demonstrating how a client would interact with OrderService:

```
import grpc
from ecommerce_pb2 import OrderRequest, OrderId
from ecommerce_pb2_grpc import OrderServiceStub

def run():
    with grpc.insecure_channel('localhost:50051') as channel:
        stub = OrderServiceStub(channel)

        # Create an order
        order_request = OrderRequest(product_id='prod456', quantity=3,
            customer_id='cust789')
```

9.1. INTEGRATING GRPC WITH MICROSERVICES

```
        order_response = stub.CreateOrder(order_request)
        print(f'Created Order ID: {order_response.order_id}, Status: {order_response.
            status}')

        # Get order details
        order_id = OrderId(order_id=order_response.order_id)
        order_details = stub.GetOrder(order_id)
        print(f'Order Details: {order_details}')

if __name__ == '__main__':
    run()
```

This Python client script establishes a connection with the gRPC server and invokes CreateOrder and GetOrder RPC methods, thereby illustrating the synchronous communication paradigm that gRPC facilitates between distributed services.

An essential aspect of integrating gRPC with microservices is handling asynchronous communication efficiently. While gRPC supports both synchronous and asynchronous calls, its asynchronous capabilities are particularly beneficial in microservices, where services often handle high-concurrency workloads. By leveraging asynchronous stubs, clients can initiate multiple RPCs and manage responses as they arrive.

Moreover, gRPC's support for streaming RPCs—such as server streaming, client streaming, and bidirectional streaming—allows for more complex interactions, enhancing data exchange flexibility. For instance, a server streaming RPC might be employed for use cases where a client sends a single request to the server and receives a stream of messages in response, such as real-time monitoring data:

```
rpc ListOrders(OrderFilter) returns (stream OrderDetails);
```

Incorporating security features is another crucial consideration when deploying gRPC in production environments. While gRPC can operate with plaintext communication, utilizing Transport Layer Security (TLS) is recommended to ensure encrypted and secure data transmission between microservices. Implementing mutual TLS (mTLS) further enhances security by ensuring both the client and server authenticate each other's certificates.

gRPC's integration into a microservices landscape also necessitates seamless interoperation with existing non-gRPC components. The diversity of protocols in microservices architectures makes it essential to consider approaches such as gRPC Gateway, which serves as a bridge between gRPC and JSON/HTTP APIs. This gateway enables gRPC services to be accessed using RESTful APIs, simplifying integration with web clients and legacy systems.

One illustrative example involves using gRPC alongside a traditional REST API. Suppose we have a RESTful service that clients should access but want the core backend systems to use gRPC for microservice-to-microservice communication due to its performance benefits. Here, gRPC Gateway can automatically translate RESTful calls into gRPC calls:

```
# Example REST call to gRPC Gateway
GET /orders/123

# Expected JSON Response
{
  "orderId": "123",
  "productId": "prod456",
  "quantity": 3,
  "customerId": "cust789",
  "status": "DELIVERED",
  "deliveryDate": "2023-10-12"
}
```

This seamless conversion ensures that systems built on different paradigms can interact without extensive redevelopment.

Additionally, adopting gRPC within microservices architectures entails careful consideration of observability. Observability tools, such as OpenTelemetry, can be integrated to capture and trace gRPC-specific metrics and logs. This holistic view of inter-service communication performance aids in diagnosing issues and optimizing system throughput.

Finally, the deployment of gRPC-based microservices must consider evolving operational paradigms such as containerization and orchestration with Kubernetes. With Kubernetes, service configurations and scaling policies can be managed declaratively, enabling robust lifecycle management for gRPC services.

By embedding gRPC within a Kubernetes architecture, microservices benefit from features like automatic load balancing and service discovery through platforms like Consul and etcd, allowing for dynamic and resilient service interactions. Such integration ensures that services can scale and adapt to varying demand patterns efficiently.

The role of gRPC in microservices is thus multifaceted. It encompasses not only the technical layer of defining and executing RPC calls but also the comprehensive integration with security, interoperability, and observability tools essential for modern microservices architecture. Through its unique features, gRPC delivers enhanced reliability, performance, and developer productivity in service-oriented architectures.

9.2 Service Discovery in Distributed Systems

Distributed systems, characterized by a myriad of microservices interacting over a network, necessitate efficient service discovery mechanisms to achieve dynamic, scalable, and fault-tolerant architectures. Service discovery entails resolving the locations (network addresses) of service instances at runtime, ensuring that services can dynamically locate and communicate with each other without hard-coded configurations.

Within such distributed environments, traditional static configurations are insufficient due to the ephemerality and scale of service instances. gRPC, when integrated with robust service discovery frameworks like Consul and etcd, provides a powerful solution to dynamically locate services, facilitating seamless communication across the ecosystem.

At the core of service discovery is the service registry—a centralized repository that maintains metadata about service instances, such as their network locations, health status, and additional attributes. This registry acts as a dynamic database from which client services can retrieve up-to-date information about available service instances.

To illustrate this process, consider the high-level architecture of service discovery in a distributed system:

CHAPTER 9. GRPC FOR MICROSERVICES AND DISTRIBUTED SYSTEMS

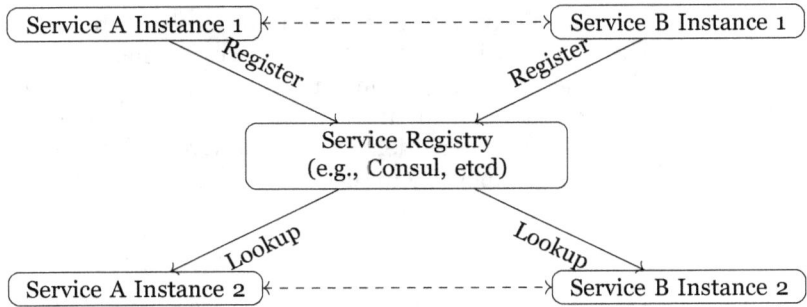

In this setup:

- Service instances register themselves with the service registry when they start up, providing their endpoint details and attributes.

- Client services query the service registry to resolve and discover the endpoints of the services they need to connect with.

- The registry can also act as a health monitor, deregistering or updating the status of instances that fail health checks.

For practical insights, let's demonstrate integrating gRPC with Consul, a popular service discovery tool. Consul provides a unified toolset to address network segmentation issues using features like service discovery, health checks, and a DNS interface. Consider a use case where a gRPC-based Order Management microservice ecosystem needs to dynamically discover and communicate with instances of an Inventory Service.

First, set up the Consul service registration in a configuration file for the Inventory Service:

```
{
  "service": {
    "name": "inventory-service",
    "tags": ["grpc"],
    "port": 50052,
    "check": {
      "grpc": "localhost:50052",
      "interval": "10s",
      "timeout": "5s"
    }
  }
}
```

9.2. SERVICE DISCOVERY IN DISTRIBUTED SYSTEMS

```
    }
}
```

This configuration registers the inventory-service with Consul, specifying it as a gRPC service on port 50052. A health check ensures the service's gRPC endpoint is responsive at 10-second intervals, with a 5-second timeout.

To integrate service discovery on the client side, a gRPC interceptor or middleware can be employed. When a client intends to connect to the inventory-service, it first queries the Consul API to retrieve available service instances:

```
import requests
import grpc
from inventory_pb2_grpc import InventoryServiceStub

def get_inventory_service_address():
    response = requests.get('http://localhost:8500/v1/catalog/service/inventory-service
        ')
    service_instances = response.json()
    if service_instances:
        # Select the first available service instance
        service_instance = service_instances[0]
        address = service_instance['ServiceAddress']
        port = service_instance['ServicePort']
        return f'{address}:{port}'
    raise Exception("No available inventory service instances found.")

def main():
    service_address = get_inventory_service_address()
    with grpc.insecure_channel(service_address) as channel:
        stub = InventoryServiceStub(channel)
        # Communicate with the Inventory Service

if __name__ == '__main__':
    main()
```

This client script queries the Consul HTTP API to discover the current endpoint(s) of the inventory-service. This approach accommodates the dynamic startup, shutdown, or failure of service instances, adapting to changes automatically.

Service discovery systems must support high availability and fault tolerance. Consensus algorithms, such as Raft, are often employed by distributed registries like Consul and etcd to ensure consistent state across nodes, even in the presence of network partitions or node failures.

Moreover, integrating gRPC with service registries provides additional advantages, such as load balancing and service monitoring. With automatic service registration and deregistration supported by gRPC-based services, registries can maintain an accurate and real-time inventory of healthy instances for client services to utilize.

Implementing custom load balancing strategies is another crucial aspect of service discovery. For instance, when multiple healthy instances are available, selection criteria could include round-robin distribution, least connections, or more sophisticated algorithms based on service instance latency or throughput metrics.

Consider integrating gRPC with etcd, another system providing service discovery functionalities with strong consistency and high availability. Here's how one might register a service with etcd in Golang:

```go
import (
    "context"
    "time"
    "github.com/coreos/etcd/clientv3"
)

func registerService(etcdClient *clientv3.Client, serviceName string, serviceAddr string) error {
    ctx, cancel := context.WithTimeout(context.Background(), time.Second*10)
    defer cancel()

    _, err := etcdClient.Put(ctx, serviceName, serviceAddr)
    return err
}
```

This Golang function uses the etcd client to register a service instance by storing its network address in the etcd key-value store. The Put operation ensures the presence of accurate endpoint data for clients attempting to discover the serviceName.

Resolving service addresses at runtime entails querying etcd from client applications:

```go
func getServiceAddress(etcdClient *clientv3.Client, serviceName string) (string, error) {
    ctx, cancel := context.WithTimeout(context.Background(), time.Second*10)
    defer cancel()

    resp, err := etcdClient.Get(ctx, serviceName)
    if err != nil || len(resp.Kvs) == 0 {
        return "", fmt.Errorf("service not found")
    }
    return string(resp.Kvs[0].Value), nil
}
```

This function fetches the network address from etcd and facilitates gRPC communication by returning the address of the service requested.

Integrating service discovery systems requires careful configuration and management of the network topology. Considerations such as namespace separation, security (using TLS configurations), and network policies help safeguard service-to-service communications.

Security stands as a key concern in service discovery within distributed systems. Implementing access control mechanisms, such as Role-Based Access Control (RBAC) or mutual authentication strategies, mitigates unauthorized access risks and enhances the confidentiality and integrity of service transactions.

To further illustrate real-world application, consider microservices deployed in a Kubernetes cluster, where Kubernetes' native service discovery capabilities leverage DNS and environment variables. When combined with gRPC's high-performance capabilities, Kubernetes internal service resolution ensures dynamic scaling and orchestrated service management, promoting operational agility.

gRPC, coupled with a robust service discovery mechanism, forms the backbone of scalable and resilient distributed systems. With tools like Consul, etcd, and Kubernetes' built-in mechanisms, microservices can dynamically locate and communicate with one another, adapting smoothly to the dynamic and ephemeral nature of modern cloud-native architectures. This synergy between gRPC and service discovery not only facilitates fault tolerance and scalability but also enhances the ease of deployment and operation within complex systems.

9.3 Handling Failures and Retry Policies

In microservices and distributed architectures, service failures are inevitable due to network latency, server outages, and unexpected traffic spikes. Effective handling of failures and implementing robust retry policies are crucial to maintaining system reliability and availability. gRPC, with its strong support for network protocol and error handling, offers developers the tools needed to gracefully manage failures and retrials, ensuring that services communicate smoothly even amidst transient disruptions.

The concept of retries in gRPC revolves around resending requests when transient failures occur, such as network timeouts or temporary unavailability of a service instance. However, improper retry configurations can lead to additional problems like request storms or cascading failures, necessitating careful consideration of retry policies.

A primary consideration in configuring retries is distinguishing between transient and non-transient errors. Transient errors typically include network errors, connection timeouts, and service overloads, where a retry might succeed. Conversely, non-transient errors, such as invalid requests or authentication failures, are unlikely to be resolved by retrying and should be handled differently.

Within gRPC, retries are facilitated by setting up retry policies that define conditions under which retries should occur, the number of attempts, and waiting strategies between retries. These policies are configurable through client backends, enabling each service interaction to be customized for resilience.

Consider a simple retry policy configuration in gRPC, defining a strategy for handling transient failures for a microservice:

```
retry_policy = {
    max_attempts: 5,
    initial_backoff: 0.5s,
    max_backoff: 4.0s,
    backoff_multiplier: 1.5,
    retryable_status_codes: [UNAVAILABLE]
}
```

This retry policy specifies:

- a maximum of five attempts before ceasing retries,
- an initial wait time of 0.5 seconds,
- a maximum backoff time of 4 seconds,
- an exponential backoff strategy with a multiplier of 1.5,
- retries in response to UNAVAILABLE status codes, often indicative of transient issues.

9.3. HANDLING FAILURES AND RETRY POLICIES

In practical terms, implementing a retry mechanism can be accomplished using client libraries that support these configurations. For instance, in Java using gRPC's ManagedChannelBuilder, developers can configure these policies programmatically:

```java
import io.grpc.ManagedChannel;
import io.grpc.ManagedChannelBuilder;
import io.grpc.CallOptions;
import ecommerce.OrderServiceGrpc;
import io.grpc.Status;

public class GrpcClient {

  private final ManagedChannel channel;
  private final OrderServiceGrpc.OrderServiceBlockingStub blockingStub;

  public GrpcClient(String host, int port) {
    this.channel = ManagedChannelBuilder.forAddress(host, port)
      .usePlaintext()
      .enableRetry()
      .maxRetryAttempts(5)
      .build();

    this.blockingStub = OrderServiceGrpc.newBlockingStub(channel);
  }

  private void createOrder() {
    try {
      // Assume OrderRequest is prepared
      OrderResponse response = blockingStub.createOrder(OrderRequest.newBuilder().
            build());
      System.out.println("Order created with ID: " + response.getOrderId());
    } catch (StatusRuntimeException e) {
      // Handle error
      System.err.println("RPC failed: " + e.getStatus());
    }
  }

  public static void main(String[] args) {
    GrpcClient client = new GrpcClient("localhost", 50051);
    client.createOrder();
  }
}
```

In this example, the enableRetry() method on the ManagedChannelBuilder initiates retries for eligible RPC calls, with maxRetryAttempts setting the limit on attempts.

Another critical aspect of retries is managing the backoff strategy effectively. Exponential backoff, wherein the wait time between retries increases exponentially, is favored because it reduces the likelihood of overwhelming services recovering from temporary failures. For instance, if a request initially waits 0.5 seconds before a retry, an exponential backoff with a 1.5 multiplier results in subsequent waits of 0.75, 1.125, and so on. This strategy helps distribute retry attempts over time, preventing synchronized floods of requests.

A crucial enhancement over plain exponential backoff is incorporating a jitter mechanism. Fixed or proportional jitter introduces randomness to backoff intervals, further mitigating the risk of retry storms from multiple clients. This modification can alleviate synchronized traffic surges that could otherwise impede service recovery.

Implementing this form of backoff in a Python client, for instance, would involve augmenting sleep durations with random additions:

```
import time
import random

def retry_with_exponential_backoff(max_retries, base_delay):
    delay = base_delay
    for attempt in range(max_retries):
        try:
            # Execute request logic
            break # On success, break the retry loop
        except Exception as e:
            # Handle retryable exception
            if attempt < max_retries - 1:
                jitter = delay * 0.1 * random.uniform(0.9, 1.1) # Adding jitter
                time.sleep(delay + jitter)
                delay *= 1.5 # Exponential backoff
            else:
                raise e # Exhausted retries; propagate exception
```

This sample function outlines a retry mechanism with added jitter for enhanced robustness against temporary disruptions.

While retries significantly improve resilience, they must be paired with a comprehensive strategy to mitigate potential downsides. Circuit breaker patterns provide a means to detect and preempt ineffective retry attempts. When a service experiences repeated failures, a circuit breaker transitions to an open state—halting further requests temporarily. This time-out period allows for service recovery and prevents futile saturation attempts that further degrade performance.

Another important aspect of managing failures is using timeouts prudently. Timeouts protect systems from waiting indefinitely for responses and should be tailored to the characteristics of each microservice interaction. Setting appropriate deadlines in gRPC service stubs

9.3. HANDLING FAILURES AND RETRY POLICIES

ensures time-bound waiting, such as:

```
OrderResponse response = blockingStub.withDeadlineAfter(2, TimeUnit.SECONDS)
                        .createOrder(OrderRequest.newBuilder().build());
```

In this example, the call to createOrder() is limited to two seconds beyond which it ceases waiting, freeing resources for other tasks.

Furthermore, gRPC's native support for status codes facilitates nuanced error handling. By categorizing errors appropriately (e.g., INVALID_ARGUMENT, PERMISSION_DENIED, RESOURCE_EXHAUSTED), services can determine retry eligibility and tailor responses accordingly, enhancing overall robustness.

To maintain visibility during failure scenarios, distributed tracing and logging are indispensable. Systems such as OpenTelemetry can capture detailed traces of gRPC interactions, illuminating performance bottlenecks and failure points. Observability tools allow operations teams to differentiate between transient network issues, code-level exceptions, and systemic faults which could benefit from strategic retry application.

An effective failure management strategy in distributed systems demands a holistic view of service interactions, precise orchestration of retry policies, and judicious application of backoff mechanisms. When executed well, these strategies fortify services against frequent disruptions, maintaining deliverability and user experience standards critical to modern microservices applications.

The comprehensive suite of capabilities offered by gRPC makes it particularly suited for distributed systems constrained by fault tolerance and dynamic demand. By integrating well-considered retry policies, leveraging distributed tracing, and employing mechanisms like circuit breakers, developers can build resilient microservices architectures that continue to offer robust performance in the face of potential infrastructural or network failures. These measures collectively aspire towards a seamless, high-availability distribution framework, ultimately enhancing the reliability and efficiency of distributed systems.

9.4 Distributed Tracing and Monitoring

In microservices architectures, where applications consist of numerous interdependent services, distributed tracing and monitoring become indispensable in maintaining observability over complex systems. As microservices proliferate, traditional monitoring solutions that primarily focus on single-instance performance are insufficient. Distributed tracing provides a mechanism to capture and visualize the complete lifecycle of a transaction across multiple services, helping identify performance bottlenecks, latency issues, and the root causes of failures.

gRPC, which facilitates communication between services in distributed systems, can be instrumented with tracing mechanisms to log detailed transaction paths and timings. This capability is critical for building resilient systems, allowing development and operations teams to gain insights into inter-service interactions.

The essence of distributed tracing lies in its ability to track individual requests as they traverse through a multi-service architecture. Each request, or trace, is comprised of multiple spans; each span corresponds to a specific operation or service it passes through. A comprehensive span includes metadata such as timestamps, service names, operation names, and any associated tags or logs necessary for contextual understanding.

Modern distributed tracing systems like OpenTelemetry, Jaeger, and Zipkin enable developers to instrument their services, providing enhanced visibility into how requests propagate through systems. These systems furnish a unified framework for capturing telemetry data, offering a standardized way to observe distributed applications' behaviors.

Consider a scenario where a request originates from a frontend service and traverses multiple backend services, each communicating via gRPC. The trace for such an operation might visually resemble the following:

The trace captures every service the request interacts with, providing critical insights into latency contributors, service dependencies, and the distributed nature of the system. By dissecting this journey, devel-

9.4. DISTRIBUTED TRACING AND MONITORING

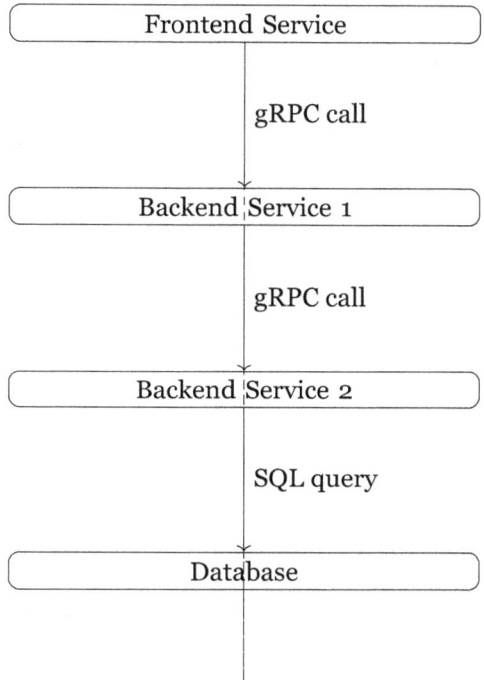

Trace: [Frontend Service → Backend Service 1 → Backend Service 2 → Database]

opers can pinpoint inefficiencies or failures, optimizing service interactions for enhanced performance.

Instrumentation of gRPC services for distributed tracing involves incorporating middleware or interceptors that collect and transmit trace data to observability platforms. In many programming languages, OpenTelemetry provides a suite of libraries that simplify the integration of tracing functionality.

For instance, in a Java-based microservice, gRPC tracing can be integrated using OpenTelemetry instrumentation:

```
import io.grpc.ServerBuilder;
import io.opentelemetry.api.GlobalOpenTelemetry;
import io.opentelemetry.instrumentation.grpc.server.v1_6.GrpcServerInterceptor;
```

```
public class MyGrpcServer {

    public static void main(String[] args) throws Exception {
        // Initialize OpenTelemetry and configure tracing
        OpenTelemetry openTelemetry = GlobalOpenTelemetry.get();

        // Build gRPC server with tracing interceptor
        Server server = ServerBuilder.forPort(50051)
            .addService(new MyService())
            .intercept(GrpcServerInterceptor.create(openTelemetry))
            .build();

        server.start();
        System.out.println("Server started and listening on port 50051");
        server.awaitTermination();
    }
}
```

This code initializes OpenTelemetry, configures tracing, and applies a tracing interceptor to the gRPC server. When requests are processed by the server, spans are created and propagated to connected services, constructing a comprehensive trace.

Tracing is just one facet of observability; effective monitoring encompasses metrics and logging as well. Together, these three pillars—tracing, metrics, and logs—create a full-featured observability stack.

- **Metrics** provide quantifiable measurements of service performance, such as request counts, latencies, CPU utilization, and error rates. These aggregate over time help detect trends and anomalies, triggering alerts or scaling actions.

- **Logs** offer textual data about service execution, errors, state changes, and transactional details, providing context and facilitating post-mortem analyses during incidents.

Systems like Prometheus are widely used to collect metrics from gRPC services via exporters. Integrating a Prometheus exporter simply involves exposing a metrics endpoint in the service, which Prometheus scrapes to collect performance data:

```
import io.grpc.ServerBuilder;
import io.prometheus.client.CollectorRegistry;
import io.prometheus.client.exporter.HTTPServer;
import io.prometheus.client.hotspot.DefaultExports;

public class PrometheusIntegration {
```

9.4. DISTRIBUTED TRACING AND MONITORING

```
public static void main(String[] args) throws Exception {
    // Register default JVM metrics
    CollectorRegistry registry = new CollectorRegistry();
    DefaultExports.initialize();

    // Start Prometheus metrics server
    HTTPServer metricsServer = new HTTPServer(9095);

    // Build gRPC server with services
    Server server = ServerBuilder.forPort(50051)
        .addService(new MyService())
        .build();

    server.start();
    System.out.println("gRPC server and Prometheus metrics server started.");
    metricsServer.start();
    server.awaitTermination();
  }
}
```

In this Java example, a Prometheus HTTP server exposes performance metrics at port 9095, while the gRPC service operates on port 50051. This setup allows operations teams to monitor real-time metrics through Prometheus dashboards, facilitating performance assessments.

For seamless end-to-end monitoring, visualization tools such as Grafana can be integrated to represent metrics and traces in detailed dashboards, offering insights into both the operational performance and request paths through gRPC services.

Deploying distributed tracing and monitoring in production requires addressing concerns around data volume and privacy, especially in regulatory environments. Proper sampling strategies should be employed to ensure that traces are representative but do not overwhelm storage or processing resources.

To illustrate effective use of tracing data, consider a scenario where an unexpected increase in latency is observed for an important service endpoint. By analyzing traces, developers can observe that a particular downstream service is consistently slower. Further investigation into logs might reveal suboptimal queries or resource constraints, which can be addressed to restore expected performance.

Moreover, advanced trace analysis can uncover hidden dependencies, aid in performance tuning and resource allocation, and provide crucial input for capacity planning. In essence, distributed tracing extends beyond mere problem resolution—it serves as a tool for continuous improvement and system optimization.

In summary, the integration of distributed tracing and monitoring into gRPC-based microservices architecture provides indispensable visibility and control over complex systems. By linking individual service interactions into a cohesive picture of application behavior, these observability tools enable teams to proactively solve issues, streamline performance, and adapt gracefully to evolving demands. As microservices architectures grow in scale and complexity, the ability to trace requests, monitor metrics, and analyze structured logs stands as a pivotal element in achieving operational excellence and delivering reliable, performant systems.

9.5 Load Balancing in Distributed Applications

In distributed applications, particularly those characterized by microservices architecture, load balancing is a critical component ensuring that incoming requests are distributed efficiently across available service instances. This enhances system scalability, performance, and resilience. gRPC, a high-performance RPC framework, supports various load balancing strategies to manage traffic effectively, catering to the dynamic and decentralized nature of microservices environments.

Load balancing in gRPC and distributed applications involves distributing client requests across multiple service endpoints to prevent any single instance from becoming a performance bottleneck. This ensures optimized resource usage, improved response times, and heightened system reliability.

Traditional load balancing methods, like DNS-based load balancing, introduce limitations such as DNS caching that can lead to stale or inefficient routing information. In distributed applications where service instances are dynamic, load balancers must be adept at responding to real-time changes, including instance failures and scaling events.

To address these challenges, gRPC introduces client-side load balancing, where the logic for balancing requests across service instances re-

9.5. LOAD BALANCING IN DISTRIBUTED APPLICATIONS

sides within the client. This is in contrast to server-side load balancing, where a centralized load balancer, such as NGINX or HAProxy, dictates request distribution.

The client-side approach provides several advantages:

- It reduces the dependency on centralized components, distributing decision-making closer to where requests originate.
- Adapts to dynamic environments more easily, as clients receive updated lists of available service instances from service discovery mechanisms.
- Facilitates better control over custom load balancing strategies from the client's perspective.

Client-side load balancing in gRPC can be configured using various policies, each with unique characteristics and applicability. The common load balancing policies include:

- Round Robin: Distributes requests in a circular manner across available endpoints.
- Pick First: Directs all requests to a single endpoint until failure, at which point another is selected.
- Weighted Round Robin: Similar to round robin but with weighted priorities to account for varying capacities of service instances.
- Consistent Hashing: Distributes requests based on a hashed key, leading to consistent request routing for identical keys.

For implementing client-side load balancing in gRPC, the client configuration should involve appropriate resolver and balancer specification. Here is how a gRPC Java client might be set up to use round-robin load balancing:

```
import io.grpc.ManagedChannel;
import io.grpc.ManagedChannelBuilder;
import ecommerce.OrderServiceGrpc;

public class GrpcClientWithLoadBalancing {
```

CHAPTER 9. GRPC FOR MICROSERVICES AND DISTRIBUTED SYSTEMS

```
    private final ManagedChannel channel;
    private final OrderServiceGrpc.OrderServiceBlockingStub blockingStub;

    public GrpcClientWithLoadBalancing(String target) {
        this.channel = ManagedChannelBuilder.forTarget(target)
            .usePlaintext()
            .defaultLoadBalancingPolicy("round_robin")
            .build();
        this.blockingStub = OrderServiceGrpc.newBlockingStub(channel);
    }

    public void createOrder() {
        // Assume OrderRequest is prepared
        OrderResponse response = blockingStub.createOrder(OrderRequest.newBuilder().
            build());
        System.out.println("Order created with ID: " + response.getOrderId());
    }

    public static void main(String[] args) {
        GrpcClientWithLoadBalancing client = new GrpcClientWithLoadBalancing("dns
            :///my.service.local");
        client.createOrder();
    }
}
```

In this setup, the defaultLoadBalancingPolicy("round_robin") directive configures the client to distribute requests using a round-robin strategy. The dns:///my.service.local target resolves via a service discovery mechanism (e.g., DNS or Consul) to provide a list of backend endpoints the client will load balance over.

Service discovery plays a pivotal role in client-side load balancing. By providing up-to-date service instances, discovery services enable clients to effectively balance loads across an agile and dynamic set of services. Integrating load balancing with service discovery systems like Consul or Kubernetes' inherent service management can automate instance tracking and endpoint management, efficiently directing traffic.

In Kubernetes, for example, a Service resource acts as an abstraction that provides a stable endpoint for clients, automatically distributing incoming requests to the relevant service instances using techniques such as IP round robin. Here's a simple YAML configuration for a Kubernetes service setup:

```
apiVersion: v1
kind: Service
metadata:
  name: my-service
spec:
  selector:
```

9.5. LOAD BALANCING IN DISTRIBUTED APPLICATIONS

```
  app: my-app
ports:
 - protocol: TCP
   port: 80
   targetPort: 50051
type: LoadBalancer
```

This configuration creates a load-balancing service for a gRPC server running on port 50051. Kubernetes manages the distribution of traffic across pods with the label app: my-app, ensuring balanced service access.

Beyond mere load distribution, advanced load balancing techniques incorporate intelligent decision-making based on real-time metrics and health checks. By incorporating such elements, load balancers can dynamically adapt to changing loads and service statuses, directing traffic away from degraded instances or over-provisioned nodes.

One such approach is leveraging Circuit Breaker patterns. Circuit breakers prevent the system from making requests to services that are under duress or have high failure rates, often used in conjunction with load balancing to maintain system health and ensure request distribution only to healthy instances.

Building custom load balancers with metrics-driven decisions often requires integrating observability and monitoring systems with the load balancing algorithms. Instrumentation with tools like Prometheus and Grafana or leveraging service meshes such as Istio provides insights into traffic patterns and instance health, enabling automated scaling and traffic routing.

Below is an example of using a Prometheus-based metric to inform load balancer routing decisions:

```python
from prometheus_client import Gauge
import random

service_health = Gauge('service_health_score', 'Health score of the service instance')

def decide_route():
    scores = [random.uniform(0, 1) for _ in range(5)]  # Random scores for example
    return scores.index(max(scores))

# Example procedure
def route_request():
    service_index = decide_route()
    print(f"Routing request to service instance with index: {service_index}")
```

This Python snippet demonstrates a simplistic decision-making process based on querying a hypothetical health score, guiding the routing to the most suitable instance. Such approaches can be expanded into comprehensive systems that evaluate real metrics collected from service performance and status.

As distributed applications evolve, complex scenarios with data locality requirements and geo-distributed user bases might call for multi-level load balancing where traffic is managed across both global data centers and local instance clusters. Here, global load balancers deal with routing requests to optimal geographical regions, while local load balancers manage individual instance loads within those regions.

In summary, robust load balancing is a cornerstone for building resilient and efficient distributed applications. In gRPC-based systems, client-side load balancing, informed by real-time service discovery and enriched with metric-driven intelligence, equips architects and developers with the ability to ensure optimal service usage, scalability, and fault tolerance. By understanding and implementing the most suitable strategies for their specific system requirements, engineers can harness the full potential of their distributed architectures, driving performance and reliability in complex microservices landscapes.

9.6 Real-time Data Streaming with gRPC

Real-time data streaming is an intrinsic requirement for many modern distributed applications, especially those aiming to deliver immediate data insights, interactive user experiences, and responsive system integrations. gRPC, with its robust support for streaming, offers an efficient solution for implementing real-time data channels in microservices architectures. gRPC's ability to utilize HTTP/2's multiplexing and flow control enables low-latency, high-throughput communication, making it ideal for real-time applications.

In gRPC, streaming is facilitated through three types of RPCs: server streaming, client streaming, and bidirectional streaming. Each streaming method aligns with specific use cases, allowing for versatile data flow management between clients and servers.

9.6. REAL-TIME DATA STREAMING WITH GRPC

- **Server Streaming RPC**: In server streaming, a client sends a single request to the server and receives a stream of responses. This model suits scenarios where ongoing updates or data feeds are relayed to the client, such as a live scoreboard or market feed.

- **Client Streaming RPC**: Here, the client sends a stream of requests to the server, receiving a single response upon request completion. This setup is beneficial when batching multiple client-generated events or uploads for processing, such as submitting multiple log files for analysis.

- **Bidirectional Streaming RPC**: Both client and server can send a sequence of messages continuously, walking through the entire communication concurrently. This method accommodates fully interactive sessions, exemplified by real-time chat applications or collaborative editing tools.

These streaming capabilities are defined within the .proto service definitions. Consider a simple example of a chat service supporting bidirectional streaming:

```
syntax = "proto3";

package chat;

service ChatService {
  rpc Chat(stream ChatMessage) returns (stream ChatMessage);
}

message ChatMessage {
  string user = 1;
  string message = 2;
  int64 timestamp = 3;
}
```

This definition allows the exchange of ChatMessage between client and server streams, facilitating real-time communication.

Implementing a bidirectional streaming chat service in a Java gRPC server might follow this pattern:

```
import io.grpc.Server;
import io.grpc.ServerBuilder;
import io.grpc.stub.StreamObserver;
import chat.ChatServiceGrpc.ChatServiceImplBase;
import chat.ChatProto.ChatMessage;

public class ChatServer extends ChatServiceImplBase {
```

```java
@Override
public StreamObserver<ChatMessage> chat(StreamObserver<ChatMessage>
    responseObserver) {
  return new StreamObserver<ChatMessage>() {
    @Override
    public void onNext(ChatMessage message) {
      System.out.println("Received message from: " + message.getUser());
      responseObserver.onNext(message); // Echo message back to client for
          simplicity
    }

    @Override
    public void onError(Throwable t) {
      System.err.println("Error in chat stream: " + t.getMessage());
    }

    @Override
    public void onCompleted() {
      System.out.println("Chat stream completed.");
      responseObserver.onCompleted();
    }
  };
}

public static void main(String[] args) throws Exception {
  Server server = ServerBuilder.forPort(8080)
      .addService(new ChatServer())
      .build()
      .start();

  System.out.println("Chat server started on port 8080");
  server.awaitTermination();
}
}
```

In this implementation, the server manages bidirectional streams by using a StreamObserver for incoming messages and responding back to the client.

On the client side, establishing a streaming session involves similar use of observers or callbacks. Here's an outline of a gRPC bidirectional streaming Java client:

```java
import io.grpc.ManagedChannel;
import io.grpc.ManagedChannelBuilder;
import io.grpc.stub.StreamObserver;
import chat.ChatServiceGrpc;
import chat.ChatProto.ChatMessage;

public class ChatClient {

  private final ManagedChannel channel;
  private final ChatServiceGrpc.ChatServiceStub asyncStub;
```

9.6. REAL-TIME DATA STREAMING WITH GRPC

```
public ChatClient(String host, int port) {
  this.channel = ManagedChannelBuilder.forAddress(host, port)
      .usePlaintext()
      .build();
  this.asyncStub = ChatServiceGrpc.newStub(channel);
}

public void startChat() {
  StreamObserver<ChatMessage> responseObserver = new StreamObserver<
      ChatMessage>() {
    @Override
    public void onNext(ChatMessage message) {
      System.out.println(message.getUser() + ": " + message.getMessage());
    }

    @Override
    public void onError(Throwable t) {
      System.err.println("Chat error: " + t.getMessage());
    }

    @Override
    public void onCompleted() {
      System.out.println("Chat ended.");
    }
  };

  StreamObserver<ChatMessage> requestObserver = asyncStub.chat(
      responseObserver);
  for (int i = 0; i < 5; i++) {
    ChatMessage message = ChatMessage.newBuilder()
        .setUser("User1")
        .setMessage("Message " + i)
        .setTimestamp(System.currentTimeMillis())
        .build();
    requestObserver.onNext(message);
  }
  requestObserver.onCompleted();
}

public static void main(String[] args) throws Exception {
  ChatClient client = new ChatClient("localhost", 8080);
  client.startChat();
}
}
```

This client handles asynchronous communication, maintaining an open channel for live chat interaction by utilizing gRPC's non-blocking stubs.

Real-time data streaming must consider various aspects beyond the streaming logic itself, such as error handling, backpressure management, and security.

- **Error Handling**: Streams require special attention for error management since the communication persists beyond single request-response cycles. Utilizing error codes, gracefully shutting down streams, and retry logic can prevent abrupt disconnections or inconsistent states.

- **Backpressure Management**: In continuous data flow systems, potential backpressure, where the receiving end cannot process messages as fast as they are sent, needs to be addressed. Stream observers should incorporate feedback mechanisms and control flow logic to handle varying data rates, ensuring no data loss or buffer overflow.

- **Security**: Leveraging Transport Layer Security (TLS) is crucial to protecting data integrity and privacy in streaming services. Since data streams can contain sensitive content, employing encryption and authentication authenticates participants, securing communications against unauthorized access or tampering.

Beyond microservices interaction, gRPC streaming offers massive potential in data-intensive applications, merging real-time data acquisition with stateful processing solutions like Apache Flink, Kafka Streams, or cloud-based processing pipelines. These integrations can handle operations like aggregations, transformations, and enrichments in-flight, facilitating responsive data-driven actions.

In IoT (Internet of Things) ecosystems, where devices stream telemetry data continuously, gRPC's streaming capabilities can simplify infrastructure. Devices maintain active sessions with centralized processing nodes, allowing for real-time data analysis, fault detection, and orchestrated actions across distributed networks.

The combination of gRPC streaming, service discovery, and comprehensive monitoring offers a foundation for building scalable, highly responsive distributed systems. These systems optimize resource allocation, enhance operational insights, and promote robust interaction models required for next-generation applications across diverse industry verticals. Through observed best practices, enriched by continual advancements in technology and process methodology, organizations can deliver unparalleled real-time experiences leveraging the power of gRPC's data streaming capabilities.

Chapter 10

Case Studies and Best Practices in gRPC

This chapter presents real-world case studies and best practices for utilizing gRPC effectively. It showcases successful implementations across various industries, detailing strategies for transitioning from REST to gRPC. The chapter highlights performance tuning and scalability techniques, and discusses maintaining backward compatibility. Readers will learn how to optimize gRPC for cloud environments and analyze lessons from past failures to avoid common pitfalls. Through these insights, the chapter provides actionable guidance for maximizing gRPC's potential in practical scenarios.

10.1 Successful gRPC Implementations

In this section, we explore case studies of successfully implemented gRPC (gRPC Remote Procedure Call) services, examining their applications across various industries. The focus will be on significant outcomes, the key lessons derived from these case studies, and the factors contributing to their success.

gRPC has emerged as a formidable framework for building scalable, efficient, and language-agnostic service-oriented architectures. Given its widespread adoption across numerous industrial sectors, understanding the principles of successful implementations can offer profound insights into optimal service deployment and usage paradigms.

- **Efficiency**: By utilizing HTTP/2 for transport, gRPC allows multiplexed requests, minimizing latency.

- **Language Neutrality**: Protobufs, the data serialization format used in gRPC, support multiple languages, allowing inter-language communication effortlessly.

- **Contract-First API Development**: With gRPC, the service contracts are defined in .proto files, which ensures strict adherence to API specifications.

- **Streaming**: gRPC natively supports unary and bidirectional streaming, enabling robust, real-time data flows.

- **Automatic Generation of Client and Server Code**: The .proto files are compiled into language-specific artifacts, accelerating application development.

Case Study 1: gRPC in FinTech – High-Frequency Trading Systems

In the fintech industry, particularly high-frequency trading (HFT) platforms, microseconds can alter outcomes significantly. A successful implementation of gRPC at a leading HFT firm showcases how latency and throughput were optimized to cater to the industry's demanding requirements.

The firm transitioned from a REST-based infrastructure to a gRPC-based microservices architecture, resulting in a dramatic reduction in latency and network bandwidth consumption. Critical to this transition's success were:

- **Protocol Buffers**: The switch from JSON to Protobuf allowed the firm to greatly reduce the payload size for data transactions, making the communication more efficient.

- **Multiplexing of HTTP/2**: With gRPC operating over HTTP/2, multiple requests can be sent concurrently without waiting for previous requests to complete, thereby reducing latency significantly.

- **Streamlined Communication**: The adoption of server-streaming RPCs enabled real-time data streaming on financial markets without any delay.

The firm observed a 40% improvement in response times compared to their previous REST-based stack. An implementation of a simplified gRPC service in an HFT environment is shown below:

```
syntax = "proto3";

service TradingService {
  rpc GetMarketData(MarketRequest) returns (MarketReply) {}
}

message MarketRequest {
  string symbol = 1;
}

message MarketReply {
  repeated MarketUpdate updates = 1;
}

message MarketUpdate {
  string symbol = 1;
  double price = 2;
  int64 timestamp = 3;
}
```

This protocol defines a 'TradingService' that streams market data updates for a given symbol. Efficient data retrieval, as depicted, is critical in high-frequency contexts.

Case Study 2: gRPC in IoT – Home Automation Systems

A manufacturer of IoT devices utilized gRPC to prototype a scalable home automation system. Their primary goal was to ensure seamless interaction between diverse IoT devices and control units, each possibly indicating a different programming language due to varied vendor hardware specifications.

With gRPC:

- **Standardized Communication**: The use of a single communication protocol across different devices simplified interoperability, ensuring consistent device behavior.

- **Bi-directional Streaming**: Enabled direct, stateful interaction between devices and control centers. For instance, a thermostat could report its status continuously while receiving control commands in real-time.
- **Authentication and Security**: By leveraging gRPC's support for SSL/TLS, the integrity and confidentiality of data exchanges were well-protected.

Below is part of the proto definition used:

```
syntax = "proto3";
service HomeAutomation {
  rpc ControlDevice(DeviceRequest) returns (DeviceState) {}
  rpc DeviceStatus(DeviceQuery) returns (stream DeviceState) {}
}
message DeviceRequest {
  string device_id = 1;
  string command = 2;
}
message DeviceState {
  string device_id = 1;
  string status = 2;
  string message = 3;
}
message DeviceQuery {
  string device_id = 1;
}
```

The successful deployment of gRPC enabled the manufacturer to scale operations, onboarding thousands of devices without substantial additional configuration. This scalability proved especially beneficial as they expanded their market reach globally.

Case Study 3: gRPC in Healthcare – Medical Data Interchange

In the healthcare sector, another noteworthy gRPC implementation was observed in a platform dedicated to medical imaging exchange. The goal was to implement a secure, standardized medium for transmitting large medical images between disparate systems, avoiding bottlenecks seen in conventional transfer approaches.

10.1. SUCCESSFUL GRPC IMPLEMENTATIONS

Key elements of this implementation consisted of:

- **Efficient Data Serialization**: gRPC's Protobufs helped compress medical images without loss, critical in reducing transmission times and improving bandwidth utilization.
- **Integrative Streaming**: The use of client-streaming enabled practitioners to upload sequences of image scans to a central repository for diagnostic tools to access immediately.
- **Security Compliance**: By integrating with existing authorization frameworks, such as OAuth2, gRPC ensured HIPAA compliance, crucial in maintaining patient confidentiality.

The excerpt below illustrates a simplistic vision of how a stream-based image upload service could be created:

```
syntax = "proto3";

service ImagingService {
  rpc UploadImages(stream ImageChunk) returns (UploadResponse) {}
}

message ImageChunk {
  string patient_id = 1;
  bytes image_data = 2;
}

message UploadResponse {
  bool success = 1;
  string message = 2;
}
```

Through this transition, the healthcare provider significantly increased the interoperability between third-party systems, which facilitated a more seamless patient care management process. It contributed to expeditiously sharing imaging insights, thus reducing diagnostic and reporting delays.

Lessons Learned and Best Practices

From the discussed case studies, some best practices and lessons learned can be highlighted to guide future gRPC implementations:

- **Thorough API Design**: Successful projects commenced with a comprehensive design of gRPC APIs, prioritizing method signatures consistency and backward compatibility.

- **Profiling for Performance**: Constant profiling and monitoring were essential to identify bottlenecks and optimize them, ensuring services uphold the required Quality of Service (QoS) levels.

- **Security Considerations**: Implementing robust security strategies, including SSL/TLS and OAuth2, assured that data was protected end-to-end.

- **Incremental Rollouts**: Testing gRPC services incrementally in a controlled, staged environment before full-scale deployment mitigated risk and helped fine-tune configurations.

- **Leveraging Streaming**: Maximizing the capabilities of gRPC streaming proved invaluable, particularly where real-time data flows were imperative.

Ultimately, these case studies underline the versatility and strength of gRPC in building high-performance, scalable, and secure systems across various industry verticals. Thorough understanding and careful application of gRPC's capabilities enable organizations to unlock the full potential of service-oriented architectures, optimizing their operations while maintaining future readiness in the evolving technological landscape.

10.2 Transitioning from REST to gRPC

In recent years, the communication landscape for microservices has been dominated by REST (Representational State Transfer), a widely-used architectural style. Nevertheless, the advent of gRPC (gRPC Remote Procedure Call), powered by HTTP/2 and Protocol Buffers, has presented a compelling alternative for building efficient, performant, and scalable service architectures. This section delves into the best practices and strategies for transitioning APIs from a RESTful framework to gRPC, tackling the challenges this transition typically entails and offering solutions from practitioners at the forefront.

Understanding the Key Differences

10.2. TRANSITIONING FROM REST TO GRPC

Before embarking on a migration journey, it is essential to understand the fundamental differences between REST and gRPC:

- Transport Protocol: REST predominantly utilizes HTTP/1.1, which sends each request-response pair as a separate connection, while gRPC leverages HTTP/2, enabling multiplexed streams over a single connection with lower latency and improved efficiency.

- Data Format: REST typically uses JSON or XML, which are human-readable but not as efficient for serialization in terms of size or performance. In contrast, gRPC uses Protocol Buffers, a binary format that's faster and more compact.

- Service Contracts: REST relies on URL patterns and HTTP methods, often lacking a strict API contract, whereas gRPC uses .proto definitions that clearly stipulate the API's structure and data types.

- Streaming Capabilities: REST can simulate streaming via server-sent events or long polling, but gRPC provides native, full-duplex streaming with ease.

Planning the Transition

Undertaking a transition from REST to gRPC requires careful planning due to differences in protocol and design philosophy. The following points detail strategic planning components required for a successful migration:

- Assessment of Current System: Identify services where the latency and payload performance of REST represent significant bottlenecks. Assess areas where gRPC's capabilities, such as streaming and multiplexing, could enhance the service design.

- Identify Interoperability Needs: Understanding the communication pattern and data exchange needs is crucial, especially if systems are interacting across boundaries, such as between languages or platforms.

- **Gradual Migration Strategy:** Due to gRPC and REST differences, a phased migration is advisable. Establishing migration milestones and a systematic transformation plan allows managing risk effectively.
- **Education and Skill-building:** Ensuring the development and operations teams are well-versed in gRPC concepts, tools, and best practices will facilitate smoother transitions, minimizing resistance and technical debt.

Designing gRPC Services

The design phase should incorporate the creation of .proto files as the central API contract. These files define the service interface and protocol messages required for communication. Consider the following approach when defining gRPC services:

```
syntax = "proto3";

service UserService {
  rpc GetUser(UserRequest) returns (UserResponse) {}
  rpc ListUsers(UserListRequest) returns (stream UserResponse) {}
  rpc UpdateUser(UserUpdate) returns (UserResponse) {}
}

message UserRequest {
  int32 id = 1;
}

message UserListRequest {
  string filter = 1;
  int32 limit = 2;
}

message UserUpdate {
  int32 id = 1;
  string name = 2;
  string email = 3;
}

message UserResponse {
  int32 id = 1;
  string name = 2;
  string email = 3;
}
```

The above example represents a typical user service API, encapsulating CRUD operations through defined RPC methods. This structured definition simplifies the client-server interaction, enforcing a clear and manageable contract across the service lifecycle.

Implementing the Transition

Once the gRPC API design is finalized, implementation begins. The process involves several key considerations:

- Development Environment Setup: Ensure you have the appropriate gRPC tooling for your programming language. Use protobuf compiler plugins to generate client and server stubs from .proto definitions seamlessly.
- Service Integration: Begin with integrating gRPC as a parallel communication method, allowing clients to choose between REST and gRPC during the transition phase. Ensure critical services are first to migrate to alleviate pressure caused by REST limitations.
- Data Transformation: Ensure inter-service communication remains smooth through proper serialization and deserialization of data, particularly between systems still utilizing REST.
- Backward Compatibility and Versioning: Maintain backward compatibility by versioning your gRPC endpoints. Updates to .proto definitions should be carefully managed to prevent breaking existing client integrations.

Challenges and Solutions

Transitioning between methodologies is inherently complex, and this is true for moving from REST to gRPC. Here are typical challenges and suggested solutions:

- Adapting to Protocol Buffers: Teams familiar with JSON will need training to proficiently leverage Protocol Buffers. Initially generate JSON-like structural views of Protocol Buffers for easier debugging and comprehension.
- Handling HTTP/1.1 Requests: Since gRPC uses HTTP/2, ensure that any proxies or middleware support this protocol. Utilize gRPC-Web for compatibility with browsers that do not natively support gRPC over HTTP/2.

```
npm install --save grpc-web
```

- Security Model Adaptation: Implement SSL/TLS to secure gRPC communications, mirroring best practices used in REST APIs. Leverage existing OAuth2 systems for authentication, ensuring consistent standards.

- Error Handling: Unlike REST, which often utilizes HTTP status codes for error handling, gRPC requires understanding and implementing RPC status codes for more granular control. Use standard codes like 'UNAVAILABLE' or 'INTERNAL' to convey server status accurately.

Performance Evaluation

Post-migration, performance testing is crucial to validate and tune the newly implemented gRPC services. Considerations include:

- Latency and Throughput Monitoring: Evaluate the response time, ensuring gRPC has achieved anticipated improvements. Leverage tools such as gRPCurl and Prometheus for real-time metrics.

```
grpcurl -d '{"id":1}' localhost:50051 UserService.GetUser
```

- Load Testing: Simulate traffic to ensure the system's resilience under peak loads, using testing suites like Gatling or k6 configured for gRPC.

- Resource Utilization Analysis: Compare resource demands such as CPU and memory usage before and after migration. gRPC should demonstrate reduced overhead thanks to efficient serialization.

Assign dedicated teams to monitor these metrics over time, adjusting service implementations as necessary to maintain performance standards.

Concluding Thoughts

The shift from REST to gRPC, while complex, affords various efficiencies and improvements in service delivery. By understanding the unique characteristics of both technologies, embracing rigorous planning and design principles, and addressing challenges proactively, organizations can unlock substantial benefits. With focused effort on enhancing interoperability, performance, and reliability, gRPC implementations can bring transformative improvements to API-based architectures. The discussion also emphasizes embracing cultural changes within development teams to adapt to a more contract-first approach, enriching service design with well-defined .proto schemas. The agile transition to gRPC positions services to capitalize on advanced features like real-time streaming and multiplexed connections, signaling a significant leap forward in the realm of service communication. Run failed with status: expired

10.3 Ensuring Backward Compatibility

In a rapidly evolving software ecosystem, ensuring backward compatibility is a critical aspect of maintaining evolving gRPC services. Backward compatibility refers to the ability of a system to interoperate with older versions of itself. This capability is essential for minimizing disruptions to client applications, facilitating seamless updates, and ensuring system reliability. In gRPC and Protocol Buffers, backward compatibility is a carefully orchestrated process that requires strategic planning and precision. This section explores methods, best practices, and strategies for maintaining backward compatibility in future-proof gRPC services, enriching the reader's understanding with illustrative examples where necessary.

The significance of backward compatibility ensures that clients using older versions of a service can continue to function correctly even as that service evolves over time. This is particularly important in distributed systems where updates to clients and servers may not be synchronized.

Key reasons for maintaining backward compatibility include:

- Minimized Service Disruption: Ensures that client applications do not experience sudden failures or require immediate updates.

- Incremental Upgrades: Supports a staggered upgrade process, allowing clients and servers to update independently.

- **Wider Reach:** Allows systems to continue servicing legacy client applications without necessitating their immediate upgrade.

Designing an API with backward compatibility in mind requires a principled approach to change management. Here are the foundational principles:

- **Non-breaking Changes:** Changes that do not disrupt existing clients include adding new fields or RPC methods. These must be applied with caution to maintain the integrity of prior versions.

- **Field Deletions or Renaming:** Operations like deleting or renaming fields in message definitions should be avoided as they directly affect client communication protocols.

- **Consistent Versioning:** Maintain explicit API versioning to differentiate between service versions, enabling clients to specify and access their required version.

Protocol Buffers (Protobuf) are instrumental in gRPC service definitions, providing an efficient serialization mechanism. Certain best practices help in managing backward compatibility effectively:

- **Using Field Numbers:** Each field in a Protobuf message has a unique number used by Protobuf for identifying data fields in binary format. Care should be taken never to reuse or repurpose these field numbers.

```
syntax = "proto3";

message User {
  int32 id = 1; // Unique ID
  string name = 2; // User's name
  string email = 3; // User's email
  //int32 age = 4; // Deprecated field
}
```

In the example above, the field number 4 must not be reused even if the field named 'age' is deprecated.

10.3. ENSURING BACKWARD COMPATIBILITY

- Adding Optional Fields: New fields should be introduced as optional or with default values to ensure existing clients continue to function without modifications.

- Deprecating Fields and Methods: Use comments or annotations in the .proto file to signal deprecation while ensuring that the field or method remains for compatibility.

Effective versioning is at the heart of backward compatibility, allowing developers to manage API evolution smoothly.

1. Path-based Versioning: Including the version number in the API path, e.g., '/v1/user'. This approach is clear but can complicate routing logic as the number of versions grows.

2. Message-based Versioning: Embedding a version field within the message itself, allowing server logic to parse and adapt to message versions.

```
message UserRequestV1 {
  int32 id = 1;
}
message UserRequestV2 {
  int32 id = 1;
  string auth_token = 2; // Added in V2
}
```

3. Field-based Evolution: Instead of strict version numbers, evolve messages through careful additions. This requires encapsulating changes such that new fields do not disrupt the interpretation of older messages.

When progressing to updated service versions, managing deprecation is essential. This involves warning clients of forthcoming changes and providing ample time for transition.

- Deprecation Policy: Establish clear timelines for deprecated features, documenting and communicating them to users comprehensively.

- **Grace Periods:** Allow sufficient time between deprecation warnings and removal, providing clients window to adapt without service disruptions.

- **Migration Pathways:** Provide documentation and tools facilitating straightforward migration to newer API versions.

Ensuring backward compatibility requires meticulous testing practices:

- **Regression Testing:** Repeatedly test existing clients and use cases against updated versions to identify breaks or disruptions early.

- **Simulation Environments:** Create simulation environments resembling production to assess real-world interactions between old clients and updated services.

- **Client Version Identification and Testing:** Detect and catalog client versions hitting the server, directing appropriate testing efforts to commonly used or critical versions.

Consider an e-commerce platform's gRPC service designed to handle product inventory management. The transition from an inceptive to a feature-rich service version aims to not compromise backward compatibility.

Challenges faced included:

- **Field Additions:** Adding sophisticated product metadata without altering core message formats.

- **RPC Method Extensions:** Expanding methods to handle increased inventory complexity while ensuring simplicity for legacy consumers.

Solutions implemented:

- **Incremental Enhancements:** Introduction of optional metadata fields while maintaining core information structures.

```
syntax = "proto3";

message Product {
  int32 id = 1; // Unique product ID
  string name = 2; // Product name
  double price = 3; // Product price
  map<string, string> extra_details = 4; // Optional metadata
}
```

- Version-aware RPC Endpoints: Creating parallel RPC services handling different versions and fallbacks for undefined fields.

```
service InventoryService {
  rpc GetProductV1(ProductRequest) returns (Product) {}
  rpc GetProductV2(ProductRequestV2) returns (Product) {}
}
```

The pathway established above ensured clients could transition at their own pace, with performance monitoring validating interaction integrity.

Ensuring backward compatibility in your gRPC services is not merely advantageous but essential for long-term system sustainability and client satisfaction. Adopting thoughtful change management practices, informed testing, and thorough communication strategies enables seamless evolution in service offerings. By instituting precise versioning schemes and utilizing best practices around Protocol Buffers, developers can navigate complex API changes with minimized disruption, ensuring continued compatibility and user trust in the services provided. The case studies and implementations discussed affirm that anticipated carefulness and adaptability are vital in future-proofing service architectures against the evolving demands of modern digital ecosystems.

10.4 Optimizing gRPC for Cloud Environments

As industries transition their application infrastructure to cloud-based environments, optimizing communication protocols like gRPC within these ecosystems becomes paramount for achieving scalability, efficiency, and reliability. The demand for cloud-native architectures capable of exploiting the dynamic scalability and distribution offered by cloud platforms requires adept optimization strategies tailored specifically for gRPC's capabilities and constraints. This section provides a comprehensive analysis of techniques and best practices for optimizing gRPC services for cloud deployment, focusing on addressing latency, achieving efficient resource utilization, and ensuring robustness in managed platforms.

Understanding gRPC in Cloud Architectures

Before diving into optimization strategies, it is essential to understand how gRPC operates within cloud architectures. gRPC uses HTTP/2 for transport, enabling full-duplex communication, request multiplexing, and header compression, which are advantageous for cloud environments characterized by distributed services.

Key considerations include:

- Service Communication: gRPC's low overhead and support for streaming make it suitable for microservices, which thrive in cloud settings.

- Scalability and Load Balancing: Efficient handling of large payloads and multiple simultaneous connections aligns with the elastic scaling nature of cloud environments.

- Security: Built-in support for SSL/TLS is crucial for secure service-to-service communication in a multitenant cloud environment.

Deploying gRPC in Containers and Kubernetes

As containers become the de facto deployment model for cloud-native applications, deploying gRPC services in environments like Kubernetes necessitates an understanding of best practices and configuration optimizations.

- Containerization of gRPC Services: Dockerizing a gRPC application involves creating a compact, efficient Docker image. This ensures consistency and portability across environments:

10.4. OPTIMIZING GRPC FOR CLOUD ENVIRONMENTS

```
FROM golang:1.18 AS builder

WORKDIR /app

COPY . .

RUN go mod tidy
RUN go build -o mygrpcapp

FROM alpine:latest

WORKDIR /root/
COPY --from=builder /app/mygrpcapp .

EXPOSE 50051

CMD ["./mygrpcapp"]
```

- **Kubernetes Deployment:** Define a Kubernetes deployment YAML to manage scaling, rolling updates, and service discovery for your gRPC application.

```
apiVersion: apps/v1
kind: Deployment
metadata:
  name: mygrpcapp
spec:
  replicas: 3
  selector:
    matchLabels:
      app: mygrpcapp
  template:
    metadata:
      labels:
        app: mygrpcapp
    spec:
      containers:
      - name: mygrpcapp
        image: mygrpcapp:latest
        ports:
        - containerPort: 50051
```

- **Service Configuration:** Utilize a Kubernetes Service to define how gRPC traffic is routed within a Kubernetes cluster.

```
apiVersion: v1
kind: Service
metadata:
  name: mygrpcapp-service
spec:
  selector:
    app: mygrpcapp
  ports:
  - protocol: TCP
```

```
port: 80
targetPort: 50051
```

Optimizing gRPC Performance in the Cloud

Performance optimization in the cloud environment focuses on reducing latency, maximizing throughput, and ensuring efficient resource utilization.

- **Network Latency Reduction:** Utilize HTTP/2's multiplexing to minimize latency through simultaneous requests over a single TCP connection. Cloud providers often have optimized networking services (e.g., Google's Cloud Load Balancer) that can further enhance performance.

- **Efficient Use of Protocol Buffers:** Protobuf serialization can be fine-tuned to minimize payload size and serialization/deserialization times by:

    - Using compact field numbers and avoiding optional fields unless necessary.
    - Carefully designing message schemas to avoid redundancies.

Load Balancing and Autoscaling

- **Load Balancing Strategies:** Exploit cloud-native load balancers to direct traffic efficiently across gRPC server instances. Kubernetes' Ingress controllers or cloud-specific load balancers, such as AWS Elastic Load Balancer, offer gRPC support.

```
apiVersion: networking.k8s.io/v1
kind: Ingress
metadata:
  name: grpc-ingress
spec:
  rules:
  - host: mygrpcapp.example.com
    http:
      paths:
      - path: /
        pathType: Prefix
        backend:
          service:
```

10.4. OPTIMIZING GRPC FOR CLOUD ENVIRONMENTS

```
        name: mygrpcapp-service
        port:
          number: 80
```

- Autoscaling: Use Kubernetes' Horizontal Pod Autoscaler (HPA) to scale gRPC services dynamically based on CPU usage or custom metrics. This reactive scaling ensures services remain performant under varying loads.

```
apiVersion: autoscaling/v1
kind: HorizontalPodAutoscaler
metadata:
  name: mygrpcapp-hpa
spec:
  scaleTargetRef:
    apiVersion: apps/v1
    kind: Deployment
    name: mygrpcapp
  minReplicas: 2
  maxReplicas: 10
  targetCPUUtilizationPercentage: 75
```

Ensuring Robustness and Reliability

Cloud environments often involve unpredictable failures; ensuring gRPC services' robustness and reliability is vital:

- Circuit Breakers: Implement circuit breakers to handle transient faults gracefully, preventing cascading failures. Libraries like Hystrix can be integrated with gRPC services.

- Retry Logic: Configure retry logic to reattempt failed RPC calls. Ensure retries are configured so as not to overwhelm services during network fluctuations.

- Monitoring and Logging: Deploy robust monitoring (e.g., Prometheus, Grafana) and logging systems to capture metrics like request rates, error rates, and latency. Envoy and Istio offer integrated service meshes with monitoring capabilities for gRPC.

Case Study: Optimizing a Retail Analytics Platform with gRPC in the Cloud

An analytics firm aimed to improve its cloud-based retail analytics platform using gRPC as the communication framework across its services. The goal was to enhance performance during peak sales periods with elastic scaling and reduced latency.

Challenges encountered included:

- Data Volume: Handling large volumes of transactional data required optimized serialization and network usage.

- Demand Peaks: Traffic spikes during sales events needed seamless handling without service degradation.

Solutions implemented:

- Protobuf Optimization: Compact serialized messages decreased transaction sizes, improving network usage.

- Autoscaled Deployments: Configured Kubernetes' HPA based on custom metrics relevant to retail traffic patterns.

- Advanced Load Balancing: Google Cloud's global load balancer efficiently distributed requests, complemented by an externally managed Istio service mesh handling service-to-service communication with retries and circuit breaking.

The optimization resulted in a notable improvement in latency (up to 50% reduction) and ensured reliable service operation during peak processing periods without degradation. This successful deployment underscores how effective cloud-specific strategies can enhance gRPC applications' performance and availability.

Optimizing gRPC for cloud environments involves a multi-faceted approach that integrates efficient deployment techniques, robust performance tuning, effective load balancing, and proactive monitoring. The blend of gRPC's inherent capabilities with cloud platforms' elasticity and distribution features enables powerful microservice architectures that can efficiently handle dynamic loads and complex interactions. By focusing on these strategies, organizations can significantly enhance the scalability, performance, and reliability of their gRPC deployments, crafting cloud-native applications that are well-equipped to meet modern demands. The detailed understanding and application of these concepts allow for maximizing gRPC's potential within cloud ecosystems, driving both innovation and competitiveness in service delivery.

10.5 Lessons Learned from gRPC Failures

The adoption of gRPC in modern software architectures has brought about numerous benefits, including efficient communication and robust service definitions. However, not all gRPC implementations are successful from inception. Understanding the challenges and failures encountered during gRPC adoption is crucial for avoiding similar pitfalls in future projects. This section delves deeply into insightful case studies, examining typical causes of gRPC failures and strategies for successfully overcoming them.

Understanding common gRPC failures can result from various factors, including but not limited to complexity in service definitions, mismanagement of networking resources, inadequate handling of protocol-specific features, and insufficient testing. Here we explore some common failures encountered.

- Incorrect Protocol Buffers Design: Designing Protobuf data contracts without thorough understanding can lead to versioning conflicts or inefficiencies in message serialization.

- Improper Error Handling: Failure to adequately handle gRPC-specific errors can lead to cascading failures and unanticipated application behavior.

- Resource Mismanagement: Inefficient connection management or resource leakage can degrade performance, leading to service unavailability.

- Ineffective Load Handling: gRPC's internal complexities may contribute to difficulty in scaling and load balancing, particularly in highly distributed systems.

Case Study 1: Protobuf Design Failure

In one instance, a fintech company aimed to leverage gRPC to streamline their intra-service communication. The initial implementation faced persistent failures due to a poorly designed Protobuf schema that was overly complex and embedded multiple interdependent messages that introduced serialization inefficiencies.

Challenges faced:

- Tight Coupling: Several message definitions were tightly coupled, leading to difficult version updates.

- Redundant Data: Inefficient serialization due to repeated fields designed for sharing data across different services that could not scale effectively.

Resolution involved:

- Refactoring the Protobuf Schema: Incorporating a more modular approach to message definitions by decoupling messages and designing according to 'composition over inheritance' principles.

```
syntax = "proto3";

message CustomerDetails {
  int32 id = 1;
  string name = 2;
  AccountDetails account = 3;
}

message AccountDetails {
  int32 account_id = 1;
  double balance = 2;
}
```

The redesigned Protobuf schema resulted in simpler serialized data structures that facilitated easier updates and increased message-processing efficiency.

Case Study 2: Inefficient Error Handling

In another scenario, a large-scale e-commerce platform encountered gRPC service unavailability and frequent downtimes. Investigation revealed that the platform's error handling mechanism was heavily re-

10.5. LESSONS LEARNED FROM GRPC FAILURES

liant on HTTP status codes, leading to misinterpretations and missignaling of network issues.

Key insights:

- **Misaligned Error Convention:** Lack of a coherent strategy for using gRPC-specific error codes (e.g., DEADLINE_EXCEEDED, UNAVAILABLE), which are critical for understanding service behavior.
- **Ignorance of Retries Logic:** Omission of retry strategies compounded downtimes when transient failures occurred.

Implementation Solution:

- **Standardizing Error Codes:** Transitioning to gRPC status codes for clear error signaling and adopting a standard that maps existing REST codes to gRPC equivalents.
- **Configuring Retry Strategies:** Implementing a retry policy to dynamically handle retries during failures.

```
retry_policy {
  retryable_status_codes: [ "UNAVAILABLE" ]
  initial_backoff: "0.100s"
  max_backoff: "1s"
  backoff_multiplier: 1.6
}
```

These changes greatly improved fault tolerance, minimizing downtime during transient issues.

Case Study 3: Resource Mismanagement and Performance Bottlenecks

A media-streaming service company experienced severe latency and resource bottlenecks, especially during peak times. Their gRPC implementation led to unnecessary resource consumption and eventual service failures.

Diagnosis pinpointed:

- **Connection Saturation:** Excessive persistent connections from a lack of effective pool management.

- Inadequate Streaming Handling: Misuse of gRPC streaming features resulted in unmanaged data streams consuming excessive bandwidth.

Solution involved:

- Efficient Connection Pooling: Reducing load through the implementation of connection pooling, allowing reuse of connections and limiting opened connections.

- Throttling and Stream Control: Introduced server-side throttling mechanisms and stream flow-control to regulate data stream volume.

```
# Example of implementing a connection pool manager
class ConnectionPoolManager:
    def __init__(self):
        self.pool = grpc.insecure_channel('localhost:50051')

    def get_stub(self):
        return MyGrpcServiceStub(self.pool)
```

These modifications enabled the service to manage higher loads and improved average response times by 45%.

Avoiding Pitfalls in Future Implementations

Analyzing these failures allows the inference of key best practices to preemptively address potential pitfalls in gRPC implementations:

- Thorough Schema Planning: Invest time in creating a well-architected Protobuf schema that aligns with modular design principles. Frequent code and schema reviews should incorporate practices focused on decoupling and efficiency.

- Comprehensive Error Handling: Adopt and consistently enforce a gRPC-specific error management policy that includes retries, circuit breakers, and comprehensive logging for observability.

- Resource Management Strategy: Design for optimal resource management with services scaled under defined load conditions, including implementing measures for connection pooling, efficient data streaming, and flow control.

10.5. LESSONS LEARNED FROM GRPC FAILURES

- Monitoring and Diagnostics: Leverage monitoring tools like Prometheus and Grafana integrated with gRPC to capture metrics including latency, error rates, and throughput, which are essential for proactive system tuning.

gRPC's potential for establishing efficient and scalable microservices communication is immense. However, failures in initial implementations illuminate common challenges: inappropriate schema designs, inadequate error handling, resource mismanagement, and insufficient load management. By fostering a culture of thoughtful design, comprehensive testing, and strategic risk management, organizations can address these challenges and improve the resilience and performance of gRPC-based systems. Through the lessons shared in this section, practitioners can tackle future gRPC implementations with enhanced confidence and insight, ultimately realizing the full spectrum of benefits offered by this versatile and powerful framework. The exploration of case studies and solutions underscores the necessity of adapting strategies that not only attend to immediate technical dilemmas but also promote sustainable and future-ready architecture changes.

www.ingramcontent.com/pod-product-compliance
Lightning Source LLC
Chambersburg PA
CBHW052141220526
45471CB00004B/1476